NOT DREAMING

THE MOREHOUSE COLLEGE
KING COLLECTION
SERIES ON CIVIL & HUMAN RIGHTS

NOT DREAMING

Martin Luther King Jr.'s Critique of America

Robert Cohen

THE UNIVERSITY OF GEORGIA PRESS | ATHENS

Athens, Georgia 30602
www.ugapress.org

Set in Sans and Arno Pro by Westchester Publishing Services

Printed digitally

EU Authorized Representative
Easy Access System Europe—Mustamäe tee 50, 10621 Tallinn, Estonia, gpsr.requests@easproject.com

Library of Congress Control Number: 2026012477
ISBN: 9780820380643 (paperback)
ISBN: 9780820380636 (hardback)
ISBN: 9780820380650 (ebook)
ISBN: 9780820380667 (PDF)

Pou imigran ayisyen yo nan Springfield, Ohio. Epi pou tout Ameriken ki te kanpe avèk yo kont kalomni rasis Donald Trump ak J. D. Vance yo.

Pour les immigrants d'origine haïtienne de Springfield, Ohio, et pour tous les Américains qui ont pris leur parti contre les calomnies et propos racistes proférés par Donald Trump et J. D. Vance.

For the Haitian immigrants of Springfield, Ohio, and for all Americans who stood with them against Donald Trump's and J. D. Vance's racist slander.

There are some things in our social system to which I am proud to be maladjusted. *I never intend* to adjust myself to the viciousness of mob rule. I never intend to adjust myself to the evils of segregation, to economic conditions which take necessities from the many to give luxuries to the few, and to the madness of militarism and the self-defeating method of physical violence. . . . Maladjustment to such principles . . . will be the only way to emerge from the bleak and desolate midnight of man's inhumanity to man into the bright and glittering daylight of freedom and justice.

—Martin Luther King Jr., speaking at New York University,
February 10, 1961
Heights Daily News, February 14, 1961

CONTENTS

FOREWORD

Professor Robert Cohen has written an important book for our times. In an era marked by rising authoritarianism and other imminent threats to democracy, Cohen's concise and accessible text invites us to reengage with the radical thought and philosophy of Dr. Martin Luther King Jr. In King's final book, *Where Do We Go from Here: Chaos or Community?*, he issued a powerful critique of American society, pointing out the persistence of what he called the "triple evils" of racism, militarism, and excessive materialism. If left unchecked, King warned, these interconnected "evils" would result in "violent coannihilation" and ultimately lead to the demise of American society. While King addressed these "giant triplets" over half a century ago, we still wrestle with these and other injustices in our twenty-first century world.

Not Dreaming: Martin Luther King Jr.'s Critique of America is particularly relevant in expanding our understanding of King's radicalism as well as our understanding of how his insight and activism might be resourced in today's world. Professor Cohen is most interested in introducing King and the legacy of organized resistance to the general public as well as to a younger generation in hopes that they will appreciate and become inspired to act against injustice on their own. *Not Dreaming* benefits from Cohen's scholarly expertise and his experience teaching King and movement history to undergraduates for more than a decade. While there is increasing pressure to censor, or teach false versions of the nation's history, Professor Cohen's book appears as a critical corrective to this trend, helping students and the public comprehend how longstanding institutionalized systems of oppression continue to persist.

Not Dreaming: Martin Luther King Jr.'s Critique of America begins with an assessment of the federal holiday established, in 1983, to honor King. Conversely, the historic national recognition of King resulted in a cooptation and distortion of his legacy, yielding an ahistorical and false version of the leader for civil and human rights. While King was heralded as a national hero, Cohen cites King's close friend and colleague, historian Vincent Harding, who perceptively called him the "inconvenient hero," one whose message challenged the status quo in its radical critique of national and global injustice. The "distorted, domesticated, and de-radicalized" version of King, Cohen notes, bears little resemblance to who King actually was: a fierce critic of racial capitalism, champion of dissent, and uncompromising advocate for nonviolent resistance.

The book's overarching framework centers around the "triple evils" King critiqued, best exemplified in three of his iconic speeches: "I Have a Dream" (1963), "Beyond Vietnam: A Time to Break Silence" (1967), and the "Mountaintop" speech (1968). The most familiar is King's "I Have a Dream" speech at the historic March on Washington for Jobs and Freedom. Here, Cohen points out that while the speech represents a powerful articulation of King's "democratic radicalism," the general tendency to overemphasize the dream segment of the speech has resulted in an obfuscation of the more radical message delivered in the first half of the address. Cohen aptly notes, "the main part of the speech was *not* about a dream of an America free from systemic racism, but an actual indictment of the racism that persists and dates to the founding of the country."

"Beyond Vietnam: A Time to Break Silence" is arguably one of King's most important speeches, yet it has been largely ignored or forgotten by most politicians and the American public. Cohen suggests that this speech, delivered in 1967 at New York City's Riverside Church, controversially voiced King's strong opposition to American militarism and neo-colonialism, as well as the escalating U.S war in Vietnam. This speech, Cohen argues, "was far too radical for much of America to embrace . . . [and] a reminder that King's commitment to nonviolence placed him well to the left of mainstream America." Also, Cohen documents the important, yet underappreciated role of King's wife, Coretta Scott, who was a staunch supporter of anti-war efforts long before King took a public stance.

King's final speech, delivered in Memphis on the eve of his assassination, brings a fuller appreciation of his strong support of union activism and his keen awareness of working-class historical agency. Here again Cohen peels back the layers of labor history to recover how African American support of mass organized resistance rendered effective organization of both the Montgomery bus boycott and the Memphis sanitation workers strike. Like King's speech at the March on Washington, the "Mountaintop" speech is best known for its dramatic ending, wherein King prophesizes his own funeral.

Finally, through deep analysis of King's most iconic speeches and insightful discussion of the complex historical narratives surrounding them, *Not Dreaming: Martin Luther King Jr.'s Critique of America* is essential reading for our times. Cohen effectively challenges us to think more deeply about Dr. King and his continuing relevance for our lives today. The book is an urgent call to action and effective reminder of our moral imperative to speak and act against injustice.

Vicki Crawford, PhD
Series Editor, The Morehouse College King Collection Series on Civil and Human Rights

NOT DREAMING

Introduction

The establishment of Martin Luther King, Jr. day as a national holiday did not come easily. It took fifteen years of Black-led organizing and petitioning, from 1968 to 1983, to make this happen. This effort was spearheaded by Representative John Conyers and Coretta Scott King, who in the wake of her husband's assassination emerged as a major civil rights leader in her own right. Stevie Wonder, the star Motown recording artist, provided a major assist by releasing a best-selling song, "Happy Birthday," in support of the holiday.[1] On one level it was appropriate that it took a mass movement, in the tradition of those MLK led in his lifetime, to finally get congressional and presidential authorization for the first holiday to honor an African American and a protest leader. And it was impressive that this victory came in the conservative Reagan era, despite the opposition of right-wingers in Congress, most notably Senator Jesse Helms of North Carolina (who kept denouncing MLK as a communist), and the initial reluctance of President Ronald Reagan himself. Despite the federal government's establishing this holiday in 1983, however, it was not until 2000 that all fifty states finally recognized MLK Day, attesting to how reluctant America was to honor King.[2]

The holiday has had at least symbolic significance in reminding America of the heroic Black-led struggle against Jim Crow. So it is a day for politicians, from mayors to presidents, to pay tribute to King and his dream of an America free of racism. At the community level, and in schools, colleges, and progressive labor and civil rights organizations, MLK Day has been an occasion to honor public service, in line with its status as the only federal holiday "designated as a day of service to encourage all Americans to volunteer and improve their communities."[3] Within the Black community it is also a time to honor and promote activism as well as to celebrate African American culture and achievement in the arts.

But for all its achievements, the King holiday has failed—and so have the nation's schools—to educate the public as to who King really was politically.

Namely, they have failed to evoke how deeply critical King was of the American social order (not just the Jim Crow South) and how radically egalitarian he was in his vision of nonviolent social democratic change at home and globally. This is in part because the movement to win MLK Day was such a struggle and encountered so much white resistance that the holiday ended up celebrating the misleading image of King as an iconic moderate, so as to appeal across lines of race, ideology, and region.[4]

Just how poorly understood MLK is by the public was recently displayed most dramatically and appallingly in the speeches and media coverage of Donald Trump's inauguration as forty-seventh president of the United States. Precious little was said in the news media, or by the U.S. political establishment, about how jarring it was to have Trump inaugurated on the day of the Martin King Luther King Jr. national holiday. Jarring because King had devoted himself to, and sacrificed his life for, the struggle against racism, hatred, and violence, and Trump's actions and rhetoric had for years supported those evils. Where were the editorials suggesting how offensive it was to King's legacy to have Trump inaugurated on King Day? That Trump's conduct attested to the continuing relevance of King's concern that America was sick with racism? This was obvious years ago when Trump became a star in Republican right-wing politics by championing the notorious "birther" lie, slandering Barack Obama, America's first African American president, by charging that he was not a U.S. citizen but a foreigner, born in Kenya (Obama was actually born in Hawaii), and so was not a legitimate president.[5] Likewise, Trump's first victorious presidential campaign in 2015–2016 centered on slandering undocumented, non-white Mexican immigrants as rapists and murderers and whipping up xenophobia. Continuing into his first term as president, Trump (in 2017) praised as "some very fine people" those who marched in a Nazi-led white supremacist demonstration in Charlottesville, Virginia, that ended with the murder of an anti-racist protester.[6] In 2020, Trump would mobilize the military, deploying tear gas to disperse a nonviolent Black Lives Matter protest near the White House. After losing his presidential reelection campaign, Trump recruited and incited a violent mob to besiege the U.S. Capitol and disrupt the Electoral College vote count on January 6, 2021, a mob that included racists wielding Confederate flags and Nazi regalia and injured more than one hundred police officers.

It would not have taken much imagination for the press to point out how contrary to King's nonviolent ethos was Trump's campaign promise (fulfilled in his first day in the White House after his reelection) to pardon the right-wing thugs responsible for the bloodshed of January 6. Or to note that Trump's victorious reelection was the culmination of the most bigoted presidential campaign in American history. Here Trump used demeaning racist and sexist stereotypes to question the intelligence of his Black opponent, Kamala Harris, and mocked her African American identity. Worst of all, from the presidential debate stage in September 2024, Trump spread the outrageous lie that Haitian immigrants stole and were "eating the dogs . . . and the cats of the people who live" in Springfield, Ohio. (The way Trump phrased this slander was itself revealing, since he did not count these Black immigrants in Springfield as "people who live there."[7]) This was the ugliest and most damaging racial comment ever made in a presidential debate, sparking bomb threats that caused the evacuations of schools and hospitals that served Springfield's Haitian immigrant community.[8]

Given his dismal record on race, it was a supreme act of hypocrisy for Trump, on his 2025 inaugural day, to try to claim the mantle of Martin Luther King. Trump had a right-wing Black minister, Lorenzo Sewell, giving the inaugural prayer that quoted Dr. King's "I Have a Dream" speech, with Sewell absurdly implying that Trump aspired to fulfill King's dream of an America free of racism.[9] Trump's inaugural address also invoked King in this way, claiming he was committed to MLK's vision of a color-blind society, grounded in merit rather than race, bringing an "end to government policy of trying to social engineer race and gender. . . . We will make his dream come true."[10] But these were just sugarcoated phrases designed to justify his campaign to destroy diversity, equity, and inclusion programs, as his stacked right-wing Supreme Court had killed affirmative action, undermining the federal government's role in battling anti-Black racial discrimination. Going still further in his first week of office, Trump pushed to end diversity programs, even in the private sector. What these programs were designed to "engineer" was an end to bigotry and discrimination. Where were the editorial writers, the TV commentators that knew enough about King to point out the absurdity of Trump's MLK Day masquerade?

Nor did the news media display any awareness of how ignorant of MLK's philosophy and activism Trump proved himself to be when, in his inaugural speech, this self-proclaimed admirer of MLK frothed with violent, imperialist rhetoric about taking the Panama Canal back from Panama. Such bellicose rhetoric was totally at odds with Dr. King's commitment to nonviolence and his opposition to colonialism.[11] Trump's xenophobic scare tactic in terming as an "invasion" the stream of undocumented, "illegal" immigrants who come to the United States in search of a better life was an equally glaring example of bigotry that clashed with King's compassionate ethos regarding poor and marginalized people in America and globally. In explaining that ethos, King declared in a sermon to his Ebenezer Baptist Church congregation in 1966:

> I choose to identify with the underprivileged. I choose to identify with the poor. I choose to give my life for the hungry. I choose to give my life for those who have been left out of the sunlight of opportunity. . . . This is the way I'm going. If it means suffering a little bit, I'm going that way. If it means sacrificing, I'm going that way. If it means dying for them, I'm going that way, because I heard a voice saying, "Do something for others."[12]

It is well to recall MLK biographer David J. Garrow's reflections, during Trump's first term as president, on the relationship between Trumpism—with its hateful white grievance politics—and King's aspiration to make America a more compassionate society. It was not hate, but as Garrow put it, "a political view of love that was so deeply central to King. Especially in our current political context . . . it cannot be emphasized enough that the real core of Martin Luther King's political theology was the utter and complete avoidance of a politics of hate." In King's view, hatred "destroys the hater," and the lesson was "never allow anyone to drag you so low as to hate."[13]

This was the exact opposite of Trump, who, in one of the earliest of his many public acts of racial hatred, back in 1989, placed a full-page ad in several leading newspapers urging New Yorkers to hate violent criminals and support the reinstatement of the death penalty. This at a time when the Central Park Five, Black and Latino youths--in a racially charged case—were wrongly accused, as evidence would show, with raping a white woman jogger in Central Park.[14] Trump's malicious ads were widely viewed as a call to execute these nonwhite youths (though the ads did not name them), and heightened racial tension in New York.[15] As the influential New York columnist Murray Kempton noted at the time, "What Donald Trump had been bold to say was 'Mayor Koch has stated that hate and rancor should be removed from our hearts. I don't think so. I want to hate.'" Kempton concluded: "Donald Trump dresses his hatred up as though it were a peacock's feathers."[16] And Trump has spent a considerable amount of his time as a presidential candidate and president doing the same.

Yet despite what should have been obvious—the dramatic difference between MLK and Trump—there was little pushback against Trump's attempt in his 2025 inaugural to hijack and distort MLK's legacy. What few objections there were tended to come from the African American community, including civil rights and MLK scholars. Most notable in this regard was Rev. Bernice King, daughter of Martin Luther King. She took Sewell, and by implication Trump, to task for misusing her father's most famous speech, noting that Sewell had not even mentioned "its clear messaging about ending racism, stopping police brutality, ensuring voting rights, and eradicating economic injustice."[17] Bernice King had never gone along with the far-fetched right-wing notion, promoted by Trump, that pretending America was a color-blind society would somehow negate the persistence of racial discrimination, without diversity and inclusion programs: "My father's dream and work included eradicating racism, not ignoring it."[18]

In retrospect, it is not surprising that such informative criticism and revealing Trump-King comparisons were so rare. Much of the TV, print media, internet, and public-school coverage of MLK's life, activism, and ideals has for decades tended to be simplistic, distorted, and redundant. With so much miseducation about King, few Americans understood King's legacy well enough to see through Trump's masquerade regarding MLK. In the pre-college classroom context, moreover, such miseducation has yielded boredom as well as ignorance. I know this from firsthand experience. I have been teaching an NYU undergraduate course on Martin Luther King Jr. for more than a decade, and enrollments are much smaller than in my popular history courses. This is because after years and years of hearing, in elementary, middle, and high school, the same "I have a dream" soundbite from MLK's 1963 March on Washington speech, undergraduates tend to think they already know all there is to know about King, who they misread as a yawn-inducing figure, a moderate accommodationist who discussed race in a dreamy way, with no sharp edges, militancy, or particular relevance to twenty-first century America. So they are often startled to learn, after reading King's speeches, writings, and interviews in my seminar, of his moral criticism of capitalism, war, imperialism, police brutality, and poverty. They discover that the man they thought of as moderate and boring was radically critical of racism in the United States and globally, and not merely militant, but among the most effective dissenting orators in American history—quite the opposite of boring. One can understand, then, why the public, news media, and mainstream political leaders, limited by their lack of such familiarity with Martin Luther King's political thought, proved unable to question Trump's distorted view of King or the president's absurd claim to be following in King's footsteps.

The roots and dimensions of late twentieth and twenty-first century America's miseducation and ignorance regarding Martin Luther King were traced most effectively, even brilliantly, decades ago by the late Vincent Harding, a leading historian of Black America, and a friend, neighbor, and political advisor to King. Harding, a Black Mennonite lay minister and pacifist, was, among King scholars, best known for his role in drafting one of Dr. King's most memorable and controversial speeches: the 1967 Riverside Church oration. With great force and drama, the speech condemned the Vietnam War and explained why, after a period of strategic silence, King decided to champion the antiwar cause at a time when most Americans and civil rights leaders supported the war. Beginning in the late 1980s, first in speeches, then in articles, books, interviews, and an online video, Harding took issue with the way King's rise to iconic status, which came as the nation belatedly honored him after the creation of the MLK national holiday, had led to an image of King so distorted, domesticated, and de-radicalized that it bore little resemblance to the historical King whom Harding knew so well, admired, and loved.[19]

The way Harding explains it, the dominant forces in America wanted to reduce King to a "convenient hero." This meant someone who spoke of interracial harmony in an abstract, idealized, and non-threatening way—an icon who did not challenge American injustices, flaws, and excesses and could somehow be harmonized with the status quo. In other words, a domesticated King, compatible with America as a militarized superpower, a capitalist behemoth, and a white-dominated social order. But Harding points out, none of this resembles King as he actually was: a nonviolent warrior for social justice; a foe of war and imperialism; a critic of American capitalism and the vast socioeconomic inequality it bred; an orator who indicted the racism that marred American history (the North's as well as the South's) and that endures into the present. Thus, to look at the real Martin Luther King is to see someone who was, as Harding labeled him, "an inconvenient hero," a dissenter in the prophetic tradition, who challenged America in deep ways that it could not handle. King had called on America, as Harding explained, to not just "give up on white supremacy" but "to move away from the great levels of materialism that have always been so much a threat to our humanity and the humanity of others" and "to look at the world not through the eyes of a dominator but the eyes of sisters and brothers to the world."[20]

King, then, was far too radical for the American political establishment, opposing its war-making, its favoring profits over people, its ghettoization and ongoing discrimination against Black Americans, its refusal (despite its status as the world's richest nation) to tackle the problem of poverty. MLK bemoaned the growing chasm between the poor and the affluent as well as America's indifference to the violence and hatred that marred its political landscape. Since King rarely did what mainstream America wanted him to do, which was to back off from his prophetic truth telling and challenges to the status quo, his scathing indictments of American racism, war-making, and economic inequality had to be muffled for its national holiday honoring him. MLK Day was not, in this regard, true to King's spirit and ideals, according to Harding, when it centered on a celebration of a few lofty lines from one speech but failed to address the radically democratic agenda King died for: his still unfulfilled vision of America as a society where equality, justice, and peace replaced racism, greed, and poverty. He had desired a nation whose sense of community and compassion prevailed, yielding a society that leaned towards an inclusive vision, akin to democratic socialism. Harding realized what had gone wrong with the King holiday quite quickly: only a year after the commemoration of King's life on the first MLK Day, Harding concluded, "It appears as if the price for the first national holiday honoring a black man is the development of a massive case of national amnesia concerning who that black man really was. . . . We Americans have chosen amnesia rather than continue King's painful, unchartered, and often disruptive struggle toward a more perfect union."[21]

One need not agree with every word Harding wrote about Martin Luther King to recognize that America ought to think more deeply about MLK's ideas, oratory, and activism than it has been doing on MLK Day and in school sessions that focus on the "I have a dream" sound bite. There is a rich field of King scholarship that should enable us to do better. There have even been three Pulitzer Prize-winning biographies of King: historian David J. Garrow's *Bearing the Cross* (1986), journalists Taylor Branch's *Parting the Waters* (1983) and Jonathan Eig's, *King* (2023).[22] Stanford University's MLK papers project has produced seven invaluable volumes of King's speeches, correspondence, and writings.[23] Memoirs of those close to King have long been available, from Coretta Scott King to Andrew Young and John Lewis, along with specialized studies on topics ranging from King's youth to his oratory, theology, his views on gender, King's civil rights organization (the Southern Christian Leadership Conference), his relationship with the FBI and Presidents John Kennedy and Lyndon Johnson, plus comparative biographies of King and Malcolm X.

The problem, however, seems to be that this illuminating writing on MLK and the volumes of his papers are not reaching nearly enough of the public. In all my years teaching about MLK, I have had only one single undergraduate who entered my class having read any of this scholarly material (or any of the books King himself wrote). This is in part an access issue. The best King biographies tend to be quite long: Garrow's was eight hundred pages, Branch's was more than one thousand pages (and that was only the first of his three volumes on the King years), and Eig's, the most concise and recent of these major biographies, still comes in at over six hundred pages. The most recent volume of the King papers, *To Save the Soul of America* (2014), is more than seven hundred pages long, even though it only covers January 1961 to August 1962. I mention this not in criticism of these books. They richly reward the interested reader and uphold high standards of historical scholarship. But they cannot educate a public that lacks the time and interest to read them. And even shorter and less honored biographies of King have failed to generate much interest, in part because they do little or nothing to connect King to twenty-first century concerns, or to the kind of thought-provoking arguments Vincent Harding made about MLK as an inconvenient hero, and the contemporary debates on King's ideas about racism and governmental programs designed to battle racial discrimination.

Perhaps the most important insight left by Harding is that the historical MLK is no museum piece, that we need to reflect upon King's thoughts, actions, and warnings—especially about racism—because they continue to be so relevant, addressing racial inequity in a nation that is still beset by it, even as it seeks to evade that harsh truth. Evidence of such contemporary relevance, and the persistent racism in America that makes it so, is all around us, visible even at the very top of our political system. We cannot avoid it if we want to be candid in explaining President Trump's 2024 electoral victory in the aftermath of the scurrilous racist lies that candidate Trump told about

Haitian immigrants in Ohio stealing and eating pet cats and dogs. Do Trump's voters share his racist nativism? Or are they simply morally indifferent to it? Either way, the fact that such racism could be displayed, and so crudely, from a soon-to-be-victorious presidential candidate in 2024—with Trump actually widening his margin of victory in Ohio that year, over his prior presidential runs—does not lead to happy conclusions about the state of race relations in the United States more than a half century after MLK's death.[24]

Nor is MLK's contemporary relevance confined to the issue of race. Twenty-first century America is much further down the road to plutocracy than it was in King's lifetime. Just look at the photos of billionaires seated near Trump at his second inauguration, including the three richest men in America, who personally accounted for more wealth than the bottom third of all Americans.[25] The gap between rich and poor has hit record levels in our century, which is why in 2011 the Occupy Wall Street movement rallied to expose and condemn the elite one percent whose economic power and influence so corrupts American democracy.[26] MLK's Poor People's Campaign and his pro-labor activism (he was slain in Memphis in the midst of a solidarity movement with that city's oppressed and striking Black sanitation workers) generated writings and speeches that illuminate the failures and inequities of American capitalism in our times as well as his.[27]

This book represents my attempt as a veteran teacher of King's thought, activism, oratory (and his relation to the Black Freedom Movement, the Left, the Right, and the political power structure of 1960s America) to introduce the public to key aspects of King's political history and legacy. I have intentionally kept this book short and sharply focused on the essential MLK. And by that I mean the aspects of King's politics and persona that are both crucial and poorly understood by the public. These are expressed through the ideas, oratory, and activism on problems that mattered deeply to MLK, that helped shape his political life, and that remain urgent today: (1) racism, (2) militarism, and (3) economic oppression and poverty. In both MLK's speeches and interviews, especially in the last years of his life, he focused on these three areas, singling them out repeatedly as the "triple evils" that afflicted America—labeling them as racism, militarism, and either "extreme" or "obsessive" materialism or "economic exploitation" that led to "poverty." He was convinced that these three evils were "tied inextricably together, and we aren't 'gonna get rid of one without the other."[28] King warned that failure to address them would move America down "a dead end road that can lead to national disaster."[29] So the focus of this book on these three evils reflects both King's elevation of them, King's priorities, and my own sense that these remain serious afflictions of twenty-first century America and that we can benefit from MLK's analysis of them.

I make no claims to being the first to see King as a perceptive social critic whose radical egalitarianism, nonviolence, and insights into the dynamics of race, capitalism, and militarism have much to teach us. In fact, my thinking on all this has been influenced by the scholarship of the King biographers mentioned earlier, along with the fine books on King's radicalism by Michael K. Honey, Thomas F. Jackson, Sylvie Laurent, and Cornel West, and many discerning studies of the Black Freedom Movement.[30] But I am setting out here to offer a book that will be shorter and more accessible than has been the case with most King scholarship and reflective of what my classroom experience suggests is the most useful way to begin to seriously engage with MLK's social criticism.

Our exploration of King will start by meeting the public where it has been stuck—on the "I Have a Dream" speech—but then going beyond its famous dream sequence and turning to the far less familiar parts of the speech that trace America's tradition of racial inequity all the way back to the Founding Fathers.[31] My approach is to contextualize that speech in relation to both the organizing of the march that made the speech possible and the other great speech of that day: John Lewis's even more radical oration, whose militancy—even after its censorship—represented the Black Freedom Movement's left wing, composed of the student activists who had led the sit-ins, saved the Freedom Rides, launched historic voting rights crusades in Mississippi and Alabama, and founded the Student Nonviolent Coordinating Committee (SNCC).[32]

We will then move on, in chapter 2, to MLK's all too rarely studied yet powerful Nation Institute and Riverside Church speeches in 1967, which embody his nonviolent faith and his bold stance against the Vietnam War, colonialism, and American militarism. This breaks with the MLK Day tendency to freeze King in 1963, when he was still battling the segregationist South (before he moved north to help lead a major offensive against racial discrimination in Chicago), which makes King seem a quaint relic since his Jim Crow nemesis back then has long since died. This has led to the right-wing pretense that MLK was addressing a problem solved, that with Jim Crow de jure segregation dead, America had become a color-blind society, a mendacious stance made possible by white blindness to racist police violence and the persistence of de facto racial discrimination and inequity in employment, education, and housing.

This type of pretense is not even possible on the topic of militarism that King addressed in his antiwar speeches during 1967 and 1968, since militarism lives on in an American empire that currently has more than seven hundred military bases across the globe. And a military-industrial complex whose arming of Israel's war on Gaza that in the wake of Hamas's terror attack against Israel, on October 7, 2023—which killed over 1,200 and trapped 251 hostages—fueled months of far bloodier state terror and a mass bombing campaign. Tens of thousands of Palestinian civilian deaths resulted, which in 2024 sparked a nationwide U.S. student antiwar movement, the largest such movement on twenty-first century American college campuses. The Nation Institute and Riverside speeches take us beyond King's role as key leader of the Black Freedom Movement, heralding his emerging role as a leading voice of the antiwar movement, a role too controversial to be commemorated at most King Day events.[33] These speeches are also significant in how open they were in their radical criticism of U.S. militarism, attesting that by 1967 King was more willing to go public with ideas well to the left of mainstream liberalism, which he had previously hesitated to dwell upon since it risked alienating powerful liberals, including President Lyndon Johnson.[34]

It was no accident that King gave his most well-known antiwar speech in a church. As you would expect with a Baptist minister, religion was a key force in shaping his politics. In our secular age, but where the loudest religious voices often come from the far right, it is difficult initially to get students to take seriously the idea that a dissident leader on the left could be so influenced by religion. From his first speech as a civil rights leader, also given in a church—the Holt Street Baptist Church—in 1955 at the start of the Montgomery, Alabama, bus boycott, to his final speech in Memphis in 1968, religious imagery, ideals, and inspiration loomed large in King's oratory.[35] And it was a religious focus with radical implications not only on war and racial justice but also on economic justice. As historian Wesley Hogan put it, in the United States "one can't think about economic justice without focusing on capitalism's organic problem: the centrality of profit. In a country where the clear majority of people are Christian, then and now, King preached about a Jesus fundamentally opposed to the profit motive. *This* King is a threat. He challenges power. In fact, his ideas fundamentally question how most pursue their daily lives."[36] And on race, the familiar King, the supposedly moderate advocate of racial integration, turns out—as the son and grandson of African American ministers—to have been raised in one of the most independent, African American-controlled institutions of the segregated South: the Black Church. As King scholar Stewart Burns stressed, MLK absorbed from that church its distinctive Black Social Gospel, with an awareness of the human propensity for evil and its distinctly Black emphasis on white America's sinful embrace of racism—"cosmic injustice," that "had to be rectified."[37] Therefore the religious dimension of King's thought, oratory, and activism must be recognized and probed.

The book's last chapter opens with a discussion of MLK's two speeches in support of Memphis's striking sanitation workers. Of these two, MLK's 1968 "I've Been to the Mountaintop" speech, in Memphis, is far better known because it was his final speech, whose dramatic ending (often broadcast as a soundbite on King Day) came close to prophesizing his assassination the next day. But when we go beyond its haunting final moments, we find his reflections on labor solidarity, economic inequality, and strategies for dealing with the greed and exploitation that continue to define a capitalist system that excels at generating, but not at distributing, wealth without even a semblance of equity. At a time when the United States has a billionaire president bent on a yet more regressive tax structure, who is supported by his even wealthier patrons with the resources to buy and sell elections, and with the labor movement in decline, the economic justice emphasized in these final MLK speeches in 1968 seems more relevant than ever.

In his last Memphis speech, King specifically named and urged the boycotting of exploitative companies and advocated for standing with striking workers then struggling for economic justice. Here King sounded much like a left-wing labor leader, while in this same speech, as a civil rights and antiwar movement leader, he celebrated the struggle against racism and the necessity for nonviolence at home and globally. Among the most striking things about King's vision and criticism of American society was how profoundly democratic they were and how seamlessly he integrated domestic and international concerns regarding justice on matters of class, race, war, and peace. In his final years, King highlighted his longstanding view that economic and racial injustice and the U.S. addiction to militarism and war were connected and must all be addressed if the nation was to progress. This critique and call for fundamental change on multiple fronts were far to the left of the Democratic and Republican parties in King's lifetime, and that is still true today.

The last topic explored in the book's final chapter is the Poor People's Campaign (PPC). Unlike the previous struggles and events discussed in these pages, this final section cannot center on an MLK speech or two because King would not live to see or speak at the (PPC)'s culminating event, its occupation of Washington, D.C., since he was assassinated the month before. This was a march on Washington without MLK. Nonetheless the statements King made as he launched, and helped organize, this multiracial encampment of poor people—seeking to prod Congress, the Johnson administration, and the public to get serious about abolishing poverty—offer some of King's most powerful moral criticism of capitalism and of America's callous indifference to the suffering of the poor.

Much like MLK at the podium, I want to avoid going on too long and desire to explain my conclusions with enough evidence to convince you but not so much as to bore or overwhelm you. This means I won't try your patience with hundreds of pages of narrative designed to cover all of King's life and work. Such comprehensiveness and detail can be gleaned from the fine, yet lengthy, King biographies mentioned earlier, which I hope this book will motivate you to read.

You can think of this book as a follow-up to Vincent Harding's effort to demystify King, to push back on those who distort King's politics and legacy. If the book accomplishes this, it will promote greater historical literacy regarding King and mass protest in 1960s America and will encourage readers to aspire to what was best in King's politics and vision. His politics and vision center on multiracial democracy and an America so committed to it that the United States would finally become a society that cherishes diversity, equity, and inclusion of those formerly marginalized on the basis of race, which is the very opposite of the surging white nationalism that in twenty-first century America seeks to demonize those ideals. Historical literacy regarding MLK and the Black Freedom Movement that he worked so hard to advance will make it easy, then, for Americans to avoid being conned by right-wing demagogues who pretend to be interested in realizing King's dream of justice and equality but misrepresent King and themselves.

It was one of MLK's gifts that he could, as in his famed "I Have a Dream" speech in 1963, look beyond an America sick with racism and dream of an

America cured of this grievous social malady. But King was also a realist, and his optimism was tempered by a deep understanding of America's long history of slavery and Jim Crow and by the violent racism he and the Black Freedom Movement encountered as they struggled against racial discrimination. Thus even when King gloried in the Black Freedom Movement's progress and the gains it made (in its heroic struggle against Jim Crow via the sit-ins, Freedom Rides, voting rights crusades, anti-racist boycotts) and sounded optimistic, asserting that "the arc of the moral universe is long, but it bends towards justice," he was not one to predict quick or easy victory over racism.[38] Indeed, reflecting on even his seemingly encouraging—and often quoted—words about the moral universe, King leaves us wondering just how long that "long arc of the moral universe" actually is, and whether it would take decades or centuries until the arc finally "bends towards justice."

Serious engagement with King as a social critic demands that we not follow the media tendency to present an MLK frozen in time at his March on Washington soundbite from 1963 and cast as merely a dreamy advocate of racial harmony. His ideas and mood evolved in significant ways in the last years of his life. Interviewed in his Atlanta Church in 1967, MLK aired a pessimism about American progress toward his dream of an America free of racism and committed to peace and justice—a pessimism that those who fixate on the hopeful segment of his "I Have a Dream" speech would do well to consider. Seeing how the Vietnam War had stalled the war on poverty, and how white America's indifference—North and South—to racism, poverty, and discrimination had fueled Black ghetto rebellions and deadly police repression, King expressed fear that his dream of interracial harmony was being trampled. In 1967, NBC News reporter Sander Vanocur asked King, "When you stood . . . that August day in 1963 on the steps of the Lincoln memorial and you said, 'I have a dream,' did that dream envision a war in Asia and in the ghettoes of the North?" King responded, "No, I didn't envision that then. In 1963 to be in the March on Washington, it meant a great deal; it was a high moment, a great watershed. . . . But I must confess that that dream that I had that day has in many points turned into a nightmare."[39]

Dream or nightmare? Or something in between? Ought twenty-first century Americans be hopeful about the racial progress as represented earlier with the election of its first Black president in 2008 and its first Black and South Asian woman vice president in 2020? Or pessimistic about its progress, given the right-wing Supreme Court's weakening of the Voting

Rights Act or its outlawing of affirmative action? What should we make of Trump's road to the White House in 2024, paved—at least in part—by his crude and cruel white grievance politics and followed by his banishment of Diversity, Equity, and Inclusion programs, his mass deportations, and abandonment of the Justice Department's role in battling anti-Black racial discrimination? King cannot answer these questions for us, but his ideas, his social criticism, arm us with historical perspective and a clarifying lens with which to view them. And so does the tragedy of King's death, his assassination, which came at the hands of a white supremacist, sparking the most widespread ghetto rebellions of the turbulent 1960s and leaving us—much like President Abraham Lincoln's assassination by a racist Confederate sympathizer a century earlier—wondering whether the largest steps forward against the oppression of Black America will continue to spark bitter and deadly resistance from white America's most hateful racists.[40] Martin Luther King's story offers much more than a dream or some out-of-context support for conservatives' fantasies about color-blindness. It provides clues to the complexities, contradictions, and tragedies of American racism and a beacon of hope for those willing to acknowledge the persistence of racism and to organize against it.

In this book I seek to help us have MLK enter our lives as a source of critical thinking about American racism, economic inequality, and militarism as well as an inspiration for our ongoing struggles for democracy, peace, and justice. But we ought not place King on a pedestal. And we certainly should not forget that it took millions of activists to bring the protest movements of his day to life and to bring progressive change to America, an organizing process that MLK assisted with but did not create. Not even MLK's most famous speech would have made much of an impact had not grassroots activists, and the great organizer Bayard Rustin, brought the largest crowd of protesters in American history to participate in the March on Washington, making this a major news event and ensuring King's speech the TV coverage and national attention that magnified its impact. On that day we can say that the movement made Martin at least as much as Martin made the movement.

Nor do we need to deny that on issues of gender—women's and gay rights—MLK was a product of 1950s America and not nearly as advanced as he was on race. His leadership style, in the Black Church tradition of charismatic pastors, was so hierarchical and male-centered that it proved almost impossible for strong Black women organizers, such as Ella Baker, to work with him for long. In private life he was flawed—not always a faithful husband—and in his academic life he committed plagiarism.[41] His defiance of homophobia was spotty, and not nearly so impressive as A. Philip Randolph's, when it came to standing up for Bayard Rustin's right as a gay man to help lead the freedom movement. But it also must be remembered that the assassin's bullet denied King the time to evolve and progress on these gender issues and that his death in 1968 came before Stonewall, before the historic women's rights victories won in the Supreme Court by Ruth Bader Ginsburg in the heyday of second-wave feminism, which came in the 1970s.

Still, King was not perfect and not a saint. He was a human being who was limited in some regrettable ways, as are all too many of us. But this does not change the fact that he was one of the most important democratic activists and inspiring orators in American history. His central role in the fall of Jim Crow and in the human rights revolution and antiwar movement of the 1960s generated oratory and writings that call us back—as Lincoln put it—to the "better angels of our nature," an urgent need in this time of Trump/MAGA cruelty, and authoritarianism. Flaws and all, King richly deserves the national holiday that Coretta Scott King did so much to make possible. But he also deserves to be remembered correctly as, in Harding's words, an inconvenient hero who criticized America as a society sick with racism, greed, exploitation, violence, and militarism, and whose calls to action challenge us to struggle for an America that is more just and democratic.

* * *

I write this book amidst the Trump era, when, at the 47th president's behest, anti-racist ideals, and even the words *diversity, equity,* and *inclusion,* are, in true Orwellian fashion, demonized and banned as discriminatory. So, as I have argued above, it seems evident that many Americans, and Trump himself, lack a basic understanding of MLK's ideas about racism and how to overcome it. And the same is true of MLK's critical outlook on American militarism and capitalism. But while much of twenty-first century America does not understand King, there is no doubt at all that King would have had no trouble understanding twenty-first century America and Donald Trump, because MLK had witnessed similar displays of bigotry by racial demagogues in his own time.

This calls to mind a conversation I had with MLK's movement comrade and admirer John Lewis, back in 2016 when he visited my MLK undergraduate seminar at New York University. I asked Congressman Lewis for his thoughts about Trump's astoundingly xenophobic presidential candidacy in the aftermath of his having achieved right-wing political eminence via racist birtherism. Lewis responded that, in his years in the civil rights movement, he and his fellow movement leaders during the 1950s and 1960s were accustomed to such crude racial demagoguery but primarily at the local or state level, especially (but by no means exclusively) in the Jim Crow South. Back then such bigoted figures never had a shot at ascending to the presidency, and, in fact, the Black Freedom Movement, as Lewis noted, had seen the federal government—both the president and the courts—as a potential ally in the struggle for racial justice. This is why MLK's writing on racial demagoguery most relevant to the Trump era was directed at state politicians rather than the White House. If we think of Trump's election victories as due, at least in part, to the white backlash against the first Black presidency and the Black Lives Matter movement, there is something strikingly contemporary about MLK's words—which appeared in his final book—about how in 1966 "the white backlash" against the Black freedom struggle "had become an emotional electoral issue in California, Maryland, and elsewhere." As he observed, "In several Southern states men long regarded as political clowns had become governors or only narrowly missed election, their magic achieved with a 'witches' brew of bigotry, prejudice, half-truths, and whole lies."[42]

King's words here, which describe Trump, though he never met or lived to see his hate-fueled political career, and Lewis's observation that racist demagoguery never managed in the civil rights movement's heyday, as it has in our era, to defile the White House, may come as a shock to those who stress American racial progress. Yes, of course, thanks in part to MLK and the movement's victories in the 1960s, Jim Crow is dead, while the Civil Rights Act of 1964 and the (now wounded and diluted) Voting Rights Act of 1965 still live--at this writing. So there has been some progress. But that twenty-first century America has twice elevated to the presidency a bigoted demagogue is a far greater electoral setback to the cause of racial justice than any King witnessed in his lifetime, a tragedy that makes MLK's insights into the nature of such racism, and into the other maladies of American politics and society, not just relevant but urgently needed.

Freedom Dream and Racist Reality

The public's understanding of MLK's place in America's history has been shaped disproportionately by the most optimistic part of his famed "I Have a Dream" speech that he delivered at the March on Washington in August 1963. Millions of Americans—and generations of students fresh out of high school—who know little or nothing else about King, will know that he was a Black civil rights leader who long ago gave a famous speech about his dream of racial harmony at a huge rally in Washington, D.C. This is because on TV, in classrooms, and the internet they have seen the black and white clips of the part of the 1963 March on Washington during which he discusses the dream and speaks longingly of a future in which his children "will not be judged by the color of their skin but by the content of their character. . . . when the sons of former slaves and the sons of former slaveowners will be able to sit down together at the table of brotherhood."[1] And this part of the speech annually gets extensive media exposure during the Martin Luther King Jr. national holiday, which reinforces the image of King as an idealistic dreamer and a moderate reformer.

On one level we ought to be thankful that Americans are exposed to the egalitarian ideal embodied in King's vision of our nation as one where racism may someday be banished. This is especially true in the current era, where white nationalism has surged in the United States and fascistic far-right movements demonizing non-whites, and especially non-white immigrants, have been on the rise internationally. It is a tribute to Martin Luther King's brilliance and democratic idealism that in 1963, a time when he and the Black Freedom Movement experienced horrendous racist violence in their campaigns for basic rights—including voting, access to public accommodations, and an end to housing and job discrimination—that King was able to see beyond this ugliness and, at the largest civil rights march and rally in American history, share a lofty and beautiful democratic dream of an America liberated from its long history of anti-Black racism.[2]

One can feel the power of this freedom dream even after King was done with the eight sentences in the speech where he specifically referred to his dream of an America liberated from racism. From the dream sentences near the speech's end, King moved into eight "Let freedom ring" sentences where he called for America to strive to end racism, letting "freedom ring" across the north and west, "but not only that. Let freedom ring" even in what had been the Jim Crow South. And then King ended dramatically by affirming that when freedom spreads—banishing bigotry across the whole nation—Blacks and whites, Americans across racial and religious lines "will be able to join hands and sing in the words of the Old Negro spiritual, 'Free at last, free at last, thank God Almighty, we are free at last!'"[3]

Here King envisioned not the form of republicanism that had defined America for so long as a white-dominated polity, relegating Blacks first to slavery and then to second-class citizenship, but rather the realization of the dissident creed of multiracial democracy pioneered by the antebellum abolitionists, Radical Republicans of the Reconstruction era after the Civil War, the founders of the NAACP in the early twentieth century, the civil rights labor unionists of the 1930s and 1940s, and the Black Freedom Movement of the 1950s and 1960s.[4] Placed in this historical perspective one could see in the speech's final sections, a radical break with America's racist past, a roadmap to an America finally becoming a genuine democracy, and King rightly elevated with this speech to the status of an American founder—much as Lincoln had been, complete with a national holiday in his honor—after he became another martyr on behalf of a "new birth of freedom," as Lincoln had put it at Gettysburg. While King was not yet offering an explicit public indictment of American capitalism (which he would in the final years of his life), his message about the deep roots and persistence of racism in the United States, as well as his demand for an immediate shift to racial egalitarianism, placed him well to the left of white America.

But if the egalitarian vision King articulated at the end of this speech was so radical in relation to the American past, why has it so often been used to characterize King as a moderate? This has as much to do with the future as the past, along with King's choice of metaphors, and white America's proclivity for denial where racism is concerned. Since King was describing (in his speech's dream segment) an American future free of racism, his words—taken out of context—enabled white America, especially conservatives, in subsequent decades and our century, to essentially ignore the racist past. And enabled white America to pretend racism, like the South's Jim Crow system, was a fading relic in a supposedly color-blind society, whose Supreme Court even began to speak of a color-blind Constitution, and to argue that such historic civil rights legislation as the Voting Rights Act, which King helped to win, was no longer necessary. Amazingly, right wing advocates have since the late twentieth century managed to convince themselves—by isolating one sentence from the dream segment of King's speech—that MLK was a conservative hero who supported their anemic approach to dealing with racial discrimination.[5]

The dream metaphor itself remains problematic. Dreaming is a passive activity. So it could be read—misread really—as implying that American society could free itself of racism without anti-racist struggle or mass protest. This is something that King never said, or even implied, in this speech at the March on Washington or anywhere else; it runs contrary to his entire experience in the Black Freedom Movement. But this has not stopped conservatives from invoking King to argue that we have somehow moved, despite King's assassination and the decline of the civil rights movement, so close to realizing King's dream that the only threat to its full realization is not persistent anti-Black bigotry but initiatives such as DEI (diversity, equity, and inclusion) programs that supposedly privilege Blacks and discriminate against whites.

The history of the "I Have a Dream" speech's reception compounded this tendency to misread the speech and MLK himself as moderate. Drew Hansen, an attorney and King scholar who authored *The Dream: Martin Luther King, Jr., and the Speech that Inspired a Nation* (2003), the most insightful history of the "I Have a Dream" speech, points out that the biggest media story of August 28, 1963, was not King's speech but the March on Washington itself.[6] It was not only the largest civil rights protest in American history but also startlingly nonviolent to a white news media that associated Blackness with criminality and so expected violence at this predominantly Black event. And while, of course, King's speech was well received, including by President John F. Kennedy who—for reasons that will be discussed below—initially opposed the March on Washington, it was not until King's assassination almost five years later that the reputation of the "I Have a Dream" speech soared.[7] It soared because in an America torn by racial violence, ghetto rebellions, and their suppression by police and National Guard, King, the martyred champion of nonviolence and racial integration, seemed moderate compared to the Black Panthers and other Black Power advocates who championed armed self-defense in the African America community. So King's "I Have a Dream" speech was *recovered*, as Hansen showed—widely reprinted in newspapers and magazines in the wake of his assassination—and King newly appreciated by the American political establishment yearning for what it saw as a less threatening brand of Black leadership.[8]

Not all those who thought of King and his "I Have a Dream" speech as moderate meant that as a compliment. As part of the Black student movement, Anne Moody, who traveled to the March on Washington from Canton, Mississippi, where she had been doing exhausting and dangerous civil rights work, was disappointed with King and the march. In her classic civil rights memoir, *Coming of Age in Mississippi* (1968), Moody wrote, "By the time we got to the Lincoln Memorial, there were already thousands of people there. I sat on the grass and listened to the speakers, to discover we had 'dreamers' instead of leaders leading us. Just about every one of them stood up there dreaming. Martin Luther King went on and on talking about his dream. I sat there thinking that in Canton we [civil rights workers] never had time to sleep, much less dream."[9]

There was an irony to all this because in MLK's years as a civil rights leader the FBI's reactionary leadership, especially FBI director J. Edgar Hoover, pegged King as a dangerous subversive. Hoover bemoaned King's close ties to radicals allegedly in or close to the American Communist Party. FBI fears of King's radicalism and its potential impact only intensified after the success of the March on Washington. William C. Sullivan, Hoover's right-hand man and the FBI's assistant director in charge of its domestic intelligence division, wrote Hoover (a month after the march) that King was "the most dangerous and effective Negro leader in the country," making him a great threat because "we are right now in the nation engaged in a form of social revolution."[10]

While Hoover and Sullivan's hatred for King led the FBI to engage in all kinds of disgraceful and unlawful dirty tricks against the civil right leader, and prodded them to vastly exaggerate the influence of Communists on King, they were not wrong to see King as a radical committed to the kind of racially egalitarian change that the FBI director loathed.[11] The FBI's guilt-by-association reasoning could be simplistic and unfair, but King's radically democratic orientation on race, economics, and global politics did mean that he was not alienated by the egalitarian ideas of others on the left and so drew close to some. And this was potentially hazardous politically in Cold War America because the hysterically anti-Communist mindset that had paved the way for McCarthyism had not died with Joe McCarthy. It was still present in the early 1960s, empowered by the U.S. House Un-American Activities Committee (HUAC), its U.S. Senate counterpart, and state legislative red-hunting committees, as well as the FBI itself. Even President Kennedy was wary of defying these purveyors of anti-radicalism, especially Hoover, given the FBI director's power and influence. So when Hoover informed JFK that people with Communist ties, including MLK's friend and advisor Stanley Levison, were active in King's Southern Christian Leadership Conference (SCLC), the president privately urged that King purge them from the movement.[12]

Since not even the president dared defy the FBI and the anti-Communist demonization it promoted, King as a far less powerful leader could not be expected to do so—at least not openly in the early 1960s. MLK well understood that being tarred as Communist could damage and even discredit the SCLC, the organizational base of his own work on behalf of racial equality. That work he thought was best served by trying to avoid being reduced to pariah status by red-baiters, which meant the SCLC would not publicly associate with the Communist Party and was cautious regarding Communist-affiliated organizations. This was, as historian Barbara Ransby notes, a "strategic" posture adopted to serve a form of respectability politics. King and the other ministers in the SCLC wanted in the early 1960s to locate their politics "squarely within the respectable American mainstream" to be able to say to white America, "We are law-abiding, God-fearing citizens, now give us our rights."[13]

King was well aware, however, of the overlap between bigoted right wingers' red-baiting and race-baiting.[14] This is one reason he often proved skeptical of red-baiting charges hurled against the civil rights movement. King, though not a Communist, was not the least bit convinced by the FBI's claims about Levison, especially since no evidence had been offered to support them. So while King seemingly deferred to the president by temporarily cutting off direct contact with Levison, MLK covertly defied Kennedy by continuing to consult with Levison via intermediaries.[15]

It is also important to understand, as King surely did, that despite all the demonization of Communists, there were good, even admirable, reasons why some of the most experienced and wisest voices near to him in the struggle for racial justice had connections, earlier in their lives, with the Communist Party (CP), the Young Communist League (YCL), or organizations supposedly in the Communist orbit. The Communist Party, the YCL, leftist-led labor unions, and so-called Communist fronts—for all their faults—had a far stronger record of opposing racism than did either major political party. The Democratic Party in the South had been the party of Jim Crow, and by the twentieth century the Republican party had long since abandoned the cause of racial justice associated with Lincoln. Thus it was little wonder that, as a young anti-racist activist, King adviser Bayard Rustin had for a time been a member of the Young Communist League.[16] Or that Stanley Levison had once been a fundraiser for the Communist Party, a role that ended more than three years before JFK ascended to the White House. Hoover, as an eager red-baiter, conveniently failed to mention to President Kennedy that this CP connection had ended.[17]

MLK's having worked so closely with such talented anti-racist advisers with Old Left ties is itself a manifestation of his radicalism and helps to explain why, at least covertly, King engaged in a form of radical political defiance, refusing, even at the request of the president of the United States, to make a pariah out of Levison by ending all contact with him over his alleged Communist ties. In fact, King would remain close to Levison—whose advice to King on political matters tended to lean towards cautiousness rather than militance—until the end of his life. It was, in fact, the FBI's discovery that MLK had not ended his ties to Levison (or moved quickly to fire the other alleged Communist in the SCLC) that led U.S. Attorney General Robert Kennedy to authorize FBI wiretapping of King.[18]

Such defiance attested to MLK's political location on the left and his failure to buy into the FBI's brand of virulent anti-Communism. Moreover, King had good reason much closer to home to reject Cold War anti-radicalism: his wife Coretta Scott King had Old Left connections. As a college student in the late 1940s, she had been a peace and anti-racist activist who played a leading role on her campus in the third-party presidential campaign of Henry Wallace. His opposition to the Cold War and Jim Crow had drawn many Communists and made his Progressive Party an easy target for anti-Communists to charge that it was a Communist front. Coretta Scott King, though no Communist, was much like her husband a democratic radical, but she was as aware as MLK, in the early 1960s, of the need to avoid any overt connection to the Old Left. As she explained in her posthumously published memoir, her pacifism had helped draw her to

> Henry Wallace's Progressive Party, which had a student chapter at Antioch. . . . For a long time, I avoided talking about my Progressive Party affiliation; The party was often accused of having links to communism, and I did not want to besmirch my reputation. Later with the battle J. Edgar Hoover was waging against my husband, I didn't want that past affiliation to become a noose around Martin's neck. But in 1948, I went to the party's national convention in Philadelphia as a student delegate. Its platform sought to end segregation, support voting rights for blacks, and provide national health insurance.[19]

MLK's democratic radicalism was very much on display in his "I Have a Dream" speech. Were it not for the stirring way King spontaneously delivered those eight sentences in the speech's dream segment, their poetic and inspiring character, and location as part of the speech's dramatic ending (or "landing," as preachers call a sermon's conclusion), the speech might have a totally different title and reputation.[20] Not one of the first 44 sentences of the speech mention any dreams or dreaming.[21] As we shall see shortly, the longer, main part of the speech was not about a dream of a future America cured of racism but rather an indictment of the racism that existed in America in 1963, dating all the way back to the founding of the United States. Indeed, if we gave the speech a title that reflected the arguments of the speech's longer opening and middle sections, rather than the shorter dream segment of the speech, it might be called the "We Have a Problem" speech (that is, racism, which needs uprooting) rather than the "I Have a Dream" speech. Or perhaps "The Bad Check" speech or "The Fierce Urgency of Now" speech since those critical and militant words were among the most memorable in King's March on Washington address.

Even before we explore the speech's important opening and middle sections, it needs to be emphasized that the four sentences right before the speech's dream sequence, and intimately connected to it, are not at all dreamy or moderate. Instead, they catalogue the "great trials and tribulations" civil rights workers faced in 1963. King spoke of their "quest for freedom" landing them in "narrow jail cells," "battered by the storms of persecution," and "staggered by the winds of police brutality." He praised the civil rights workers' "redemptive . . . suffering," encouraging them to go back to the deep South to continue the battle against Jim Crow and also to return "to the slums and ghettos of our northern cities" and battle against racial discrimination there.[22]

King ends this civil rights worker narrative segment, and then bridges to the dream segment, by expressing concern that their demanding and dangerous civil rights organizing might leave them demoralized. He urged them to recognize that "somehow this situation," with the racist system they were challenging "can, and will be changed." And he urged that they "not wallow in the valley of despair."[23] To further encourage their continued activism in the movement, he told his fellow civil rights organizers, "My friends . . . even though we face the difficulties of today and tomorrow, I still have a dream."[24] In other words, if you look at the speech's structure and sequence, it is evident that King's immediate goal in spontaneously describing his dream of an America free of racism was to encourage the civil rights workers he had just praised and addressed with such concern not to lose hope, insisting that the future might well bring the new birth of freedom for which they had worked and sacrificed so much. At his most lyrical, King offered this powerful egalitarian vision not to be dreamy or utopian but to define what the prize was, urging his fellow civil right workers, as the freedom song put it, to keep their eyes on the prize. MLK's attempt at such uplift was—as he knew only too well—badly needed by civil rights workers, who had faced death threats, racist terrorism, police harassment, and arrest when they organized against racism.

And just as King concluded his speech's dream segment by affirming his faith that a just God would help make this dream of racial justice and equality a reality, he again linked that dream, and this faith of divine support of it, to the ongoing work of Black Freedom Movement activists. Indeed, here King sought to bolster their morale by assuring them that "with this faith we will be able to hew out of the mountain of despair a stone of hope. With this faith we will be able to transform the jangling discords of our nation into a beautiful symphony of brotherhood."[25] This is not to suggest that King was *only* directing the dream segment—and his whole speech—to movement activists. He understood that he was speaking to the nation via the news media coverage of the march. But it was the enormous rally crowd, filled with grassroots civil rights activists, that he was addressing when he ended his speech's dream segment by affirming that, armed with their faith in the coming triumph of the anti-racist movement, "we will be able . . . to struggle together, to go to jail together, to stand up for freedom together, knowing that we will be free one day."[26]

What this means is that when we look at the way the "I have a dream" segment of King's March on Washington speech was prefaced and concluded we can see that he was not offering his dream of racial justice as a passive act or a sunny abstraction but rather as a fighting faith to inspire the protest, the civil disobedience, necessary to overcome the freedom movement's racist foes.

Nor did King sound moderate in the speech's dream segment when he referred to foes of the movement. He spoke of Mississippi as "a state sweltering with the heat of injustice, sweltering with the heat of oppression." And King referred to Alabama's "vicious racists" and "its governor having his lips dripping with the words of interposition and nullification."[27] King's dream involved the concrete goal of achieving such success in overcoming racism that even so violent a center of resistance to the civil rights movement as Mississippi would be "transformed into an oasis of freedom and justice."[28]

In other words, the dream segment of King's March on Washington speech has been widely misunderstood as moderate, sentimental, and disconnected from militant anti-racist struggle. The evidence, the plain language in that segment (and the meaning of the sentences prefacing and following that segment), which contradicts this moderate image has been ignored. But this is only half of the problem with the way the speech has been misunderstood by the public and misrepresented by politicians. The other half derives from what we might call the soundbite temptation—a tendency to judge the whole speech based on its telegenic "I have a dream" conclusion, which is the only part of the speech that consistently gets airtime and attention. It is like judging an entire feature film only on the basis of its last minute or so.

There is a political dimension to this soundbite temptation and to its impact. Americans are mostly, and have long been, well to the right of MLK politically, so most people focus on the part of the speech that seems not to question the nation's political assumptions. This takes us back to the useful labels Vincent Harding (friend and advisor to MLK) developed, that American memory has distorted and domesticated King, converting him to a "convenient hero" and losing touch with who he really was as a radical thinker and social critic. Convenient because in this diluted form King just reflects back on America its flattering self-perception, unlike King as he really was: Harding's "inconvenient hero" challenging America to confront and address its serious social problems. Applied to King's March on Washington speech, this led to a distorting rush to focus—and focus exclusively—on the dream segment, which imagined America free of racism, and skipping over the most challenging parts of the speech that, as Harding noted, offer a "presentation of the ways in which blacks have been treated so unjustly and his cataloguing of that injustice." This yields a fundamental misreading of both the speech and of King himself because, as Harding explained, spotlighting only the dream leaves Americans "not talking any more about the injustices, the struggle that is necessary to overcome the injustices," which was the subject of most of King's speech.[29]

At the opening of King's March on Washington speech, he quickly turned to Black history. This was MLK discussing not a dream but the historical reality African Americans confronted with slavery and emancipation. Speaking from the steps of the Lincoln Memorial, King praised Abraham Lincoln for issuing the Emancipation Proclamation, "a momentous decree [that] came as a great beacon light of hope to millions of Negro slaves who had been seared in the flames of withering injustice. It came as a joyous daybreak to end the long night of their captivity."[30] But the promise of freedom met with disappointment because anti-Black racism persisted, denying Blacks political rights and economic opportunity not only in the distant past but into the present. In 1963, a century after the Emancipation Proclamation, African Americans were still not free. "The life of the Negro," King observed, "is still sadly crippled by the manacles of segregation and the chains of discrimination. . . . The Negro lives on a lonely island of poverty in the midst of a vast ocean of material prosperity . . . an exile in his own land."[31] A situation that King characterized as "appalling."

The historical viewpoint King opened his speech with, and the imagery and language in it, were deeply critical of America and its long history of anti-Black racism. He offered the kind of criticism that has been banned from schools in red states in our own time, when conservatives have contested and invested considerable effort to suppress critical race theory (CRT) and The 1619 Project's historical review of American slavery, holding that such deeply considered indictments of America for its anti-Black racism are "divisive" and might hurt the feelings of, and psychologically damage, white students.[32] By pointing out the unfulfilled promise of the Emancipation

Proclamation and the endurance of racism a century later, King, much like critical race theorists, presented racial discrimination as systemic and, even after slavery, a permanent feature of American society from 1863 to 1963 at least (though he did have faith that mass protest and federal legislation could one day overcome the racist past). In this narrative, King both established the endurance of racism and highlighted the severity of its oppressiveness into mid-twentieth century America, using the harsh imagery of slavery when he spoke of "the manacles of segregation and the chains of discrimination."[33] And like The 1619 Project, King began his account of American history not with the Founders and their liberal revolution against monarchy in 1776 but rather with America at it most illiberal: its chattel slavery and the unfulfilled promise of the Emancipation Proclamation.

This was not the first time that King, who since his youth had been well-schooled in African American history, brought into his political discourse the Emancipation Proclamation and its failure to yield racial justice. In May 1962 (more than a year prior to the March on Washington), King wrote President John F. Kennedy on the need to follow up on Lincoln's Emancipation Proclamation. He urged Kennedy to use the approaching centennial of the Proclamation in 1963 as the occasion for issuing a Second Emancipation Proclamation, abolishing racial segregation as dramatically as Lincoln had acted to abolish slavery. In fact, King sent President Kennedy a draft of this proposed document, which his lawyers had spent more than six months preparing. King asked the president to "proclaim all segregation statutes of all southern states to be contrary to the Constitution, and that the full powers of his office be used to avoid their enforcement."[34]

Had Kennedy issued this proclamation, which King saw as a "logical and compelling short cut to racial justice," it would have, as King biographer Taylor Branch noted, shaken "American politics and reverberate[d] throughout the world."[35] But President Kennedy, who came into office as a cautious moderate on race—who dared not even mention the civil rights movement or a civil rights agenda in his inaugural address—never issued such a proclamation. Fearful of alienating white Southern voters and segregationists who chaired key Congressional committees, JFK failed even to respond to King's letter proposing a Second Emancipation Proclamation.[36]

The historical segment of King's March on Washington speech went even further back than Lincoln to the Founders. Much like his discussion of the Emancipation Proclamation, King presented the Constitution and

Declaration of Independence as freedom-oriented documents that America had failed to honor with regard to Black freedom and racial justice. King credited "the architects of our republic" with composing the "magnificent words" they embedded in the Constitution and Declaration of Independence, but he complained that "the unalienable Rights of Life, Liberty, and the pursuit of Happiness" that the Founders promised had been denied to African Americans.[37] King compared this unfulfilled promise, America's default "on this promissory note" for freedom, to a "bad check" that had been foisted upon Blacks. King expressed his refusal "to believe that the bank of justice is bankrupt . . . that there are insufficient funds in the great vaults of opportunity of this nation."[38] And so the Black Freedom Movement and its great march had, in King's words, "come to cash this check—a check that will give us upon demand the riches of freedom and the security of justice."[39]

In this "bad check" part of King's historical discussion, he was accusing America—and albeit only implicitly, by extension, its Founders—of criminality. After all, passing a bad check constitutes fraud, and fraud is a crime. And in the historical discussion King offered, as we have seen, of America's revered founding documents, the Declaration of Independence and Constitution, though perhaps inadvertently, became part of this fraud since they made promises that went unfulfilled: they offered the text for the bad check. This is a powerful indictment of America as first a slaveholding republic and later a segregated and racially discriminatory nation. It contradicts white America's self-perception of the nation as a beacon of liberty and democracy, the conceit of American exceptionalism.

Yet it is also true that this radical critique was expressed diplomatically, as inoffensively as was possible, toward white America and its heroes. King did not *explicitly* accuse James Madison or the Constitution's other authors, or Thomas Jefferson and his co-authors of the Declaration of Independence, of fraud. And, as we have seen, he even praised as "magnificent" the Constitution's words about liberty and opportunity. So it may not have been them or the documents they wrote but rather "America" (whatever that means) that in King's view bore prime responsibility for not sharing in the liberties enumerated by the Founders, denying freedom to African Americans, and thereby "defaulting on the promissory note" drafted. The language King used to identify the key culprits in the "bad check" crime was so imprecise that you must read it very carefully to realize that his indictment includes the Founders, as well as the nation they helped create, for falling short of the republic's liberal founding documents. This critique is powerful and radical yet expressed with much more subtlety than his condemnation later in the speech (in the "I have a dream" segment) of Alabama's "vicious racists." In the speech he never denounced the Founders, even the slaveholders among them, as vicious or racist. This reflects a strategic decision by King rhetorically and politically.

King wanted to see the founding document's liberal rhetoric and America's democratic ideals—which much of the Black Freedom Movement embraced and championed—finally applied to Black Americans, so it would have made no sense to discredit their authors by explicitly calling them out as racists or hypocrites. This same kind of rhetorical restraint recurs near the end of King's March on Washington speech, where—shortly after the "I have a dream" sentences—MLK looked forward to the day when America finally lived up to its egalitarian ideals, so "all of God's children [regardless of race] will be able to sing with new meaning" the patriotic song "My country 'tis of thee, sweet land of liberty, of thee I sing, Land where my fathers died, land of the pilgrim's pride, From every mountainside, let freedom ring!"[40] And then, as we have seen, King used the "Let freedom ring" phrase (in eight sentences) to herald the spread of racially inclusive freedom across America. So King was interested in invoking America's democratic ideals on behalf of racial justice, and while eloquent in pointing out the nation's hypocrisy in failing to live up to those ideals, he did so in a way that was not dismissive of those ideals or their authors. Also, later in the speech, King warned against Blacks seeking "to satisfy our thirst for freedom by drinking from the cup of bitterness and hatred."[41] Thus while MLK would offer a powerful critique of America's grim history of racial discrimination, he phrased that critique carefully so as not to come across as rancorous. And since the March on Washington came as Congress was finally considering the Kennedys' long-delayed civil rights bill, it made no sense to MLK to risk alienating JFK and leaders on Capitol Hill by harshly denouncing America's founders and their ideals.

Even so, careful as King was not to mock the Founders, his "bad check" metaphor and the historical evidence used to back it show that he was not a moderate accommodationist. He was a dissident whose understanding of African American history—an understanding shared by those in his inner circle, who he consulted on the speech—ran deep. This Black historical sensibility led him to a far more critical reading of U.S. history than the one then in vogue among most white Americans in 1963 (and even in our own century) who, if they thought about slavery and Jim Crow at all, regarded such injustices as fleeting aberrations in America's glorious democratic history rather than as the deep, enduring flaws in that history, which King saw and condemned.

MLK's understanding of the history of American racism was far deeper and more brutally candid than he indicated in his "I Have a Dream speech which, as mentioned above, he modulated so as to be able to invoke the Founders' liberal ideas on behalf of Black freedom. In his books, however, MLK did not hold back on this. For example, in King's second book, *Why We Can't Wait* (1964), he wrote that "our nation was born in genocide when it embraced the doctrine that the original American, the Indian, was an inferior race." This had led to a "national policy to wipe out its indigenous population." And rather than face this hard truth about early American racism, white America "elevated that tragic experience into a noble crusade," and the nation's "literature . . . films . . . drama . . . folklore all exalt it."[42] Similarly, in his last book, *Where Do We Go from Here: Chaos or Community?* (1967), King criticized the Founders far more directly than in the "I Have a Dream" speech. This book characterized George Washington as "a fourth-generation slaveholder" who, though privately expressing sympathy for slavery's abolition, "never made a public statement condemning slavery," and "when he died he owned, or had on lease, more than 160 slaves."[43] As to Washington's fellow Founders, who "we cherish as our authentic heroes," they "were so enmeshed in the ethos of slavery and white supremacy that not one ever emerged with a clear, unambiguous stand on Negro rights."[44]

* * *

Although MLK, then, could have—if he desired—done more in his "I Have a Dream" speech to confront white America with its racist past, the history that he did cover from that podium was in its own way quite hard-hitting. So much so that, as Vincent Harding correctly observed, the parts of King's March on Washington speech that rarely get discussed on MLK Day catalog the injustices Black Americans faced in the past and continue to face. And it is not only his critical presentation of this injustice that is so striking but also the impatience King displayed with white incomprehension of the

Black demand for freedom, which in the movement was not a demand for freedom next month, next year, or next century, but for freedom *now*. Undoubtedly recalling demands from the Kennedy administration and other white moderates for a "cooling off" period after the Freedom Rides and the racial conflict in Birmingham, King, only a few minutes into the speech, said that the marchers had come to Washington "to remind America of the fierce urgency of now." MLK rejected the idea of a "cooling off" period to calm the waters on race and delay further Black protest, warning against "the tranquilizing drug of gradualism." Instead, he insisted, "Now is the time to make real the promises of democracy."[45]

Later in the speech, King returned to this kind of impatient juxtaposition of white incomprehension and Black understanding of racial inequality and to the need for mass protest to be liberated from that inequality. In fact, the speech's most extensive description of the racist oppression confronting Black America came as King responded to "those who are asking the devotees of civil rights 'When will you be satisfied?'"[46] He began answering this question by citing the issue that over a half century later would ignite the Black Lives Matter protests, the most widespread anti-racist demonstrations in twenty-first century America: police brutality. "We can never be satisfied as long as the Negro is the victim of the unspeakable horrors of police brutality."[47] Next he said that Blacks could not be satisfied so long as their "bodies heavy with the fatigue of travel cannot gain lodging" because the color line barred them from motels and hotels. Job and housing discrimination, Black children "stripped of their selfhood and robbed of their dignity" by "whites only" signs, and the denial of the right to vote, all made it impossible for African Americans to be satisfied, to prematurely end their agitation for basic human rights. Going further on the failure of the American political system, King held that it was not only the denial of Black voting rights in the South that was the problem but also the cowardice of politicians in the North to address the issue of racial discrimination. As King put it, "We cannot be satisfied as long as a Negro in Mississippi cannot vote and a Negro in New York believes he has nothing for which to vote."[48]

King concluded listing the unfair treatment, the discrimination, Blacks faced with an answer to the question of when African Americans would be satisfied. That would happen when "justice rolls down like waters and righteousness like a mighty stream."[49] This gorgeous phrase's origins were biblical, from the book of Amos. It was natural for King as a preacher to cite a biblical justification for the Black Freedom Movement's quest for justice. And this was a way of making his radical indictment of racism seem somehow mainstream, as if you were in church or Sunday school discussing the difference between righteousness and sin. Here again, then, we find King exposing racism as a radical critic of America, yet doing so in a way that minimizes its offensiveness to whites, aligning that criticism with the nation's reverence for Christianity and the Bible.

Later in the speech, King again offered a kind of hybrid form of support for ongoing Black protest, expressed in a way that, while radically pro-agitation, would also be reassuring to whites. This was in the speech's brief section on nonviolence, stressing the need for the movement to avoid violence, bitterness, and anti-white hatred. Yet at the same time King praised "the marvelous new militancy which has engulfed the Negro community."[50] Thus unlike moderates, King regarded Black militancy as admirable and necessary. Not only that, he warned white America that it would be a mistake to assume Blacks would calm down and acquiesce to the racially discriminatory status quo and that "the Negro" had been engaged in protest merely because of the need to "blow off steam." Those holding such assumptions were in for "a rude awakening." As a prediction or perhaps promise, he declared, "The whirlwinds of revolt will continue to shake the foundations of our nation until the bright day of justice emerges."[51]

With regard to economic injustice, near the start of his "I Have a Dream" speech, King mentioned the immorality of Black poverty being allowed to persist in a nation as rich as the United States. This connected with the March on Washington's economic agenda—its now largely forgotten initial focus on class as well as race, demanding that the federal government battle poverty and eliminate unemployment by creating a massive jobs and anti-poverty program and by supporting the rights of labor. This reflected the march's roots in the labor movement and the fact that the very idea for the march came from the dean of Black labor and civil rights leaders, A. Philip Randolph. A generation earlier, on the eve of the United States' entry into World War II, Randolph, founder of the Black labor union called the Brotherhood of Sleeping Car Porters, launched and led the March on Washington Movement, whose threat to hold a mass Black march on Washington demanding an end to job discrimination in defense plants (as well as an end to segregation in the military) compelled President Franklin Roosevelt to create a Fair Employment Practices Commission, tasked with ending racial discrimination in the defense industry.[52] Though the economic demands of the 1963 March on Washington have been largely forgotten by the public, since the issue of racism proved so central to the speeches of King and others who addressed the marchers, the need for federal intervention against economic inequity and unemployment was also a high priority. This was reflected in the very name of this great mass protest, which was the March on Washington for Jobs and Freedom.[53] In fact, labor unions brought bus, train, and planeloads of members to Washington, D.C., forming a disciplined, organized core for the march.

Try as conservatives might to claim King's speech for their vision of America as a color-blind society, for which militant anti-racist agitation and government intervention against discrimination are not needed and are counterproductive, too much in his most famous oration just does not fit into their misreading of King's speech. His praise for such agitation, his criticism of the federal government for providing too little anti-racist intervention since the American republic's founding, push in the exact opposite direction of white America's right wing and its condemnation of such intervention on anti-statist grounds. In fact, the speech's most effusive praise for America comes in that rare moment when the government finally takes anti-racist action, striking out against racial slavery with Lincoln's Emancipation Proclamation, which offered "a great beacon light of hope" for Blacks by elevating their human right to freedom above the property rights of treasonous Confederate slaveowners. But as we have seen, King expressed disappointment that this had not been followed by sufficient government action to ensure the protection of Black rights, resulting in century of racial discrimination.

As to conservatism, regarding race, what was there to conserve in a nation with such a long history of trampling Black political and legal rights, perpetuating racial discrimination that hampered Black economic opportunity? That at its founding passed a bad check to Black America on the promise of freedom? There was no place at all in King's "I Have a Dream" speech for the empty-headed nostalgia of Donald Trump's "Make America Great Again" (MAGA) slogan so beloved by his MAGA movement. In fact, King made it clear that claims of American greatness were a spurious national conceit that clashed with the nation's endemic racial discrimination. America could only *become* great if it ended its racist behavior, as King concluded near the speech's end: "If America is to be a great nation, this [vision of a society liberated from its racist past] must become true."[54] And if you reflect on the Black spiritual lyrics with which King so dramatically ended the speech, they invoke a memory of America's past as constituting the equivalent of a *long* prison sentence for Blacks, from which they needed to be freed. That when such liberation from the racist past would *finally* be won by the freedom movement, Americans of all races and religions could *at long last* together sing [emphasis added]: "Free *at last*! Free *at last*! Thank God Almighty, we are free *at last*!"[55]

Thus far we have dealt only with the words King spoke in his most famous speech. It was, however, not just the words but the way he delivered them from the podium that mattered. Ever since King's years as a young student, his poetic sensibility, ability to draw on the Black Church tradition of dramatic and emotional preaching, and his compelling baritone had left people impressed with his oratory. His experience both in church pulpits and at movement rallies had afforded him many opportunities to hone his impressive speaking skills. And since much of white America had never heard him speak before, his March on Washington speech seemed yet more powerful and dazzling. Few knew that King had used the improvised dream metaphor segment in at least three prior speeches.[56] Of course, it was not only the speech's delivery that was powerful. So was the beauty of King's dream, his ability to envision American democracy with racism removed, and Blacks being treated equally in a more perfect union.

But being attracted to the dream at the end of the speech must not prevent us from paying attention to the bulk of the speech that focused on the grim historical reality of American racism and those courageous activists battling against it. When you add up King's critique—the "bad check" and failed promise of even America's greatest freedom documents, from the Declaration of Independence to the Emancipation Proclamation, to ensure freedom and equality to Blacks; his cataloging of Black oppression, from disenfranchisement and police brutality to Jim Crowism and Black poverty; his praise for militant anti-racist protest; and his rejection of calls for gradualism in favor of immediate Black freedom, "the fierce urgency of now"—it constitutes both a call to anti-racist action and a radical review of America and its racism, past and present. Yet this was radicalism that came off as less alienating to non-radicals because of the skillful way King used biblical imagery, invocations of God, a minister's call to righteousness, and even lyrics from the patriotic song "My Country, 'Tis of Thee" (also known as "America") to give the message a softer tone and a mainstream-like veneer, but it was radicalism all the same.

This leads to the question of radical in relation to whom and what? Certainly when compared to discourse in white America, King's speech was radical. Its searching criticism of American racism to this day is overlooked, and the focus is on the most idealistic part of the speech's conclusion envisioning a racism-free America. But in a Black context, of other civil rights movement leaders who addressed that enormous, majority Black, March on Washington crowd, it was not King's speech that was seen by movement organizers as the most radical but rather that of John Lewis, chairman of the Student Nonviolent Coordinating Committee (SNCC). This was in part because Lewis—who collaborated with several of his comrades in drafting his speech, which reflected SNCC's revolutionary spirit—spoke of the movement as a "serious revolution."[57] Lewis critiqued as inadequate the civil rights bill that President Kennedy had belatedly introduced, mocked both the Democratic and Republican parties for harboring foes of civil rights legislation, dwelled upon the exploitation of Mississippi's Black sharecroppers, and in the speech's initial draft angrily dismissed calls for delay and patience in the struggle for racial equality by denouncing patience as "a dirty and nasty word." And quite dramatically, Lewis in that first draft pledged that the movement would "march through the South, the heart of Dixie, the way Sherman did . . . and burn Jim Crow to the ground—nonviolently."[58]

The radical reputation of Lewis's speech derives, above all, from the fact that he was the only March on Washington speaker who generated a censorship dispute. After seeing an advanced copy of Lewis's speech, Washington D.C.'s Catholic archbishop, Patrick O'Boyle, objected to its inflammatory tone and said he would not give the opening invocation at the March's rally if Lewis delivered that speech. At the urging of A. Philip Randolph, the March's senior leader and organizer, Lewis reluctantly agreed to last-minute changes that removed several of the speech's most hard-edged phrases.[59] But the speech as finally delivered retained much of SNCC's militant spirit, offering scorching criticism of America's institutional racism and exploitation of impoverished Blacks.

There is no question, then, that Lewis's speech was seen as the most radical one at the March on Washington, but it would be a mistake to conclude that King's was not. Their speeches were in important respects similar. Most of their differences were over the style and tone of their rhetoric, and they differed in their tactical approach to dealing with the Kennedy administration. Style and tone led to Lewis's conflict with the archbishop, who was most offended by Lewis's harsh words about patience, since Catholics regard it as a virtue. But King's speech had made the same point as Lewis, rejecting gradualism as a "tranquilizing drug" and explaining why Blacks could no longer wait for their freedom, which they demanded immediately. Lewis and King even used similar arguments against gradualism, as when both cited how intolerable police brutality was. However, their language differed. Lewis was heavy-handed with the adjectives he chose to denounce the very idea of patience, while King, as a more memorable phrase-maker, composed "the fierce urgency of now" to explain why Blacks could not abide any delay in attaining their rights. This was merely a rhetorical difference, a distinction without a difference. Similarly, both Lewis and King supported a militant struggle to overturn America's white supremacist tradition. Lewis's speech was more explicit in characterizing it as a social revolution, though King in his books and other writings had also used the word "revolution."[60]

On the Kennedy administration, Lewis was willing at the March on Washington to criticize the president, his leadership team, and party, as well as the proposed civil rights act's loopholes, while King was not. This was not because MLK was too moderate to challenge Kennedy or was in the pocket of the Democratic Party. In fact, the year before the March on Washington, King had published in *The Nation* an article titled "Fumbling on the New Frontier" that offered major criticisms of the Kennedy administration's civil rights record, characterizing it as "cautious and defensive."[61] King charged that in the area of executive initiatives on behalf of civil rights, President Kennedy had become "increasingly feeble," signaling "the chilling prospect . . . of a general administration in retreat." While crediting Kennedy's Department of Justice with blazing "some new trails . . . in the sensitive areas of [Black] voting and registration" in the South, he took JFK to task for "backing away from" his campaign promise to issue "an Executive Order to end discrimination in housing" and for failing to invest his political capital in disempowering the Jim Crow South's Senate filibuster caucus, so as to pave the way for major civil rights legislation.[62]

King's critical take on the Kennedy administration's initially weak civil rights record was also evident in his response to the famously stormy meeting that occurred in May 1963 between President Kennedy's brother, Attorney General Robert F. Kennedy, author James Baldwin, and a group of prominent African Americans who Baldwin had invited. Here Jerome Smith, a young Freedom Rider, who had been assaulted and badly injured by white supremacists in the South, rebuked the attorney general for his administration's lethargy on civil right. Smith shocked Kennedy by saying he would not fight to defend the United States and that if he picked up a gun it would be against racists who attacked him. Smith said that even being in the same room with Kennedy "made him want to vomit."[63] The meeting ended in discord, word of it leaked out, and it was front page news in *The New York Times* the next day. Among those present at this meeting was famed singer and civil rights activist Harry Belafonte, who worried that the meeting and the publicity it generated had damaged the movement by alienating Kennedy. This is why Belafonte told MLK, who had phoned to inquire about the meeting, that it been a "disaster." But as Belafonte noted in his memoir, "[W]hen I relayed Jerome Smith's fighting words, Martin had a different view. 'Maybe it's just what Bobby needs to hear,' he said. 'He's going to hear a lot more of it if the President keeps dawdling on that civil rights bill.'"[64]

By mid-June 1963, however, prodded by the media coverage of the racist violence that King and the Black Freedom Movement faced in the Birmingham struggle, and by the obstinate segregationist resistance to the federal court orders integrating the University of Alabama and the University of Mississippi, President Kennedy finally shifted on civil rights, making a televised address defining Black rights as a moral issue, which represented a first step in introducing legislation later enacted as the historic Civil Rights Act of 1964.[65] This is not to say that by June 1963 JFK had totally dropped his cautiousness on civil rights. In fact, Kennedy—out of concern that a mass march on Washington might alienate needed votes in Congress for the civil rights legislation—initially urged the civil rights leadership to cancel the march, something that King and the other key leaders refused to do, though JFK eventually came to support the march.[66]

The crucial point for King, however, was that Kennedy, by the summer of 1963, had finally responded to the freedom movement by introducing a civil rights bill that constituted a major attack on the Jim Crow system and on racial discrimination nationally. This left King disinclined to criticize the Kennedy administration in his "I Have a Dream" speech. In this sense one could say that, unlike Lewis, King was speaking as more of a pragmatic radical, one who wanted to preserve his fragile alliance with JFK on civil rights legislation that, with all its limitations, looked to be the most significant federal action on Black rights since the Reconstruction era. It is also true, however, that despite his reservations, Lewis in his March on Washington speech did mention his "support of the administration's civil rights bill," so he was not devoid of pragmatism.[67]

Whether politically prudent or not, with regard to the Kennedy administration, it was John Lewis who spoke truth to power in his March on Washington speech. Among the reservations Lewis mentioned about the Kennedy administration's civil rights bill was that it would "not help the thousands of black people" in the South, "who want to vote"; that the bill offered "nothing to protect the young children and old women who must face police dogs and fire hoses in the South while they engage in peaceful demonstrations"; nor would it "protect the hundreds and thousands of" civil rights workers arrested on trumped up charges. "What about the three young men, SNCC field secretaries who face the death penalty for engaging in peaceful protest? . . . We must have legislation that will protect the Mississippi sharecropper who is put off his land because he dares to register to vote."[68]

Going beyond the issue of civil rights legislation, Lewis chastised the Kennedy administration for not waging a war on poverty to aid "the homeless and starving people of this nation" and for its indifference, or worse, to the abuse of civil rights workers in the deep South. Lewis charged that nine SNCC organizers in Albany, Georgia, were "indicted not by the Dixiecrats, but by the federal government for peaceful protest." "What did the federal government do when Albany's deputy sheriff beat attorney C. B. King and left him half-dead? What did the federal government do when local officials kicked and assaulted the pregnant wife of Slater King, and she lost her baby?" Lewis accused Kennedy's party and its Republican opposition of lacking leaders willing to "stand up for" racial justice and equality. "For the party of Kennedy is also the party of [Mississippi's segregationist Senator John] Eastland. The party of [New York's liberal Republican Senator Jacob] Javits is also the party of [Arizona Senator Barry] Goldwater [who opposed civil rights legislation]. Where is our party? Where is the party that will make it unnecessary to march on Washington?" And unlike King, who ended his speech with a dream and a chance to imagine an America free of racism, Lewis ended by demanding that America face it racism, past and present, and remake the Jim Crow South in "the image of God and democracy." Calling upon America not to dream but to "Wake up . . . Wake up!"[69]

There was one issue, however, to which neither Lewis nor King had themselves woken up in 1963. With regard to gender, both men's speeches were disappointing. And so was the leadership of the march when it came to valuing the voices of women in the movement. In this chapter I could not compare King's speech with that given by a woman leader of the movement because initially no woman was invited to speak at the march by its male leadership. And when prominent women in the movement complained, the response was to allot so little time to NAACP organizer Daisy Bates that she was able to do little more than express solidarity with the march.[70] Neither King nor Lewis said a word in their March on Washington speeches about gender inequity nor on what we would today call LGBTQ+ rights. In the lead-up to the march, however, homophobia did become an issue. Strom Thurmond, South Carolina's militantly segregationist senator, engaged in ugly gay-baiting of Bayard Rustin in the hopes of ousting him from movement leadership and disrupting the planning of the march. To their credit, thanks to the leadership of A. Philip Randolph, both King and the other march leaders backed their colleague and would not remove Rustin from his key role.[71]

Lewis's speech is a useful reminder that, prominent as he was, King was only one of the important leaders of the Black Freedom Movement, both nationally and locally. By 1963 there were, especially in SNCC and the Congress of Racial Equality (CORE) ranks and in the Black student movement, anti-racist organizers who were as dedicated as King to the freedom struggle, with some even more radical than King. The key point is that we ought not view MLK in isolation from the mass protest movement that made possible his emergence as a national leader. King's great talent, especially as an orator, strengthened the freedom movement, but without that movement, the fame, movement victories, and historic civil rights legislation associated with MLK would never have occurred.[72]

To take just one example, King's "I Have a Dream" speech in 1963 was not the first speech he gave at a major civil rights event in Washington. Back in May 1957, on the third anniversary of *Brown v. Board of Education of Topeka*, King spoke from the Lincoln Memorial at the Prayer Pilgrimage for Freedom, a civil rights march held to urge federal intervention on behalf of racial integration and Black rights. King's speech on behalf of voting rights, "Give Us the Ballot," was powerful, but coming as it did, when the civil rights movement was in something of a lull, the event drew a smaller than expected crowd of twenty-five thousand, and the speech attracted relatively little news media attention.[73] This was quite a contrast to the 1963 March on Washington, held in the wake of Birmingham's dramatic civil rights struggle, whose brutal police suppression (with police dogs and high-powered fire hoses used against nonviolent protesters) and the movement's hard-fought victory generated national media coverage and a huge wave of civil rights protests across the United States. This electric political atmosphere and the grassroots voting rights work that SNCC and CORE initiated in the deep South helped pave the way for the enormous crowd of more than two hundred thousand that joined the March on Washington in August 1963. The unprecedented size of the event is what gave King's "I Have a Dream" speech the national news coverage lacking in 1957, adding to his fame as the civil right movement's most eloquent and charismatic leader.

This is important because it means that a narrow biographical focus on King cannot do justice to the civil rights movement's multilayered history. The national movement was composed of scores of local movements, many of which connected with the regional and national civil rights organizations, SNCC, CORE, the NAACP (and its youth branches), and not necessarily with King and his SCLC.[74] For big national events, like the March on Washington, they all came together. But such events were rare, and it is somewhat misleading to think—as the March on Washington video clips seem to suggest every MLK Day—that the freedom movement centered on such mass rallies and media events. Actually, most crucial movement organizing was neither televised nor telegenic. It occurred below the radar screen of the news media, such as the door-to-door canvassing done by voting rights workers seeking to recruit Southern Blacks to take the risk of entering hostile, white-controlled courthouses and attempt to register to vote.[75] SNCC organizers did this kind of organizing while embedded in deep South Black communities and living with local Black families. Their largest events were not mass rallies in D.C. but rather intimate African American community meetings held in local Black churches.

None of this detracts from MLK's importance but rather enables us to put into context his leadership role in this enormous, complex mass movement. That context comes to mind when one considers the way King biographer Taylor Branch subtitled his three-volume history on the era of King's civil rights movement leadership: *America in the King Years*. This new way of labeling this era of America's history is appealing, since it suggests that the moral agenda of America on human rights and racial justice in the wake of the *Brown* decision, from the Montgomery bus boycott up until King's assassination, was set by MLK and not presidents Eisenhower, Kennedy, and Johnson. This is a novel and useful way to break with traditional textbook U.S. history—wedded to the presidential synthesis—that named eras after their presidents and their domestic and international agendas. And it is true that MLK labored to push all three of these presidents—most successfully with JFK and LBJ—to move more quickly and sweepingly on civil rights than they would have on their own. But it is problematic to ascribe that moral impetus and influence to King alone.

After all, the Black student movement's direct action through sit-ins in 1960 helped revive mass Black protest with the largest civil disobedience campaign in American history. In 1961 CORE ignited the most serious racial crisis in the Kennedy presidency's first year by launching the Freedom Rides. SNCC's intrepid volunteers saved the Freedom Rides by replacing the CORE riders who were injured by racist thugs. This crisis pressured Kennedy to finally get the Interstate Commerce Commission to bar racial discrimination in interstate bus travel. The NAACP won desegregation orders for the University of Mississippi in 1962 and the University of Alabama in 1963, and their progress, combined with the integration struggle King led in Birmingham, yielded the crises pushing JFK to finally make civil rights a legislative priority. SNCC initiated the early 1960s Mississippi voting rights crusade and Freedom Summer in 1964, and its voter registration work in Selma, Alabama, paved the way for King's historic voting rights campaign there. The Selma struggle yielded the televised racist police brutality on the Edmund Pettus Bridge on "Bloody Sunday" (March 7, 1965), sparking a national political crisis and leading LBJ to demand a legislative response that resulted in the Voting Rights Act of 1965. Although it was more succinct for Branch to call these the King years, it is more accurate to call them the King-SNCC-CORE-SCLC-NAACP years.

Black America's political diversity was not limited, however, even to these central organizations of the civil rights movement. It also encompassed Black nationalists, best represented in the early 1960s by the Nation of Islam—"the Black Muslims"—that Malcolm X represented with such incendiary eloquence. In fact, this wide political spectrum enabled King to represent himself, despite his radical social criticism, as mainstream, reasonable, and open to negotiation and even compromise (on tactical questions but not on the ultimate goal of eliminating racial discrimination). This side of King could make him seem moderate to white liberals wary of Malcolm's angry anti-white rhetoric. Even more so because the way King advocated the inclusive ideal of racial integration assured whites that America, despite its flaws, could make progress on racial justice and, as the motto of King's SCLC indicated, have its soul redeemed if it rejected racism. This helped to give King crossover appeal beyond Black America to non-racist whites and is why so keen an observer of the civil rights movement as David Halberstam referred to King as "the great and shrewd centrist of the movement," the pragmatist who could "brilliantly appeal to white America."[76]

Although King did not utter Halberstam's word "centrist" in his March on Washington speech, that speech's use of the Bible, patriotic song, the country's founding documents, and especially the "I have a dream" and "Let freedom ring" segments can all be viewed as having crossover appeal. King came closer to explicitly embracing that centrist identity several months before the March on Washington during the Birmingham civil rights crusade. In his "Letter from Birmingham Jail," written in April 1963 and rebutting local, white "moderate" religious leaders who had criticized that crusade as extremist, MLK at one point denied this charge by placing himself and his nonviolent movement in the center of the Black political spectrum. On one side of that spectrum was, King explained, a segment of middle-class African Americans, characterized by "complacency," that "as a result of long years of oppression" had been "drained of self-respect" and so "adjusted to segregation."[77] At the political spectrum's other end were Black nationalists, so afflicted by "bitterness and hatred" that they came "perilously close to advocating violence." Thus King argued that "I stand in the middle of" those "two opposing forces in the Negro community," emulating neither "the 'do-nothingism' of the complacent [n]or the hatred and despair of the black nationalist," but instead working to end Black oppression through "the more excellent way of love and nonviolent protest."[78]

Yet King could not be satisfied with this kind of centrist identity, since he knew all too well that his embrace of an ethos of nonviolence and love and use of mass civil disobedience to battle racial discrimination placed him far to the left of mainstream American politics. This is what King had in mind, in his "Letter from Birmingham Jail," when he went on to defend extremism, if it was extremism in defense of love, as was the case with Jesus who preached "Love your enemies" (Matthew 5:44), or in defense of justice and righteousness, as Amos did with his words "Let justice roll down like waters and righteousness like an ever-flowing stream" (Amos 5:24). And as Lincoln also did, when he argued in his "House Divided" speech (1858) that "the nation cannot survive half-slave and half free." Although he was "initially disappointed" that his white clergy critics in Birmingham had categorized him as an extremist, when King recalled that Jesus, Amos, and Lincoln had been extremists on behalf of love and justice, he noted, "as I continued to think about the matter I gradually gained a measure of satisfaction from the [extremist] label. Perhaps the South, the nation, and the world are in dire need of [such loving,] creative extremists."[79]

On some level, however, it was less King's self-definition—in all its complexity, both radically egalitarian in its politics and seemingly mainstream in its Christian universalism—than the white observer's own political orientation that determined whether MLK was seen as centrist or extremist. For those fearful Birmingham clergy that King addressed in his open letter from jail, he had seemed extreme in his civil disobedience campaign demanding an immediate end to Jim Crowism. But for such liberals as James Reston, the famed *New York Times* columnist who wrote the front-page article on King's March on Washington speech, it was King's idealistic "I have a dream" segment—not the speech's indictment of America's long history of racism—that linked him to and "echoed" the best of the nation's reform tradition, from Roger Williams's call for religious liberty and Samuel Adams's pleas for political liberty to William Lloyd Garrison's advocacy of abolitionism, Henry David Thoreau's opposition to coercion, and Eugene V. Debs's cries for economic equality.[80]

Front-page stories, of the sort that Reston wrote on King's oratory, can be seen as evidence that Taylor Branch's use of the phrase "King era" is not as big a break with the presidential synthesis as it might seem at first glance. Branch does depart from the textbook tendency to label eras with concepts connected to presidents of the United States, like Kennedy's New Frontier, articulated as a presidential candidate in July 1960, and Johnson's Great Society, introduced on university campuses in May 1964. But as the late SNCC and Mississippi Freedom Summer leader Robert P. Moses explained in an oral history interview, King was, in important respects, perceived by the news media and the American public as the president of the Black Freedom Movement, who generated news coverage whenever he traveled or spoke, much as the president of the United States did.[81] This was especially true in the wake of the March on Washington and King winning the Nobel Peace

Prize in 1964, an honor that none of the three Cold Warrior presidents of the King era ever received. So the "King years" term is not inappropriate, as long as it does not obscure the full range of movement activists and leaders—including Black nationalist dissenters such as Malcom X, who derided the March on Washington as the "farce on Washington"—and their role in shaping the struggle for racial justice.

* * *

King's leadership in the movement, his Noble Peace Prize, his tragic assassination, his martyrdom on behalf of social justice, the national holiday and national memorial that honor him in the nation's capital, signal his rise in the late twentieth and twenty-first centuries to a celestial status, equivalent to that of the founders of the American republic. This means that King's words have a great deal of cultural and political capital. And so they are invoked to support, to legitimate, all kinds of political causes. This is especially so with regard to the "I Have a Dream" speech, which has become so iconic and widely quoted that it is as closely associated with King and American democracy as the Declaration of Independence is with Thomas Jefferson and the Constitution is with James Madison.

This canonization has, as we have seen, its positive side in honoring one of America's greatest champions of social justice. But it has also led to an absurd misreading and distortion of King's ideas, and especially his speech. MLK lived for almost five years after that public address. If our understanding of King is limited to that one speech in August 1963, we miss how the tragic and polarizing events between 1963 and his death in April 1968 impacted his ideas, public discourse, and oratory. These included the horrific racist bombing of 16th Street Baptist Church in Birmingham that killed four young African American girls, only weeks after the March on Washington; the assassinations of Medgar Evers and President Kennedy; the voting rights workers murdered in Mississippi before and during Freedom Summer; the Selma voting rights marchers viciously assaulted on "Bloody Sunday" by Alabama police on the Edmund Pettus Bridge; the Selma activists murdered before and after that assault; the ugly racist assaults he and the Chicago Freedom Movement experienced; and the escalation of the Vietnam War. King witnessed the tragic persistence of racist violence in the final years of his life, most notably the bloody suppression of the ghetto riots, summer after summer, and the growing white backlash against the civil rights movement. These ghastly events greatly disturbed King, who as we have seen earlier feared that a country sick with racism and violence was turning his dream of a democratic, just, peace-oriented America into a nightmare of chaos, war, and inequality.

That is why "chaos" was the first word King chose in subtitling his last book, *Where Do We Go from Here: Chaos or Community?* (1967). In this book, which offers a powerful corrective to the miscasting of King as a naïve and dreamy moderate, MLK offers a radical critique of white America and the "stone walls of white resistance." And finding that while sympathetic to the need to "eliminate barbaric conduct" against Blacks by Southern sheriffs, such white sympathy disappeared when Blacks, north and south, pushed for equality. And even former allies of the movement, King wrote, "quietly disappeared. . . . It appeared that the white segregationist and the ordinary white citizen had more in common with one another than either had with the Negro."[82]

Whether one characterizes it as pessimistic, realistic, or both, King in his last book fretted, much as a twenty-first century critical race theorist would, about racism as a permanent feature of American society. As he observed, "[W]ith each modest advance the white population promptly raises the argument that the Negro has come far enough. Each step forward accents an ever-present tendency to backlash."[83] This seemed a very troublesome dynamic to King, especially since in his view—based on more than a decade of intensive civil rights organizing—only "a minority of whites . . . genuinely want authentic equality."[84] The years following the March on Washington had shown King that America had moved further away from the dream he had described there, and the only hope was for a broader movement to challenge and defeat the "'triple evils' of racism, materialism, and militarism."[85]

Remembering King's "I Have a Dream" speech from 1963 while forgetting his subsequent five years of leadership, speeches, and writings is unfortunate. The chapters that follow will hopefully help readers overcome this problem by discussing his key post-1963 speeches on war, labor struggles, and economic inequality. But probably the worst distortions of the "I Have a Dream" speech have come from right-wing ideologues and politicians who spin a single sentence near the speech's ending and read it out of context, ignoring the rest of the address, so as to make it seem as if this somehow proved that MLK would have agreed with their war on affirmative action and diversity, equity, and inclusion programs, which were designed to battle racial discrimination. The sentence they always focus on is from the dream sequence in which King expresses the hope that one day, in an America free of racism, his children would "not be judged by the color of their skin but by the content of their character."

Conservatives love that line, since they see it as indicating that, like them, King thought his aspiration for a world free of racism was somehow self-executing—that if we just ignored race and racism and had no government (or private sector) programs that acknowledged race and racism in order to intervene to combat racial discrimination, America would somehow magically emerge as a color-blind society.[86] But King never believed that. His own understanding of American history, and his experience as a civil rights leader, left him convinced that a non-racist society could not emerge in the United States without extensive, energetic, and sustained government intervention, encouraged and allied with mass movements for racial equality.[87] This was because he knew from bitter experience the strength and persistence of American racism, and how it generated hatred and violence.

King's "I Have a Dream" speech told us that what was needed was *more* such government intervention against racial discrimination, which was why, as we have seen, King had lobbied President Kennedy to issue a Second Emancipation Proclamation, abolishing Jim Crowism and why civil rights activists continued to demand such intervention. In 1963 the Black Freedom Movement was a long way from winning such intervention in the form of affirmative action and DEI initiatives, but the idea that King would ever oppose such government action to halt anti-Black discrimination is a right-wing fantasy. His speech attests that he welcomed government intervention against racial discrimination and recognized how necessary it was in order to overcome America's racist past.

There is also considerable evidence from King's subsequent writings—most notably in *Why We Can't Wait*, the book he published in 1964 as he reflected on the March on Washington and the Birmingham struggle—that he supported government compensatory programs for Blacks to redress past discrimination, much like affirmative action and DEI programs of later years. In fact, the case King made for such government intervention on behalf of African Americans in the last chapter of this book was extensive, clear, and enthusiastic. King found that "special measures for the deprived have always been accepted in principle by the United States" and cited the

Marshall Plan through which the United States funded the rebuilding of western Europe as one example. He argued that the GI Bill providing benefits for World War II veterans offered a powerful example of special compensation. To make up for the "deprivation of certain advantages and opportunities" those in the armed forces experienced when they were overseas fighting for their country, the government subsidized their education, health care, and loans for housing, along with "a strong social climate which for many years favored the preferential hiring of veterans in all walks of life."[88] King advocated for a similar compensatory program for Blacks (as well as for other economically disadvantaged groups) who had been unjustly denied wages under slavery and then experienced decades of discrimination. He saw this as a matter of fairness, "atoning for the injustices" America "has inflicted upon her Negro citizens."[89]

Alex Haley, in his 1965 MLK interview, posed several questions whose premises resembled those of Trump and other twenty-first century right wingers, suggesting that it was somehow unfair, would cause white resentment, and constitute a form of reverse racism (discriminating against whites) if the federal government established programs that accorded special preferences to African Americans. Haley asked King if he thought it fair "to request a multibillion dollar program of preferential treatment for the Negro, or any other minority group?" "I do indeed," answered King.

> "Can any fair-minded citizen deny that . . . for two centuries the Negro was enslaved, and robbed of any wages?—potential accrued wealth which would have been the legacy of his descendants. *All* of America's wealth today could not adequately compensate its Negroes for his centuries of exploitation and humiliation. . . . Within common law, we have ample precedents for special compensatory programs, which are regarded as settlements. American Indians are still being paid for land in a settlement manner. Is not two centuries of labor, which helped build this country, as real a commodity?[90]

Both King's book *Why We Can't Wait* and his interview with Haley refute conservatives' claims that King shared their warped version of color blindness, which serves to blind them to the ongoing problem of racial discrimination. But one really does not have to read beyond the text of the "I Have a Dream" speech to know that King would never have sided with Donald Trump and other foes of DEI and affirmative action, who seek to abolish anti-discrimination programs and replace them with nothing. Every anti-racist struggle King led in the years leading up to the speech taught him three lessons that the American right wing prefers to ignore. These are 1) that racism is deeply embedded in American society; 2) mass protest and great political leverage are needed to overcome racism even at the local level; and 3) the federal government's intervention is important, and often necessary, to provide such political leverage. These lessons were clear from King's first action against racism in the Montgomery bus boycott of 1955–56. There King and the boycott movement faced relentless racist resistance by Montgomery's white leaders, their police force, and white supremacist terrorists whose bombings targeted King's home as well as other boycott leaders. The white leadership thought it could defeat the boycott through police repression, divide and conquer tactics, the eventual exhaustion that would come from months of boycotting the buses Montgomery's Black working class traditionally used to commute. But thanks to strong organization and leadership, the solidarity held for the remarkable 13-month-long boycott. The final victory came when the *federal government*, through its Supreme Court decision in *Browder v. Gayle* (1956), ruled Montgomery's Jim Crow bus system was unconstitutional.

These same lessons held in King's major civil rights victory shortly before the March on Washington, in the Birmingham integration struggle of 1963, and in his biggest win after the march, the Selma voting rights struggle of 1965. In both cases presidential intervention arrived and proved decisive, though it took crises generated by white supremacist violence to force that intervention. These two campaigns paved the way for historic civil rights legislation: the Civil Rights Act of 1964 and the Voting Rights Act of 1965. In the face of the violent racist resistance from local and state officials in the South, it was natural for King to look for such federal intervention. There would be no reason at all for King to have trusted that large corporations, universities, or other white-dominated institutions could be counted on to end their racially discriminatory practices voluntarily, without federal intervention, and remedies like affirmative action, DEI, or some mechanism for forcing compliance. King never gave a hint of holding any such trust and with good reason. Nor should we. Indeed, a 2025 *Wall Street Journal* report found that, despite DEI programs, most senior managers in the corporate world today are still white men.[91]

In light of all the misunderstanding it has caused, it is tempting to conclude that King's "I Have a Dream" speech requires a name change.

Wouldn't Americans, and especially conservatives, better understand King and American racism if they looked to the speech to learn about racial realities? Wouldn't it be better if America went beyond the dream sound-bite version of the speech and actually read the address? Obviously it would. But realizing how difficult it is to challenge such a popular title, I would simply ask you to read the entire speech and consider whether "Bad Check" or "Fierce Urgency of Now" are more accurate titles for the speech than its common name. Of course, it is hard to imagine conservatives being comfortable with such incendiary new titles—though in both cases they are King's own words. Perhaps it all comes down to the choice Vincent Harding left us with, whether we want King to continue to be misrepresented as a conveniently domesticated hero or studied as the radical social critic and social justice leader that he actually was.

If the radicalism of MLK's speech at the March on Washington seems surprising, this may be not only because of how misunderstood King has been by much of the public but also because the radicalism of the march and its organizers have been largely forgotten. It is true that some on the left, such as SNCC leader James Forman, complained that March organizers had diluted its radicalism when they jettisoned earlier plans to deploy mass civil disobedience in Washington and when they asked John Lewis to tone down his speech.[92] But the decision to shelve civil disobedience was tactical not ideological, the idea being that disruptive methods were not needed and that a less confrontational organizing strategy would draw more participants, creating the largest civil rights demonstration in American history and thus have a huge impact. As to John Lewis's speech, even Forman conceded that it ended up being a "strong indictment" of both American racism and of the Kennedy administration's failure to combat it vigorously. Both he and Lewis saw the speech as conveying SNCC's radically critical perspective on race in America.[93] Indeed, the justifiably angry tone of Lewis's voice and the sense of urgency his words and radical analysis conveyed from the podium leave no doubt that Archbishop O'Boyle's intervention had failed to muffle SNCC's message on behalf of an anti-racist social revolution.[94]

Moreover, at a time when white-dominated political gatherings, such as the major party conventions, were the norm and whites nearly monopolized TV air time, it was quite a departure to have Black speakers—especially such scathing critics of the racist status quo as Lewis and King—covered by the national TV networks. And as has been mentioned earlier, it was the leftist A. Philip Randolph, a Black democratic socialist labor and civil rights leader, who conceived of the idea of the March on Washington. His protégé Bayard Rustin, a veteran civil rights leader, gay radical pacifist, and ex-Communist, was the key organizer of the march. Randolph and Rustin played central roles in formulating the march's demands, which were both socially democratic and anti-racist. These demands (not dreams) would be read by Rustin from the podium at the march. He asked and received the enormous crowd's roaring affirmation for them. Rustin explained to the crowd that their approval was needed, so that when the movement's leaders met with President Kennedy after the march, they could speak on behalf of all its participants. Rustin called them "the demands of this revolution." Among these eight demands were effective civil rights legislation, "no compromise, no filibuster," an immediate end to segregated education and housing, the creation of job-training programs and an end to unemployment, a "strong" Fair Employment Practices Commission to prevent racial discrimination in hiring, and a raise in the federal minimum wage.[95]

Columnist Murray Kempton, who had been a revolutionary in his youth, could hardly believe that so leftist an agenda was aired at a nationally televised event, which is why he singled out Rustin's reading of the demands as the most radical part of the March on Washington rather than any of the speeches. Kempton reflected upon the march a few days after.

> The moment in that afternoon which most strained belief was near its end, when Rustin led the assemblage in a mass pledge never to cease until they had won their demands. A radical pacifist, every sentence punctuated by his upraised hand, was calling for a $2-an-hour minimum wage. Every television camera at the disposal of the networks was upon him. No expression one-tenth so radical has ever been seen or heard by so many Americans.[96]

With this dissident political context in mind, one could say that it would have been surprising if MLK had *not* been radically critical of America's long history of inequality and racism in his March on Washington speech.

* * *

Even though we have started with MLK's "I Have a Dream" speech as an introduction to his views on racism, its place in American history, and the best way to challenge racism, there were several points in this chapter where other King sources were used to illuminate his thinking about racism. That is because King's ideas about racism were so rich and complex that they cannot be fully understood from one brief speech delivered on a stage shared with so many others. To do justice to King's thinking about racism, one really needs to review not only his major speeches, sermons, and most revealing correspondence but also the three major books he wrote: *Stride Toward Freedom: The Montgomery Story* (1958), *Why We Can't Wait* (1964), and *Where Do We Go from Here: Chaos or Community?* (1967).[97] So we should regard with skepticism any claim that because King's "I Have a Dream" speech is his most famous therefore his thinking about racism can be judged solely on the basis of that one speech or its most celebrated sentences near that speech's conclusion.

Since we lack the space here to review all of King's writings on racism, I want to call your attention to the best concise summary of MLK's ideas about racism, by King scholar Brandon M. Terry. In an insightful essay, grounded in an extensive reading of King's writings and speeches, Terry argues convincingly that MLK's theory of racism has three essential components.[98] The first is psychological: that racism is "deeply entangled with 'irrational fears' of losing economic or social standing, of an unknown future, and above all, of revenge and retaliation." Since such fears are irrational and can result in "strange psychosis and peculiar cases of paranoia," which can yield racist violence, King did not believe that "rational argumentation or moral suasion" were by themselves "sufficient tools to undermine racism."[99]

The second part of King's view of racism is both historical and America-focused. Terry labels this "sociopolitical," and it was very much in evidence in the "bad check" section of King's March on Washington speech. American racism cannot be upended unless we refute the myth that American history has been shaped by "the ideology of freedom and equality, while racism is just an occasional departure from the norm on the part of a few extremists." The reality, King held, is and has been the "'congenital deformity of racism that has crippled the nation from its inception." But the "democratic sprit" opposing racism was, in King's view, "equally real" and preserves the hope for achieving a more perfect union free of racism.[100]

Finally, for King the third crucial aspect of racism—and one that has considerable strategic importance for those working to free America from its racist past—is, as Terry so aptly puts it, that racism "arises from cognitive and empathetic failures."[101] That the inhumane practices associated with racism, ranging from slavery, Jim Crowism, and disenfranchisement to genocide, are grounded in "the arrogant assertion that one race is the center of value," and only this superior, white race "contributed to historical progress and it alone can do so in the future." This yields "blindness to the capacities" of those in the subordinated races. So for King a key part of confronting and overcoming racism is to critique, contradict, and refute its "legitimating ideas . . . the stereotypes . . . and stigmas that underpin racial domination."[102]

Above all this meant, as King explained in *Why We Can't Wait*, attacking white America's self-serving myth of Black passivity, the assumption that the African American was "a creature who could quietly endure, silently suffer and patiently wait." This is a key reason why the militant and disciplined Black protest movement that demanded equality was so important and potentially liberating, since it demonstrated to America that Blacks had no less historical agency than whites and thereby "dissolved the stereotype of the grinning, submissive Uncle Tom." In other words, through its own public assertiveness in demanding equality, the Black Freedom Movement was forcing white America to recognize that Blacks did not constitute an inferior race destined for, and accepting of, submission to white domination. In King's view, then, the movement heralds liberation from racism by pushing the nation to "recognize blacks as co-creators of a democratic society" and in the process enhances Black self-respect.[103]

Terry's summary confirms what much of King scholarship and MLK's own speeches and books document: that King was a serious thinker about the causes, character, and consequences of racism and about the challenges and possibilities of working to overcome racism. His knowledge of Black history and his own movement and personal experience enabled him to reckon with racism's depth, complexity, and persistence while also retaining the faith that a democratic and nonviolent protest movement could, through a process of struggle, bring liberation. If we read King's "I Have a Dream" speech from start to finish and in context, we can move beyond the simplistic image of King as merely a dreamer and draw from his ideas a usable past, a critical lens to understand and struggle against American racism in our own time.[104]

As a final inducement to read King's most famous speech from start to finish, and to recognize that it was about far more than a dream, we ought to consider that those closest to MLK did so. We have already discussed

Vincent Harding's plea that we not skip over the speech's critical account of America's history of anti-Black racism. But Coretta Scott King also reminds us, in her memoirs, that the speech had more to it than a hopeful ending about a world free of racism. She does this in several ways. First, she takes us back to the night before the March on Washington when, in their hotel room, Martin drafted the speech and had trouble keeping it short enough to fit into the "eight minutes he had been allotted" by the march organizers. In discussing this drafting process, Coretta lets us know that its initial focus was not on dreams for the future but rather on historical realities of race and Black history, beginning with Lincoln, whose memory MLK was planning to evoke, as she put it, by opening the speech "with Lincolnesque phrases" similar to those in the Gettysburg address: "Five score years ago, a great American, in whose symbolic shadow we stand today, [rallying for freedom, outside the Lincoln Memorial] signed the Emancipation Proclamation." "Martin then," she notes, "inserted language pertaining to" America's failure to make good on the promise of emancipation, "issuing blacks a check that 'has come back marked insufficient funds.'"[105]

Coretta does not deny that the "I have a dream" phrase that MLK ended up using in the speech would prove electrifying. But she reminds us that the dream segment was not part of his planned speech, which was why in their hotel room that night as she "listened and watched him insert, delete, state, and restate his premises" she "did not hear the famed 'I have a dream'" phrase. And, in fact, Coretta suggested that part of the reason the media made so much of that phrase was that it seemed new to journalists, a perception that reflected their ignorance of MLK's prior oratory. As she pointed out, "[H]e had used that phase so eloquently at Detroit's Cobo Hall the previous June. Since that had been a smaller audience, however, the press in Washington treated the 'dream' flourish as new."[106]

There have been varied accounts as to what provoked MLK to break away from the text of his prepared March on Washington speech and to spontaneously insert the speech's dream segment. Coretta Scott King's views on this center on an earlier part of the speech itself, and the crowd's powerful reaction to it, in a dialogical process that she believed inspired MLK's shift towards this spontaneity. The part of the speech that she saw as having this impact was one of its most militant segments, which MLK launched by "remind[ing] America of the fierce urgency of now," that Blacks were unwilling to wait for their freedom. That "now is the time to make real the promises of democracy. . . . Now is the time to lift our nation from the quicksands of racial injustice."[107] According to Coretta, when MLK "got to the rhythmic part of this "'Now is the time'" refrain, "the crowd caught the timing and began shouting 'now' in cadence. Their response lifted Martin to new heights of inspiration. In a moment of transformation, he turned aside his manuscript, and the 'I Have a Dream' rhetoric, which was not on paper but was tucked inside him, began to roll off his tongue."[108]

Whether or not Coretta is right about this connection between these two segments of his speech, her account is a reminder that MLK's speech did have a militant as well as a utopian segment. That before MLK had even decided to insert the dream rhetoric, the crowd had responded enthusiastically both to his claim that racial oppression was real and evil and to his demand that it end immediately. She was implicitly making the point that the speech's militancy ought not be forgotten. And, its anti-racist militancy had certainly not been forgotten by Coretta. She knew that the speech's meaning was distorted when its demand that racial injustice end "NOW" was erased and replaced with only an invitation to dream.

MLK's advisor and friend Andrew Young made a similar point in his memoir, *An Easy Burden: The Civil Rights Movement and the Transformation of America* (1996). In discussing MLK's speech, Young did not see the need to quote the famous lines, to replay the "now familiar cadences," from King's dream segment. Instead, he offered a lengthy (sixteen-line) quote from the speech's "bad check" segment.[109] For Young it was not the dream but rather this "bad check" discourse, documenting the broken promises to Black America regarding freedom and equal opportunity, that best defined political reality in the United States for decades to come. As Young explained, "more than thirty years" after the March on Washington that "bad check" MLK described so graphically in 1963 "continues to plague this nation."[110] Here Young was thinking especially of "the despairing and often violent underclass in our cities," made up of those "who went to redeem their promissory note at the bank of opportunity only to have it returned marked 'insufficient funds.'"[111]

So for Young, much as for Harding, America's misreading of King's speech constitutes an extension of the nation's refusal to address the inequity and injustice that MLK spent the bulk of his speech, and the last thirteen years of his life, confronting. "America," in Young's estimation, "has accepted Martin's happy vision of equality without applying its full resources to enabling the dream to become a reality for all citizens. We are content to be swept away by the beautiful dream and are unwilling to recognize the painful realities that keep the dream from coming true."[112]

Viewed collectively, the memoirs of Andrew Young, Coretta Scott King, and Vincent Harding enable us to see that, among those closest to MLK, his "I Have a Dream" speech was memorable not merely for its ageless vision of a world without racism but its always timely recognition of racism's persistence, and its urging of action against anti-Black racism here and now. They interpret the speech in this way because of their awareness as African Americans of Black history and their personal encounters with racism, an understanding that MLK shared. Indeed, while the speech is famed for its universalism (its culminating dream of transcending race), for those who lived through the oppression on the Black side of the color line, the speech also resonated in evoking that oppression, which King knew so well because he not only battled it but *had experienced it.*

Among the most powerful examples of this is when King, as we have seen, twice in the "I Have a Dream" speech, denounced police brutality—with its "unspeakable horrors"—in a way that would certainly make uncomfortable the right-wing "Blue Lives Matter" foes of twenty-first century America's Black Lives Matter movement. Here King spoke, much as the BLM activists would after the Minneapolis police murder of George Floyd in 2020, drawing on an awareness that Black communities saw the police acting contrary to the way white conservatives imagined, not as virtuous agents of law and order but—too often—as lawless purveyors of racist violence and injustice. This was for King not some theoretical matter but an evil he had witnessed and experienced personally. As King scholar Jeanne Theoharis explains, MLK

> had numerous experiences of police abuse, and the terror he felt in police custody was palpable. Arrested twenty-nine times over his shortened life, he had to fight his own fear of the police and what they would do. Over the years, police . . . half-nelsoned and slammed him down on a counter, choked him, kicked him in the back, picked him up by his pants, and shackled and chained him to a police car floor for hours. . . . He made common cause with Black people across the country around police

> brutality. . . . King didn't see the problem of police as a few bad apples but a structural one . . . where police and the courts act as "enforcers" [of racial tyranny].[113]

The challenge, then, in reading MLK's most famous speech is to try to hear—as much of white America has not—an enduring indictment of American racism and a painful evocation of its oppressiveness by a Black man who had lived it, as well as his hope for an America emancipated from this grim history.

Against War and Militarism

A little more than a decade ago, when preparing to teach my first undergraduate MLK seminar, I read many articles on Martin Luther King Jr.'s final years, but none resonated in quite the same way as David Halberstam's "The Second Coming of Martin Luther King," published in *Harper's Magazine* (August 1967).[1] This reflected, in part, the insightful reporting Halberstam did while traveling for ten days with King at a crucial transitional time, when MLK had recently broken decisively with President Johnson over the Vietnam War. He had opened a second front in his work for social justice, moving from the Jim Crow South to the Black ghettoes of the North—starting with Chicago in 1966—in his nonviolent war on racism and poverty. This article's impact on me was likely intensified by my own interaction with Halberstam, with whom I had a long telephone conversation back in 1996 about a conference I was helping to plan at the University of Georgia on the civil rights movement's impact on small Southern towns. Halberstam offered numerous smart suggestions, reflecting the work he had been doing on *The Children,* his evocative group biography of Nashville's most intrepid Black student protesters of the 1960s, whose sit-in movement and other activism he had covered as a cub reporter for the *Nashville Tennessean.* Several of these students would become SNCC leaders and worked closely with MLK. Halberstam brought this same depth of knowledge and insight to his "Second Coming" article, in which he argued for a radicalized King, a change Halberstam attributed to MLK's need both to speak for the alienated northern Black ghetto communities and to compete with Black Power advocates of defensive violence. He also noted the lasting impact of King's frustrating experiences in the freedom movement battling the white power structure.[2]

In support of this reading of MLK's radicalization, Halberstam noted that King and his aides employed a leftist frame of analysis, depicting impoverished Black ghettoes as a case of domestic colonialism. Halberstam cited some strikingly radical King quotes from the time they had spent together in spring 1967. King had, for example, told Halberstam that "For years I labored with the idea of reforming the existing institutions of society, a little change here a little change there. Now I feel quite differently. I think you've got to have a reconstruction of the entire society, a revolution of values."[3] On race, King indicated to Halberstam that his views of whites had changed "deeply," becoming more skeptical in the aftermath of the violent white resistance he encountered in the Chicago struggle against discrimination. When he started his civil rights work in the South, during the 1950s, he believed most Americans could be swayed to the cause of racial justice, that the freedom movement "was touching the conscience of white America," and that only parts of the white South and a small scattering of Northern racists stood in the way. But Chicago convinced him that foes of racism were few in white America and most were college students. "Most Americans," King had realized, "were unconscious racists."[4]

I found this argument by Halberstam thought-provoking but not entirely convincing. After all, when Coretta Scott King first met Martin, years before he emerged as a civil rights leader, he aired a critical view of American capitalism and the vast economic inequality it bred and on that basis voiced his preference for democratic socialism.[5] In his youth MLK had experienced upsetting racist incidents, not only while a high school student in Georgia but also up north in New Jersey and in Pennsylvania when he was a divinity school student at Crozer Theological Seminary.[6] Among the most disturbing racist experiences Coretta experienced in her youth, which she surely shared with her husband, was being barred by a segregationist school official in Ohio from her public school student-teaching placement and finding that the president of her college—Antioch—was unwilling to intervene. (She had heard that he owned a black dog he had named "Nigger."[7]) Moreover, the work of King scholar Jeanne Theoharis, *King of the North: Martin Luther King Jr.'s Life of Struggle Outside the South* (2025) shows that, long before MLK brought the SCLC to Chicago in 1966, he had been aware and publicly critical of Northern racism, supporting local movements against racially discriminatory housing and employment and against anti-Black police brutality.[8] So it is difficult to believe that King did not recognize the depth of Northern racism until the last years of his life and that some new radicalization process had been necessary to provoke that recognition. Such evidence, from MLK's student days and early years as a civil rights leader, left me inclined to suspect that King had always been radical and in his final years—even if moving somewhat further to the left—had finally felt free to be more open and candid in articulating that radicalism.[9]

Halberstam's article did, however, help set the terms for historians and biographers to debate the ways King had and had not been changed by his experiences as a movement leader. Indeed, Halberstam's article would in time help seed the most influential framework King scholars used for understanding MLK's political evolution, which is best articulated in the phrase from King biographer David J. Garrow: "from reformer to revolutionary."[10] In the final years of his life, after coming to the painful realization that the civil rights legislation he had helped win—which seemed so historic in 1964 and 1965—did little to improve the lives of poor Blacks in the rural South and in urban ghettoes, MLK shifted his thinking leftward. Initially conducting his advocacy work on the premise that civil rights legislation could end Black oppression, King ultimately saw the persisting limitations imposed on Black Americans, which made him realize that his approach was inadequate and that only a sweeping, holistic brand of radicalism, centered on systemic economic change, could liberate impoverished Blacks. And so MLK became openly anti-capitalist, deploying rhetoric calling for major, even revolutionary, change that aimed for a "radical redistribution of economic and political power in the United States."[11]

This lens for understanding King's evolution has much to commend it, especially since it is grounded in quotes from King himself, some of which Halberstam had reported on. And it is certainly the case that in his final years King spoke repeatedly of the Black Freedom Movement having entered a second and more challenging phase after the Voting Rights Act of 1965. He moved from championing constitutional rights (won via civil rights legislation, with no budgetary sacrifice in Washington) to crusading against poverty and economic inequality (that would require unprecedented federal anti-poverty expenditures). But to characterize the movement King helped lead from 1955 to 1965 against the powerful Jim Crow system as reformist seems problematic. The goal of toppling the enduring racist social order of the United States' most reactionary region had a revolutionary cast to it. Thus, as Vincent Harding points out, the movement's "so-called reformist ideas and programs," and even its "normal political activities, such as voter registration . . . when Black people were involved . . . in the South became essentially and fundamentally radical" and bred a white supremacist massive-resistance movement far more vehement and violent than what one might expect a merely reformist movement could generate.[12] In discussing racist resistance, which gained momentum nationally and pushed American politics rightward after the ghetto rebellions of the mid-1960s, King termed it a "counterrevolution," which begs the question of how their could have been a counterrevolution if the freedom movement was anything less than revolutionary.[13] As late as 1967, King still referred to the movement that won the civil rights and voting rights acts as having accomplished a "civil rights revolution."[14] The "reformer to revolutionary" lens also misses King's support of anti-colonial revolutions, which he had expressed publicly since the 1950s.[15]

The case for MLK, even in his early movement years, as more of a revolutionary than a mere reformer was summarized effectively by historian (and former MLK papers editor) Clayborne Carson, who saw King as a precursor of anti-capitalist liberation theology, which later "enabled activists around the world to redefine widely held spiritual beliefs that are often used as supports for the status quo."[16] Carson argued that MLK's radicalism was founded upon the "African American variant" of Social Gospel Christianity, in which King incorporated democratically "socialist ideas," critical of the "gulf between superfluous wealth and abject poverty'" under capitalism, while embracing anti-racist, "anti-colonial sentiments spurred by the African independence movements," and it sought to "combine social gospel Christianity with Gandhian ideas of nonviolent struggle."[17] Carson noted that the famed West Indian socialist intellectual C. L. R. James, in reflecting on King after meeting with him in London in 1957, viewed him as a revolutionary, similar to Kwame Nkrumah, leader of Ghana's nonviolent independence movement. To James, the direct-action campaigns that resulted from King and Nkrumah's nonviolent and egalitarian ideals demonstrated "tremendous boldness . . . strategic grasp and . . . tactical inventiveness," which were "fundamentally revolutionary."[18]

The radical tendencies, the socially democratic orientation, in King's early thought can also be discerned in his first book *Stride Toward Freedom: The Montgomery Story* (1958) in which, unlike moderate social reformers, he proved willing to acknowledge the value of Marx's insights into the capitalist system's flaws. Though not uncritical of Marx, as King scholar Adam Fairclough put it, in this book MLK "praised Marx for revealing 'certain truths' and 'raising basic questions' about the economic injustices of traditional capitalism—remarks that his publisher urged him, without success to omit . . . [MLK's] criticisms of capitalism had been hiding in plain sight."[19] Still, there is no denying that late in his life King was more often openly and deeply critical of American capitalism, militarism, and imperialism than he had dared to be in the tense Cold War years of the 1950s. As King scholar Thomas F. Jackson notes, in stressing the role of capitalist interests in driving U.S. military interventions, during his final years MLK "became more overtly Marxist" in his "view of American foreign policy."[20]

It certainly seems plausible to argue, in the Halberstam-Garrow mode, as Gary Dorrien does in his impressive study *Breaking White Supremacy: Martin Luther King Jr. and the Black Social Gospel* (2018) that, due to his encounters with anti-Black racism and violence in the Freedom Movement, "King was more angry and radical in 1960 than in 1955, more angry and radical at the end than ever. In his last years he was more of both than anyone around him, while cultivating a public image of neither."[21] And yet this claim of neat chronological progression is hard to square with King's words back in 1963, in his "Letter from Birmingham Jail." Think, for example, of how irate was the letter's longest (gargantuan, actually) sentence, which filled 26 lines, describing the evils and pain Blacks faced, including lynching, police brutality, economic exploitation, and segregation, and featured his five-year-old son's questioning why "white people treat colored people so mean."[22] Here MLK, who wrote the letter (as King scholar Jonathan Reider put it) "in a furious state of mind," sounded as if he was "a man on fire."[23] It is, then, hard to credit the notion that King was angrier in his final years than he was when he vented such fury at anti-Black racism in his most famous piece of writing back in 1963.

Another important aspect of Halberstam's reporting on King resonated with me, as a veteran of the Vietnam era antiwar movement, on a personal level. This was the section of his article on MLK's new role in 1967 as a key voice against the Vietnam War. Halberstam had played a prominent role in the national debate about Vietnam with his critical, Pulitzer Prize-winning reportage on the war for *The New York Times*, in his scathing account of the early stages of the war in his first book, *The Making of a Quagmire* (1965), later in his biography of Ho Chi Minh, *Ho* (1971), and in his best-seller, *The Best and the Brightest* (1972), indicting the decision-making that had led America into the Vietnam disaster. So at a time when much of the media scorned King for opposing the war, Halberstam did not share that scorn, as seen in his account of MLK's speech at UC Berkeley in May 1967.

By May 1967, the Berkeley campus was a national center of the antiwar movement, especially its dynamic and militant student wing. Having offered a powerful indictment of the Vietnam War just a month earlier in his Riverside Church speech, MLK received a hero's welcome at Berkeley. An estimated seven thousand students packed Cal's Sproul Plaza, some hoisting signs urging MLK to run for president on a peace ticket with Benjamin Spock, the pediatrician and best-selling author of baby and child-care advice books. King reciprocated the students' admiration, praising Berkeley as "the conscience of our nation."[24]

The most dramatic moment in King's Berkeley visit came after the rally. King, in response to press questions, indicated that he was not going to run for president. But then a graduate student stepped forward and pleaded with King to reconsider: "You're a world figure . . . the most important man" in the antiwar movement. "You're the only one who can head a third-party ticket. And so, when you make your decision, remember there are many of us who are going to have to go to jail for many years [resisting the draft and the war]. This is a very serious thing . . . the most serious thing in our lives. . . . So please weigh our jail sentences in the balance when you make your decision."[25] King was "stunned" by this appeal. Halberstam noted, "I have watched King with dozens of people as he nods and half listens, and this is the first time I have ever seen anyone get to him. King responded to the student, "Well you make a very moving and persuasive statement."[26]

This Berkeley student's view of King's importance and moral authority was similar to my own view when I was a student, though I was younger and became a high school antiwar activist in the Nixon era after MLK had been assassinated. My family had been divided generationally over the Vietnam War: my uncles were World War II and Korean War veterans who denounced criticism of the war as heretical and un-American. So our extended family gatherings at times turned into angry debates between them and my older brother who opposed the war. These disputes, and the disillusionment about the war expressed by my neighbor who had served as a Marine and been wounded in Vietnam, got me reading books about the war by Halberstam, Bernard Fall, and other foreign correspondents. This led me first to criticize the war and then to organize against it in school as a part of the national moratorium against the Vietnam War in 1969.[27] Still, I found it unnerving to encounter adults in my blue-collar Brooklyn neighborhood who denounced the peace movement and called its activists traitors who should be shot. So I remember feeling comforted and supported, validated, when I learned of MLK's opposition to the war, since I viewed him as a heroic figure and understood that his resistance to the war reflected his high ideals as a minister. This was no mere abstraction, and in fact, for years after his death, King's image strengthened the peace movement. I vividly remember the antiwar buttons and posters featuring photos of MLK and quotes from his speeches against the war. Most of all, as a student activist, I was moved by the motto on those buttons and posters: "Honor His Memory." The message suggested that, in opposing the unjust war in Vietnam and by joining the peace movement and its demonstrations, we were following in King's footsteps and keeping alive his nonviolent ethos, his dream of a just and peaceful world.[28]

Such student activist reverence for King's antiwar leadership suggests that even though he took a high-visibility public stance against the Vietnam War quite late in his life—starting the year before his assassination—this was for many of King's admirers no sideline or add-on but was deeply appreciated and meaningful. And for King it was a role that he, as a relentless advocate of nonviolence, embraced eagerly after a long period of hesitation. This peace work left King feeling liberated from his earlier politically repressed silence on a war he always loathed.[29] This is why his historic antiwar speech on April 4, 1967, at Riverside Church in New York City, is sometimes referred to as "A Time to Break Silence" (though the speech is also titled "Beyond Vietnam" or a combination of the two: "Beyond Vietnam: A Time to Break Silence").[30] It is a mark of King's stature and broad vison of social change that, by the time of his death, he was a leading voice not for one but rather multiple dissenting mass protest movements: anti-racist, labor, anti-poverty, and antiwar.[31]

King's Riverside Church speech was not just one more speech; it was cherished by antiwar activists, including SNCC organizers in the Black Freedom Movement's left wing. For example, John Lewis noted that he

> had heard Dr. King speak many, many times, and I had no doubt that this speech was his finest. It was deep, comprehensive, thoughtful and courageous. It was about what we were doing in Vietnam, but beyond that it was about what we were doing on this *earth*. He was saying that those bombs that were being dropped in Vietnam would detonate here, that they were being dropped on the hopes and dreams of the American

> people. And he was so right. We are still recovering today from the spiritual wounds inflicted by that war.[32]

Similarly, during a 50th anniversary commemoration of the speech that my MLK seminar and I organized at NYU in 2017, Asia scholar James Peck argued that King's "Beyond Vietnam" speech was of such great value, with its critique of American militarism, that he wished we could declare a five-year moratorium on playing those "I Have a Dream" speech excerpts on MLK Day and in their place America would listen to King's powerful indictment of the Vietnam War.[33]

Such a shift away from the "I Have a Dream" speech and towards the "Beyond Vietnam" speech has not occurred (and is unlikely to occur in the future) because the United States is too addicted to the use of military force abroad and gun violence at home to focus on King's peace advocacy and nonviolent faith. How can the nation with the world's most enormous military deal not only with King's antiwar speech but also with his nonviolent and anti-imperialist view of international relations? Instead, America avoids this part of King's politics and ethics so consistently that it seems to have developed a case of amnesia about it. As Vincent Harding explained in 1987, reflecting on the official U.S. government ceremony honoring King and upon the placement of a bust of MLK in the Capitol Rotunda: "Surely nothing could be more ironic than having George [H. W.] Bush, the former head of the Central Intelligence Agency, the probable White House overseer of the Contra [counterrevolutionary military] actions [in Nicaragua], speaking words in King's honor. Or was it more ironic to watch the representatives of the Marine Corp, carrying fresh memories of [the U.S. invasion of] Grenada . . . playing 'We Shall Overcome,' while the bust of the prince of nonviolence was placed in the Capitol rotunda, without a word being spoken about nonviolence?"[34] On the day of this event, Harding pointed out that were MLK alive he would not have been drawn to this ceremony with the Marines but would instead join "the veterans who were sitting outside on the Capitol steps to protest American policy toward Central America."[35]

The other crucial reason King's Vietnam speech has been much less remembered by the public than his "I Have a Dream" speech is that the Vietnam speech does not offer the hopefulness found at the end of the March on Washington speech. Instead there is a chilling indictment of America's brutality in waging an unjust war and a candid, depressing assessment of how the war reflected skewed values in American politics and of the war's damage to the cause of democratic change. So unlike the dream speech, the Riverside Church speech's critical view of America's moral and political failures simply could not be evaded, and in that sense the speech was just too radical for veneration outside of the peace movement.

That King gave a speech on the war that was too radical for much of America to embrace is worth reflecting on. It is a reminder that King's commitment to nonviolence placed him well to the left of mainstream America in his own time (and today). The fact that King had his friend Vincent Harding write the first draft of his Riverside Church speech is quite telling.[36] In 1960s America, two places that served as leading centers of radical antiwar criticism were universities and historically pacificist churches. And Harding, a history PhD who would rank among the most eminent historians of the Black experience, chaired the history department at Spelman College and also served as a lay pastor in a Mennonite church, constituting a prominent peace activist who bridged both worlds.[37]

Though the student wing of the civil rights movement, SNCC, is known for being the first civil rights organization to come out against the war, and did so in January 1966, well before that time Harding had tried, back in August 1965, to get King's SCLC (to which Harding belonged) to oppose the war.[38] Reminding the SCLC of its opposition to colonialism, Harding, in his open letter to the organization, accused the United States of "acting like a colonial power" in Vietnam. "Our nation is wrong in what it now does in Vietnam, and has been wrong for more than two decades. . . . We as a nation are called upon to repent of the arrogance that took us into Vietnam in the first place."[39] It took not only trust and friendship but also a virtually identical view of the war for King in December 1966 to have Harding, who stood in the vanguard of antiwar activists in the civil rights movement, compose a first draft that King planned to use in crafting the final version of his Riverside Church speech.

If we focus on MLK rather than on the SCLC, it is evident that his early antiwar impulses link him to his young radical counterparts in SNCC. Thus the disdainful words about the Vietnam War that MLK chose, amidst one of the most tragic moments of the Selma voting rights struggle in March 1965, closely resembled those of SNCC's voting rights leader Robert P. Moses, as he responded to equally tragic racist murders during Mississippi Freedom Summer. Speaking at the site of the Black church in Neshoba County in

August 1964, whose burning Michael Schwerner, James Chaney, and Andrew Goodman had come to investigate, Moses bitterly noted that the Klan's killing of these three voting rights activists was made possible by Washington's willingness to send troops to Vietnam and failure to defend civil rights workers struggling for democratic rights in Mississippi.[40] Seven months later, MLK made this same point when presiding over the funeral of Jimmie Lee Jackson, who had been killed by racist police in a nonviolent voting rights march of the Selma movement. King insisted that Jackson "was murdered by the timidity of a federal government that is willing to spend millions of dollars a day to defend freedom in Vietnam but cannot protect the rights of its own citizens." [41] King made these remarks at a time when public opinion polls indicated that only 19 percent of Americans favored ending Vietnam War.[42]

This naturally raises the question of why King, if he shared Moses's and Harding's early opposition to the war, waited until 1967 to shine a national spotlight on his antiwar views via his Riverside Church speech. Actually King, as early as 1965, had made other public statements critical of the Vietnam War and its escalation. In March 1965 at Howard University, he had argued that the Vietnam War "had accomplished nothing."[43] Then in July, King told a Virginia SCLC meeting he was "not going to sit by and see the war escalated without saying anything about it" and insisted that the war must be stopped. "We must even negotiate with the Vietcong. We're not going to defeat Communism with bombs and guns. . . . We must work this out in the framework of our democracy."[44] Indicating his openness to the campus antiwar movement's nonviolent tactics, King spoke of helping to organize peace rallies and teach-ins to promote a negotiated end to the war. But the combination of internal resistance from the civil rights community and heavy pressure from President Lyndon Johnson and his allies made it impossible in 1965 for King to act on these early antiwar statements and to add peace activism to the agenda even of his own organization, the SCLC.

King in 1965 had not only called for a halt to U.S. bombing in Vietnam but also offered to facilitate negotiations to end the war via letters he planned to send out to North Vietnam President Ho Chi Minh, the United Nations' secretary general, and others, appealing for such negotiations. But when, in August 1965, he sought to enlist the SCLC in support of such antiwar moves, he found it unwilling to endorse antiwar work. Instead the SCLC passed a resolution, written by King's movement colleague Bayard Rustin, affirming that it was a single-issue organization "to secure the full citizenship for the Negro citizens of this country." Rustin wrote that the SCLC lacked the "resources to assume the burden of two major issues."[45]

Other civil right leaders echoed these arguments about the need to steer clear of the war issue. The key reasons for this refusal to go along with King's antiwar initiative was fear of antagonizing the public and the president. At this point, Americans were still largely united in support of the anti-Communist crusade in Vietnam. To moderate civil rights leaders it seemed reckless to risk alienating President Lyndon Johnson, who was escalating the war but had been a crucial, immensely powerful ally to the Black Freedom Movement, having recently overseen the enactment of the historic Voting Rights Act and the Civil Rights Act.

This fear of aggravating President Johnson was grounded in political reality. The president was furious at King in 1965 for criticizing the war. Johnson had one of his Senate allies, Thomas Dodd of Connecticut, attack King in the press for meddling in foreign affairs, alleging that this was an area in which King sorely lacked expertise and implying that the only issue a civil rights leader had knowledge of was domestic race relations. Dodd even suggested that King's offer to facilitate negotiations with Ho Chi Minh violated the Logan Act, barring private citizens from assuming the federal government's role in conducting U.S. foreign policy. And in a phone call, the president applied heavy pressure on King to end his antiwar activity: Johnson complained that King had left members of Congress with the impression that "you are against me in Vietnam," and he warned, "You better not leave that impression."[46]

Lacking a base of support in the SCLC, even among most of his advisors, for his ideas about linking the civil rights and antiwar movements in 1965 and facing such hostility from LBJ, who as president had so much potential to further assist the civil rights movement, King retreated. MLK privately acknowledged in September 1965 that he did not "have the strength to fight this issue [of Vietnam] and keep the civil rights fight going."[47] So King, in late 1965, stopped publicly advocating an alliance between the civil rights and antiwar movements and did not make antiwar speeches. This is not to say he gave up his antiwar principles or cut off all links to the peace movement. In fact, in 1966, when SNCC veteran Julian Bond was denied his seat in the reactionary, white-dominated Georgia state legislature on account of his antiwar views, King joined the protests, though he did so more on free speech concerns than antiwar grounds.[48] Coretta Scott King, meanwhile, served as an informal representative for MLK at peace movement events.

MLK, however, was never comfortable with his retreat from the antiwar barricades, since he deemed it his moral obligation as a minister, advocate of nonviolence, and as Nobel Peace Prize laureate to speak out against the Vietnam War. When King dramatically announced in his Riverside speech an end to his retreat from antiwar activism, this is why he found it so personally liberating. Despite the political price he would pay for antagonizing war hawks, King realized he was now, at last, acting on his deeply held nonviolent principles rather than bowing to the pressure not to do what he knew to be right.[49]

King was not the only one disappointed by his earlier reticence regarding antiwar activism. Others in the peace movement, who knew how much the movement struggled to overcome public indifference and hostility and needed King's voice, experienced this same sense of disappointment. So the emotions evoked by the Riverside speech over this delayed entry into the antiwar movement, a mix of regret, joy, and relief, were reflected in the audience as well as at the podium that night. Thus James Fraser, who as a graduate student attended the speech, recalled how he experienced the meaning and emotions of that historic event:

> The evening was electric. It was also an odd mix. For many of us in the anti-Vietnam war movement, King's speech seemed to be coming late. We had wanted him to speak out on the war for some time. I think we completely overlooked the incredible sacrifice he was making as a civil rights leader in making that speech and challenging the whole war effort in Vietnam as he did. He had worked long and hard . . . and ultimately successfully . . . to build strong connections to the Johnson administration—and the administration's embrace of civil rights was very real and far stronger than any previous government. Now he was severing those ties and he knew it. . . . I did not appreciate that night how much moral courage the move took and how much criticism King would endure from his allies for doing so.[50]

Fraser was not wrong to argue that it took courage for King to come out so strongly against the war with the Riverside speech, when it meant incurring the wrath of LBJ and so many shapers of American public opinion, who in 1967 still supported the war. But King did not see it that way. Instead, he felt guilty about what, near the start of this Riverside Church speech, he termed "the betrayal of my silences," meaning the way he had abandoned the idea of pushing the Black Freedom Movement to embrace the antiwar cause for almost two years, from fall 1965 through the beginning of 1967. With this in mind, King told his SCLC colleagues in May 1967 that "My name wouldn't have been written in any book called *Profiles in Courage*."[51]

Actually, most King scholars argue that by 1967 MLK had far less to lose by taking a strong stand against the war than had been true two years earlier, in part because his relationship with President Johnson had deteriorated.[52] LBJ and a rightward-leaning Congress by late 1966 were losing interest in further civil rights legislation, as white America and its political leaders responded to the ghetto rebellions with disdain and repression rather than compassion. LBJ's War on Poverty had lost momentum, a casualty of the massive military expenditures on the Vietnam War. King's criticism of this had fueled such tensions with Johnson that his aides limited MLK's role at a White House Conference on Civil Rights in 1966, and King had broken two meeting dates with the president.[53]

Other SCLC leaders increasingly agreed with King's view that the war was incompatible with progress on civil rights and ending poverty. Thus in April 1966 the SCLC board passed its first antiwar resolution. James Bevel, a close aide to King, had become deeply engaged with the peace issue and relentlessly urged King to do the same. Bevel's eagerness to embrace the antiwar cause—intensified by his conviction that it was God's will that he do all possible to end an evil war—led him, by the end of the year, to take a leave of absence from his SCLC work to direct the Spring Mobilization to End the War in Vietnam.[54]

Ultimately the moral issue pushed King to stop limiting his public criticism of a war he had always loathed and to risk a complete break with LBJ and other Cold War liberals over Vietnam. In January 1967, while at the airport enroute to Barbados for a working vacation, King opened a copy of *Ramparts* magazine that featured a story, "The Children of Vietnam," illustrated with disturbing photos of Vietnamese victims of U.S. bombings and napalm. Bernard Lee recalled that he and King were about to eat when King viewed the article. "[He] froze as he looked at the pictures. He saw a picture of a mother holding her dead baby, a baby killed by our military. Then Martin pushed the plate of food away from him. I looked up and said 'Doesn't it taste good?' and he answered 'Nothing will taste any good to me until I do everything I can to end that war.' That's when the decision was made."[55] Whether or not Lee was correct in citing those *Ramparts* photos as pivotal, MLK's reaction to them was shaped by his nonviolent faith and his longstanding view that the Vietnam War was unjust, brutal, hurting the cause of social justice at home, and had to be stopped.

The part of MLK's move towards becoming a voice for the antiwar cause that is most difficult to sort out—and has not gotten the attention it deserves from King biographers, who have been almost exclusively male—is the role that Coretta Scott King played in it.[56] Coretta's antiwar activism dated back to her student days, when she had opposed U.S. Cold War policy. At MLK's request, she had spoken at a 1965 SCLC retreat on why this civil rights organization should come out against the Vietnam War. She participated that year in a large antiwar rally at Madison Square Garden and was its only woman speaker. In the next two years, when MLK had retreated from public antiwar activism, Coretta continued her participation in the peace movement as a member of the Women Strike for Peace, attending peace movement events.[57] King aide Bernard Lafayette thought that Coretta's antiwar activism in this period and "long before it . . . had a lot of influence on Martin Luther King coming to . . . [the] conclusion" that he needed to come out strongly against the war.[58]

However, in her memoir, Coretta suggested that her antiwar activism may have made it easier for her husband to delay his own. "Until 1967, Martin had been content to leave it to me to march, protest, and mount public challenges to the war in Vietnam. With my history of antiwar activism, it was easier to assuage his conscience about not being more strongly involved himself. We were always a team, so he felt that 'Well, at least one of us is involved.'"[59]

It may be that both Coretta's view and Lafayette's were accurate. MLK admired Coretta's peace activism and saw it as representing him too, which helped him rationalize his not taking on a public antiwar role. Yet at the same time he felt guilty that she was acting to stop an unjust war while he was not. If you read between the lines of his statement to a news reporter on this, you can feel both her influence and his guilt about his not being at her side in those antiwar protests: "I decided I would leave it to my wife to take the stands and make the meetings on the peace issue, but I came to the conclusion that I could no longer be a silent onlooker, but that in some real way, I had to be an involved and concerned participant."[60]

Although, as we have seen, King's most high-impact speech highlighting his antiwar stance came in New York City's Riverside Church in April 1967, he actually gave his first speech totally devoted to the Vietnam War more than a month before that, at a Nation Institute meeting in Los Angeles's Beverly Hilton, on February 25, 1967. This first antiwar speech was titled "The Casualties of the War in Vietnam" and offered a scathing account of the war's impact upon Vietnam and the United States. King began this speech by virtually replicating the images of the death and destruction wrought by the U.S. military that so disturbed him in the "Children of Vietnam" article and that he felt was also both physically and psychologically damaging to American soldiers. Here King spoke of the war's "nightmarish physical casualties," captured in TV news footage and in the press.

> We see the rice fields of a small Asian country being trampled at will and burned at whim. . . . Grief stricken mothers with crying babies clutched in their arms as they watch their little huts burst forth into flames. . . . Fields and valleys . . . painted with humankind's blood. . . . Young men . . . sent home half men, physically handicapped and mentally deranged. Most tragic of all is the casualty list among children. Some one million Vietnamese children have been casualties of this brutal war. A war in which children are incinerated by napalm, in which American soldiers die in mounting numbers, while other American soldiers . . . in unrestrained hatred shoot the wounded enemy as they lie on the ground, is a war that mutilates the conscience. These casualties are enough to cause all men to rise up with righteous indignation and oppose the very nature of this war.[61]

For King the killed and wounded in Vietnam were, however, only one part of what made the war so catastrophic. He believed "the casualties of principles and values are equally disastrous and injurious" and in the long run even "more harmful" because they were "self-perpetuating." And unless these were "healed," further bloodshed was inevitable. So in this first antiwar speech, King spent a good deal of time exploring the ways the Vietnam War revealed how America had lost touch with the best in the democratic and liberal traditions. He began with international law and how U.S. military intervention in Vietnam violated the UN Charter respecting the use of force against the "territorial integrity" and "political independence . . . of any state." King noted that though the United States justified its use of military force on the grounds that it did so to defend South Vietnam from

North Vietnamese aggression, this charge was never brought to the United Nations. "Instead we unilaterally launched an all-out war on Asian soil." This act of U.S. military aggression undermined the United Nations, violated international law, and alienated most of America's allies, who refused to join the United States in waging "this ugly war," leaving the United States "morally and politically isolated."[62]

King's critical view of the war was informed by his conviction that that the United States was waging a deplorable neocolonial war against Vietnamese nationalists fighting for their independence. This critique represented a radical dissent from the claim of President Johnson and his allies that the war was a noble democratic crusade to prevent a Communist takeover of Vietnam. Equally radical was the charge MLK made that seeing events in Vietnam through that Cold Warrior lens was a product of America's "paranoid anti-Communism" rather than the facts on the ground in Vietnam. King suggested that anti-Communist dogma as well as America's wealth and self-absorption left its political leadership unable to understand the insurgency of Vietnamese peasantry: a "failure to feel the ache and anguish of the have nots."[63]

MLK demonstrated a strong grasp of the history of American antiwar dissent, which he used in his "Casualties of War" speech to counter accusations that opposing U.S. military intervention was unpatriotic and un-American. King cited the opposition to the U.S. war with Mexico, whose outspoken critics included such great Americans as Abraham Lincoln, Henry David Thoreau, and Ralph Waldo Emerson. Their dissent, MLK held, proved how wrong it was of war hawks to urge the suppression of anti-Vietnam War dissent on the grounds that "American tradition forbids criticism of our government when the nation is at war." King warned that unless such political intolerance was resisted, "the principle of dissent" would become a "casualty of the war in Vietnam," as there had already been "an ugly repressive sentiment to silence peace seekers."[64]

King also made effective use of history in this speech to back his claim that U.S. intervention in Vietnam reeked of colonialism. He offered a pointed summary of U.S. support of France in its "attempted re-conquest of her former colony [Vietnam]," after World War II, including U.S. funding much of the French war in Vietnam, right up to the French defeat at Dien Bien Phu.[65] This occurred despite the fact that, when proclaiming their national independence, Ho Chi Minh's government had quoted the American

Declaration of Independence. "The greatest irony and tragedy," explained King, "is that our nation, which [in its revolution of 1776] initiated so much of the revolutionary spirit of the modern world is now cast in the mold of being an arch anti-revolutionary." Going even further, King perceived a white-supremacist tinge to the Vietnam War. To King, colonialism was little more than Jim Crowism on the international stage. "We are engaged in a war that seeks to turn the clock of history back and perpetuate white colonialism."[66]

For King the war looked even worse when you considered its domestic impact. He told the Nation Institute audience that the Vietnam War was so expensive that it had left woefully little funding available to support the Johnson administration's anti-poverty work. So as the war in Vietnam escalated, according to King, LBJ's War on Poverty in the United States de-escalated to a mere "skirmish against poverty." In support of his claims, King cited data showing that "we spend $322,000 for each enemy we kill, while we spend in the so-called war on poverty about $53 for each person classified as 'poor.'"[67]

King thundered against the hypocrisy and arrogance of America's wartime rhetoric about battling for freedom. He pointed out that similar U.S. anti-Communist rhetoric was used to support tyrannical, racist regimes in South Africa and Rhodesia and that our ally South Vietnam was governed by dictators. King also found it arrogant for the United States to profess being "concerned about foreign nations while not setting our own house in order." He offered the following as evidence: "Many of our Senators and Congressmen vote joyously to appropriate billions of dollars for war in Vietnam, and these same Senators and Congressmen vote loudly against a Fair Housing Bill to make it possible for a Negro veteran of Vietnam to purchase a decent home. We arm Negro soldiers to kill on foreign battlefields but offer little protection for their relatives from beatings and killings in our own South."[68]

None of these antiwar arguments were unique to King. Their significance lies not with their originality but with their radicalism. King's indictment of the war as imperialist, racist, and hypocritical was quite similar to SNCC's stance on the freedom movement's left wing.[69] What was new here was that King, as the movement's greatest orator, its only Nobel Prize winner, and its most eminent leader—even as he faced new challenges from the Black nationalists and the violent ghetto rebellions—had begun to accord sustained attention to the war, loaning his prestige to an antiwar movement that badly needed it. And he suggested the possibility of strengthening that movement by aligning it with the civil rights movement: "Those of us who love peace must organize as effectively as the war hawks. As they spread the propaganda of war we must spread the propaganda of peace. We must combine the fervor of the civil right movement with the peace movement. We must demonstrate, teach, and preach until the very foundations of our nation are shaken. We must work unceasingly to lift this nation that we love to a higher destiny, to a new plateau of compassion, to a more noble expression of humaneness."[70]

King's sweeping indictment of the war in this speech did not significantly differ from SNCC's antiwar position, but his religious sensibility enhanced that indictment's moral power. His gifts in crafting and delivering memorable phrases—some from the Bible—conveyed his arguments more forcefully and successfully than similar statements from SNCC, which was in its Black Power stage in 1967. Even as his "Casualties of War" speech resembled a jeremiad warning about the dire consequences of militarism, King couched his criticism in a language of patriotism: "I oppose the war in Vietnam because I love America. I speak out against it not in anger but with anxiety and love in my heart and above all with a passionate desire to see our beloved country stand out as a moral example to the world. I speak out against this war because I am disappointed with America . . . with our failure to deal positively with the triple evils of racism, extreme materialism, and militarism. We are presently moving down a dead-end road that can lead to national disaster."[71]

In ministerial terms, King was making the case for a moral choice between the sinful arrogance of war and the redemption of the nation through peace. He sought a new commitment to social justice, an integrated vision of a more humane society that addressed the country's failures at home and abroad and would work to end those "triple evils" that afflicted it.

> Our nation has not yet used its vast resources of power to end the long night of poverty, racism, and man's inhumanity to man. Enlarged power means enlarged peril if there is not a concomitant growth of the soul. Constructive power is the right use of strength. Our arrogance can be our doom. . . . Ultimately a great nation is a compassionate nation. We are challenged in these turbulent days to use our power to speed up the day "when every valley

> shall be exalted and every mountain and hill shall be made low: and the crooked places shall be made straight, and the rough places plain."[72]

Given the power of this first antiwar speech, its vision, and the ambition it articulated, it may seem remarkable that it did not create a greater stir. King was not merely calling for an end to war via a critique of the political bankruptcy that the Vietnam debacle embodied but was combining this with a call for a renewed commitment to battling racism and inequality and for a coalition of America's most controversial protest movements—the peace and Black Freedom movements. Had the speech been given at a higher-visibility venue or event, it likely would have made the kind of splash that King's Riverside Church speech did six weeks later.

Before Riverside, in late March 1967, King participated in his first antiwar march, in Chicago, attended by some five thousand people, where he declared that the war displayed to the world America's "barbarity."[73] By now, at the urging of Bevel (his only aide obsessed with ending the war), King was considering the idea of speaking on a larger political stage, in New York City, at the peace movement's planned mass spring mobilization march and rally. But agreeing with the advice of his advisors, King would first make his most famous antiwar speech in a religious setting.

MLK's decision to deliver his statements in a church reflected his choice of ministerial morality over being cautious and politic in the manner of moderate civil rights leaders. Had King operated in the world as calculating, self-interested politicians did, he would have kept quiet about Vietnam—continuing the retreat he had felt compelled to make in 1965 to avoid sailing against the winds of public opinion, defying the president on the war, and risking the damage to the SCLC. But ultimately this was, as we have seen, a moral question for King. On some issues, such as whether to oppose the Vietnam War, King explained,

> cowardice asks the question, Is it expedient? And then expedience comes along and asks the question, Is it politic? Vanity asks the question, Is it popular? Conscience asks the question, Is it right? There comes a time when one must take the position that is neither safe nor popular, but he must do it because conscience tells him it is right. I believe today that there is a need for all people of goodwill to come with a massive act of conscience and say in the words of the old Negro spiritual "We ain't gonna study war no more."[74]

So for King, the resolution of the moral question raised by the Vietnam War connected with his religious beliefs, and the church location helped make that plain. As Vincent Harding put it, "Martin chose Riverside because he wanted to make a religious statement. . . . He wanted the speech to represent his convictions as a faith leader and not just as a civil rights leader. At the deepest level Martin was a pastor to this country. The country was going wrong and he needed to speak prophetically about it."[75]

There were also tactical considerations that led to Riverside. Radical as King was in relation to mainstream America on the war and politics more generally, he (and his advisors) had a culturally conservative streak that led to a form of respectability politics. King, for example, dressed formally in dark suits, and so did his aides. Journalist Calvin Trillin, seated on an airplane behind King and three aides, noted their formal attire, and wrote that "except that all of them are Negroes and that the men were wearing buttons in their lapels that said S.C.L.C. FREEDOM NOW, the group might have been thought to consist of a corporation executive off to make a sales conference speech accompanied by efficient, neatly dressed young assistants brought along to handle arrangements and take care of the paperwork."[76]

In this same spirit, what could be more respectable than King as a minister, giving a speech from the pulpit of one of New York's most elegant and historic churches, in an event sponsored by clergy—in this case, Clergy and Laymen Concerned About Vietnam (CALCAV)? The church location was also selected for King's speech, according to King aide Andrew Young, so as to ensure that far-left sectarian groups, that often appeared at mass antiwar rallies, could not shape the event and to prevent having countercultural youths convert the event into some kind of weird spectacle, making it easier for critics to red-bait or hippie-bait the protest in order to dismiss or demonize King. And unlike other rallies, where King might have to keep his remarks brief, King could take as much time as he wanted in this church event, attended by some three thousand people. But despite these attempts at respectability politics, the powerful antiwar message of King's Riverside Church speech would provoke a storm of angry denunciations from supporters of the Vietnam War.[77]

Those denunciations, which we will assess below, are not surprising given the profound alienation of King from U.S. policy in Vietnam, which he expressed in even more elaborate and pointed form at Riverside than he had in his first antiwar speech in Los Angeles. What may have been almost as objectionable to King's critics was the introspective way King began his Riverside speech, explaining his choice to come out against the war in moral terms. Here King expressed regret over "the betrayal of my own silences," referring to his earlier retreat from antiwar activism—which, as we have seen, was caused by pressure from President Johnson and his allied war hawks. King spoke of the need to break his silence on the war, of its cruelty, and of how the billions of dollars wasted on the Vietnam debacle made impossible the funding of adequate anti-poverty programs, disrupting the quest for social justice. He took on critics who insisted that, as a civil rights leader, he ought to focus only on the struggle for U.S. racial justice and avoid getting involved in foreign policy debates. King argued that the attempt to divorce domestic from global concerns reflected a "tragic misunderstanding," which missed their interconnectedness. Owing to massive military expenditures in Vietnam, Washington's anti-poverty program had been "broken and eviscerated as if it were some idle plaything of a society gone mad on war." This, King explained, hurt low-income Blacks and whites alike, leaving him "compelled to see the war as an enemy of the poor and to attack it as such."[78]

It was not only this damage to anti-poverty programs that was his concern as a civil right leader but also the cost in human lives among the Black poor, who he claimed were dying in disproportionate numbers on Vietnam's battlefields. And dying supposedly to "guarantee liberties in Southeast Asia which they had not found in southwest Georgia and East Harlem." Black and white soldiers were killing and dying together for a nation that, in their student years, had kept them apart in segregated schools. "[On TV] we watch them in brutal solidarity burning the huts of a poor village, but we realize they could hardly live on the same block in Chicago. . . . I could not," King explained, "be silent in the face of such cruel manipulation of the poor."[79]

King's commitment to nonviolence led him to "an even deeper level of awareness" of the war's damaging impact and his need to oppose it. He spoke of his work in the ghettoes in the past three summers of racial unrest, where he urged young Blacks—angered by the poverty and discrimination they faced—to work for social change nonviolently rather than embracing violence. Such appeals, King explained, were undermined by the expanding war in Vietnam, as Black youths responded to his pleas for nonviolence by asking, "What about Vietnam?" "They asked, and rightly so . . . if our own nation wasn't using massive doses of violence to . . . bring about the changes it wanted." Noting that this justifiable question "hit home," King, in one of the most controversial lines in the Riverside speech, added that "I knew that I could never again raise my voice against the violence of the oppressed in the ghettos without having first spoken clearly to the greatest purveyor of violence in the world today: my own government."[80]

Alluding to those who asked him, "Aren't you a civil rights leader?", as if such leadership made it inappropriate for him to play a role in the peace movement, King referred them to the motto of the Southern Christian Leadership Conference: "To Save the Soul of America." This was no narrow civil rights motto. It described a desire to make America a just, humane, and democratic society, which was necessary since racial integration would be a dead end if it meant integrating into a white society sick with violence and militarism. And on this need for an American renewal, King cited the famed Black poet Langston Hughes:

> O, yes, I say it plain,
> America never was America to me,
> And yet I swear this oath—
> America will be![81]

In another of this speech's memorable and controversial lines, King warned, "If America's soul becomes totally poisoned, part of the autopsy must read 'Vietnam.'" To prevent such a tragedy, antiwar activism had become necessary: "Those of us who are yet determined that 'America will be' are led down the path of protest and dissent, working for the health of our land."[82]

King's willingness to quote Langston Hughes in this speech seems significant politically. King had long admired Hughes's poetry, and his 1941 poem "I Dream a World" may have been an inspiration for King's use of the dream metaphor in his March on Washington speech. But almost certainly owing to the Cold War and its anti-Communist legacy, from 1960 to 1965 King avoided publicly quoting Hughes, who earlier in his career was reputed to have been a Communist sympathizer.[83] At Riverside, however, King quoted and named Hughes. It is possible that the Hughes quote had initially been inserted into the speech by Vincent Harding, who helped with its initial draft and was a Hughes admirer.[84] But the fact that King kept Hughes's words and name in the speech—or added it himself—may well have been his way of rejecting the reflexive anti-Communism that had framed Washington's view of events in Vietnam and that the Johnson administration used to justify the war and its escalation. King seems to have symbolically made this same point in a subsequent speech honoring the great African American intellectual and activist W. E. B. Du Bois at the centennial celebration of his birth, even though in the Cold War years the U.S. government had treated DuBois as a pariah because of his late-life conversion to communism.[85]

As in his "Casualties of War" speech, at Riverside King insisted that the key to understanding the conflict was as a struggle for Vietnamese independence, first against France's (United States-backed) quest to "re-colonize" Vietnam, and then against the United States. America had replaced France, in what had become a neo-colonial crusade, under the banner of anti-Communism. But King's indictment of the war was even more pointed in his Riverside speech than it had been in his "Casualties of War" speech. He now spoke of "the madness" of the war, in which America's supposed quest for freedom in Vietnam had begun with the United States propping up the South Vietnamese regime of Ngo Dinh Diem, who King characterized as "one of the most vicious dictators of modern times." King adopted a Marxist-inflected class analysis of the insurgency in South Vietnam, describing a conflict between the United States-backed government in Saigon representing the landlord class versus the peasantry. "What," asked King, "do the peasants think as we ally ourselves with the landlords and refuse to put into any action our many words about land reform?" The answer to that question helped explain why, after Diem's overthrow he was succeeded by a steady stream of dictators, who King characterized as "corrupt, inept, and without popular support."[86]

King was scathing on the war's brutality. He spoke at Riverside of how U.S. forces would "herd" peasants into "concentration camps" and how much death and destruction the U.S. bombing raids had wrought, "with at least 20 casualties from American firepower for one Vietcong-inflicted injury. . . . So far we may have killed more than a million of them, mostly children." He charged that "we test out our latest weapons" on the Vietnamese peasants, "just as the Germans tested out new . . . tortures in the concentration camps of Europe." Such mass violence, King charged, "left nothing to build on, save bitterness."[87]

Linking the Vietnam tragedy to the pattern of counterrevolutionary U.S. interventionism across the globe, King, in another Marxist formulation, argued that it had economic roots in American capitalism. The "need to maintain social stability for our investments," King explained, "accounts for the counterrevolutionary action of American forces in Guatemala. It tells why American helicopters are being used against guerillas in Cambodia and why American napalm and Green Beret forces have already been active against rebels in Peru."[88]

In King's eyes, the Vietnam War was symbolic of such selfish materialistic interventionism and was "but a symptom of a far deeper malady within the American spirit."[89] Unless America's excessive materialism was curbed, the Vietnam War would be followed by endless U.S. military interventions. The main task ahead would be to get the United States "on the right side of the world revolution" of formerly colonized nations. This would require, in perhaps the most revolutionary passage of his Riverside speech: "[W]e as a nation must undergo a radical revolution of values. We must rapidly begin the shift from a thing-oriented society to a person-oriented society. When machines and computers, profit motives and property rights, are considered more important than people, the giant triplets of racism, extreme materialism, and militarism are incapable of being conquered."[90] It would take this "radical revolution in values" to motivate Americans "to question the fairness and justice" of American policy at home and abroad.

Readers will notice the most striking similarity in these first major speeches that he devoted entirely to opposing the Vietnam War. In Los Angeles in February 1967, MLK spoke of the "triple evils of racism, extreme materialism and militarism." Then in New York, that April, he denounced the "giant triplets of racism, extreme materialism and militarism." This was not new for King. Back in March 1965, he had used a similar analytic framework in his Howard University speech. Although not entirely devoted to Vietnam, it did air some of his earliest public criticisms of the Vietnam War. As King biographer David J. Garrow noted, even that early, in 1965, when MLK spoke of "the three evils of racism, poverty, and violence," this was already "a standard theme" for King.[91] Garrow was correct. In fact, years before the U.S. war in Vietnam had escalated—before LBJ's presidency, with its commitment of hundreds of thousands of U.S. combat troops to Vietnam and its unleashing of the deadly Rolling Thunder bombing campaign—MLK had sounded this theme. For example, in May 1962 King spoke at the United Packinghouse Workers of America (UPWA) annual convention and urged its members to "maintain a keen sensitivity to these social evils that pervaded our nation. . . . The evil of war, the evil of economic injustice, and the evil of racial injustice."[92] This attests that MLK was not a mere single-issue leader; it reflects a systemic analysis of the United States as a society that was more of a warfare state than a welfare state, far more oriented towards global hegemony and corporate profits than to ridding America of racism and poverty.

King's leftist critique of American imperialism and capitalism, and the sympathy he expressed for the anti-colonialist cause, could and would be misread by Vietnam War hawks as evidence that his Riverside speech was pro-Communist. But King made it clear at Riverside that the "revolution in values" he advocated was democratic (more akin to democratic socialism). And he argued that this "positive revolution in values is our best defense against Communism. War is not the answer. Communism will never be defeated by . . . bombs. We must not engage in negative anti-communism, but rather in a positive thrust for democracy . . . [and] in behalf of justice. We must with positive action remove those conditions of poverty, insecurity, and injustice, which . . . seed . . . communism."[93]

As part of his call for resistance to the war, King at Riverside urged those subject to the draft, who regarded the Vietnam War as "dishonorable" and "unjust," to consider filing for conscientious objector status. He cited with pride the more than seventy students at Morehouse College, his alma mater, who had followed this path.[94] And he urged religious leaders to file for conscientious objector status, rather than take a ministerial exemption, to demonstrate their opposition to the war. King also called for the U.S. government to halts its bombings, declare a unilateral ceasefire, negotiate an end to the war, and set a date to remove all foreign troops from Vietnam.

Though the speech drew much applause from the crowd of some three thousand who attended the Riverside Church event, most of whom were antiwar, the larger national response troubled King. While King had expected criticism from his traditional foes on the right, he was shocked by the extensive, bitter attacks from moderates and liberals, including some former political allies in the news media, politicians, and even fellow civil rights leaders. *The New York Times*, which had supported the historic civil rights legislation King helped make possible, ran a scathing editorial on "Dr. King's error," described as King's attempt "to fuse two problems, the war and civil rights, when those problems are distinct and separate. By drawing them together Dr. King has done a disservice to both." The newspaper objected to King's "comparing American military methods to those of the Nazis," which it denounced as a "slander," and the editorial accused King of "whitewashing Hanoi" and of facile thinking about the war.[95] *Life* magazine offered a similar rebuke, charging that King's speech "sounded like a script from Radio Hanoi" and citing the NAACP board's unanimous vote that it was a serious mistake to merge the civil rights and antiwar movements.[96] Similarly, John Roche, LBJ's academic liaison, told the president that King "has thrown in with the commies."[97]

As Roche's red-baiting comment and the similar *Life* editorial make evident, some of the attacks on King were fueled by a simplistic anti-Communist assumption that MLK's opposition to the war derived either from sympathy with or naivete about Vietnam's Communists. A subsequent, mid-April news analysis by Gene Roberts of *The New York Times*, who in 1968 would become the *Times* Saigon bureau chief, offered another kind of anti-radical criticism of King on the war. Roberts believed that over the preceding year Black Power advocates had divided and weakened the civil rights movement: their militancy and radicalism alienated moderate civil rights leaders and the public. The movement had become, in Robert's estimation, "fragmented and directionless." His hope had been that King could help the movement end this supposedly damaging Black Power phase, unifying moderates and militants, so that the struggle for racial justice could restore its earlier momentum. Roberts thought King's opposition to the war made it impossible for MLK to play such a unifying role, since that opposition aligned King with the inept, divisive Black Power radicals, who had long opposed the war. King had, in this way, "sacrificed his middle ground position among civil right leaders," undermining his own influence with them.[98]

Implicit in most of the criticism of King's antiwar activism was the assumption that, as a civil rights leader, he had gotten out of his lane by commenting on international affairs. His expertise was on domestic race relations, so he should leave foreign affairs to the experts in Washington. In this vein, John Roche's confidential memo to the president, blasting the Riverside speech, characterized King as "inordinately ambitious and quite stupid (a bad combination)."[99] There were, according to King aide Andrew Young, racial overtones to at least some of this disrespectful and heated criticism of King: "Martin gave a brilliant rationale for his position on the war in Vietnam. And as a Nobel Prize winner, we expected people to take it seriously, but to disagree with certain specifics. We didn't get that. We got, instead, an emotional outburst attacking his right to have an opinion. It was almost, you know, 'Nigger, you ought to stay in your place.'"[100]

Such attacks on MLK, whether characterized as condescending, racist, or both, were clearly inaccurate. To think that King was ignorant or poorly informed about international relations three years after he had won the Nobel Peace Prize was absurd. Indeed, King had been giving speeches on global affairs since the late 1950s. King scholar Lewis V. Baldwin has edited an entire book of King's speeches on international issues, *"In a Single Garment of Destiny": A Global Vision of Justice* (2012), documenting that King had thought deeply, and certainly for many years, about such issues as global poverty, apartheid, and the independence struggles of former colonies. At the invitation of Kwame Nkrumah, he had attended Ghana's independence ceremonies in 1957.[101] One could easily make the case that King had a better understanding of anti-colonialism and Third World revolution than did the Johnson administration, which tended to see them through the sometimes-distorted Cold War lens that presented virtually every event on the global stage as shaped by Communism versus anti-Communism. King rejected as "narrow and provincial" the idea that he ought not comment on Vietnam or anything other than domestic racial issues.[102]

Later MLK went even further in his critique of U.S. global policy, asserting in his posthumously published essay "A Testament of Hope" that the failure of U.S. policy toward Vietnam and the entire Third World reflected the white monopoly on the shaping of U.S. foreign affairs.

> The implications of true racial integration are more than just national in scope. I don't believe we can have world peace until America has an "integrated" foreign policy. Our disastrous experiences in Vietnam and the Dominican Republic have been, in one sense, a result of racist decision-making. Men of the white West . . . have grown up in a racist culture. . . . They don't really respect anyone who is not white. But we simply cannot have peace in the world without mutual respect. I honestly feel that a man without racial blinders—or, even better, a man with personal experience of racial discrimination—would be in a much better position to make policy decisions and to conduct negotiations with the underprivileged and emerging nations of the world (or even with Castro, for that matter) than would an Eisenhower or a Dulles.[103]

For King, then, the Black experience bred a kind of cosmopolitanism and compassion, an understanding of the aspirations of formerly colonized nations—like Vietnam—that white policymakers often lacked. There has been, King explained, "a kind of collective experience—a kind of shared misery in the black community—that makes it a little harder for us to exploit other people." Were African Americans given access to foreign policymaking, King concluded, "American Negroes can be a bridge between white civilization and the nonwhite nations of the world because we have roots in both."[104]

Like most American antiwar critics, King stressed the abuses of the U.S. side while saying little about those committed by the other side. He also tended to underestimate the influence of Communists in the South Vietnamese insurgency's National Liberation Front. But these, and other, flaws in his reading of the war were minor compared to those of President Johnson and most of his advisers. King understood, as they did not, that the United States was fated to lose the Vietnam War because it sided with the widely loathed foes of a nationalist revolution that was popular in Vietnam, even though the United States government despised its Communist leadership.

King was also right about the disastrous impact the Vietnam War would have on the quest for social justice at home. The war first divided liberals from the New Left, then polarized the nation, and finally undid the Johnson presidency. After all, it was a peace candidate, Senator Eugene McCarthy, whose strong showing in the 1968 New Hampshire Democratic primary—made possible by antiwar student volunteers—who prompted LBJ to end his presidential campaign. Nixon's subsequent capture of the White House would push the Supreme Court and American politics on the rightward trajectory that still shapes, and mars, the U.S. political landscape. It was King, not Johnson, who recognized from the start of U.S. escalation of the Vietnam War that, aside from its cruelty and futility, war was, as historian Richard Hofstadter put it, "the nemesis of the liberal [reform] tradition."[105]

While King's Riverside speech was of great importance to the antiwar movement, in aligning King—his great oratorical skill, prestige with the Left, and status as a Nobel Prize winner—with the crusade to end the Vietnam War, the peace movement still faced a daunting uphill climb. King understood this. As one attendee at the Riverside speech put it, "There was a sadness to the speech—this was not the rhetoric of 'We Shall Overcome,' with any confidence that we [in the antiwar movement] would overcome any time soon."[106] Neither the public—including the Black community, of which only a quarter supported MLK's antiwar position according to polling data—nor most of the nation's media or political leadership had given up on the war effort.[107]

In discussing the relationship between the civil rights movement and the antiwar movement, King usually avoided the idea of a complete or what he called a "mechanical merger" between the two protest movements. This was, in part, because he knew that both movements were preoccupied with their own issues. But he thought collaborative actions were possible and desirable, as he explained in his press conference at the UN, after addressing the spring mobilization's huge antiwar march, on April 15, 1967: "The priorities of the civil rights movement and the peace movement are from a content point of view inextricably tied together. In the final analysis there can be no peace without justice and no justice without peace. . . . The spirit of the civil rights movement should certainly imbue . . . and thereby strengthen the peace movement."[108]

King understood the resistance to a merger with the antiwar movement on the part of such major civil rights groups as the NAACP and the Urban League, whose leadership still preferred their singular focus on civil rights. Other obstacles included the Black nationalist politics of younger activists, who were wary of working with the white-dominated antiwar movement, and the SNCC's and the SCLC's dislike of the New Left's sectarian divisions. The antiwar movement also had its own single-issue orientation and a white parochialism that limited its interest in anti-racist activism.[109] And for Black freedom activists, the struggle against racism was so consuming, especially in the wake of the white backlash against the civil rights and Black Power movements, that there were simply not enough hours in a day, or funds, for civil rights organizations to devote much time to building the antiwar movement. This even proved true of King himself, who spent the final year of his life working primarily not in the antiwar movement but rather in his Poor People's Campaign against poverty. In the aftermath of the ghetto riots, he tried to show that nonviolence remained the best route to progressive change, and in his pro-labor organizing in Memphis for the striking sanitation workers, that effort ended with his assassination.

This question of how much time King spent on antiwar organizing was raised in a hostile manner by those who supported the war and viewed it as inappropriate for a civil rights leader to help lead the peace movement. For example, in an interview in the summer of 1967, King was asked why he was "spending more time today speaking out against the war in Vietnam than raising funds for job training for Negroes which they so desperately need." King replied: "I don't spend that much of my time on the peace question or Vietnam. . . . Ninety-five per cent of my time is still spent on the civil rights struggle."[110] And King challenged the premise of this question by pointing out that it would be both immoral and impractical for him, as a religious leader and civil rights leader, to pretend that the war was none of his business.

> I'm a clergyman. I was a clergyman before I was a civil right leader, and when I was ordained to the Christian ministry, I accepted that as a commission to constantly and forever bring the ethical insights of our Judeo-Christian heritage to bear on social evils of our day. And I happen to think that war is one of the major social evils facing mankind. . . . It would be foolhardy for me to work for integrated schools or integrated lunch counters and not be concerned about the survival of the world in which to be integrated.[111]

It would be a mistake, however, to assume that the limited time King could devote to the antiwar movement lessened the significance of his antiwar position and role. He became co-chair of Clergy and Laymen Concerned About Vietnam (CALCAV), the nation's leading religious organization against the war. Along with the prominent antiwar activist and best-selling child-care author Dr. Benjamin Spock, in 1967 King announced in Cambridge, Massachusetts, the launch of one of the most important antiwar organizing efforts staffed by student peace activists: the Vietnam Summer campaign. This project took the peace movement off campus, into hundreds of communities, canvassing ordinary Americans against the war.[112] King was a vocal critic of the federal indictment of antiwar leaders Dr. Spock and Yale Chaplain William Sloan Coffin Jr., in January 1968, on charges of counseling young people to resist the draft.[113] That same month King traveled to northern California's Santa Rita Detention Center to visit his friend Joan Baez, the famous young folk singer, who (along with her mother and manager) was among those jailed for participating in an anti-draft sit-in at the Oakland Army Induction Center. Before leaving Santa Rita, King made a short speech supporting draft resistance and encouraging those drafted who opposed the war to seek conscientious objector status.[114]

King used his connections with the labor movement to make the antiwar case. In fact, it is hard to think of another peace activist who had the kind of reach that MLK did, since he spoke to and was admired in the labor movement, the student antiwar movement, the civil rights movement, and in the pacifist churches. Among King's most powerful antiwar speeches was one he gave in the fall of 1967 to dissident labor organizers in the National Leadership Assembly for Peace, who sought to get the nation's most influential labor federation, the AFL-CIO, to end its Cold Warrior militarism and come out against the Vietnam War. Here King stressed, as always, the unjust, brutal, and imperialistic character of the war while also pointing to the political reaction and indifference to the need for egalitarian social change that the war bred at home. Highlighting the importance of the Leadership Assembly's attempts to align the labor and antiwar movements, King explained, "with an amazing tenacity and boldness . . . millions of ordinary people, eminent scholars, distinguished senators, journalists, businessmen, professionals, students, and political leaders . . . have protested the war."[115] But the voice of organized labor had been missing. "The absence of that one voice was all the more tragic because it may be the decisive one for tipping the balance toward peace. . . . For too long the moral flame has been flickering, not shining," unlike the labor movement's "dynamic days of growth" in the New Deal era. MLK believed the Leadership Assembly's antiwar activism was a hopeful sign: "[It] reaffirms that the trade union movement is part of forward-looking America. . . . That no matter what the formal resolutions of the higher bodies [in the labor movement] may be, the troubled conscience of the working people cannot be stilled. This conference speaks for millions. You here today will be remembered as those who had the courage to speak out and the wisdom to be right.[116]

Thanks to King's role as a magnet for the media, he was able to spotlight religious opposition to the war in a uniquely effective way. As he did with his front page *New York Times* interview on the war, which appeared two days before his Riverside Church speech and whose headline indicated that civil disobedience might, in King's view, be necessary to end the war.[117] President Johnson quickly and angrily realized, from the moment King embraced the peace movement, that MLK was his most important antiwar critic. Consequently, LBJ turned on King, privately referring to him—despite their prior collaboration on historic civil rights legislation—as a "goddamned nigger preacher."[118] King's civil rights organizing then, while limiting his time for antiwar work, did not undermine the prominence of his voice as an antiwar critic in his final year. It was not MLK's anti-poverty and civil rights organizing but rather his assassination that kept him from looming even larger in the peace movement. King would not live to see the withdrawal of the last U.S. ground troops from Vietnam in 1973, or the fall of Saigon in 1975, events that proved how prescient he had been in predicting that, despite its massive military might, the United States would lose its imperialistic war in Vietnam.

Late as it was, King's embrace of the antiwar movement still required a degree of political courage since, as we have seen, it angered not only LBJ and civil rights leaders previously aligned with him but also the most influential newspapers and news magazines that had been important supporters of his civil rights campaigns. And King created this political hurricane against the advice of most of his advisors, choosing to take all these political risks as a matter of conscience instead of political expediency. Less well known, however, is the fact that King's antiwar stance also involved physical courage, since his critique of the war, rejection of its anti-Communist premises, and denunciation of U.S. militarism led superpatriot extremists to heckle and threaten him as "a traitor." This emotionally fraught, demonizing, label could lead to violence from intolerant right-wing militants who convinced themselves that King was undermining the war effort, which in their view endangered American troops in Vietnam and gave aid and comfort to the enemy. King's most trying encounter with such hostility came only a few weeks before his death, in a Grosse Pointe, Michigan, speaking engagement.

Grosse Pointe was an affluent white suburb of Detroit with a long record of resisting racial integration. It was thus a place where the vocal and extreme Detroit-based superpatriot group, Breakthrough, thought it could rally support. This organization and its far-right leader, Donald Lobsinger, had battled against neighborhood racial integration in Detroit. Its leaders were outraged that Grosse Pointe's Human Relations Council had invited King to speak and furious about his antiwar, anti-racist, and anti-poverty leadership.[119] Lobsinger's organization issued a hate-filled leaflet seeking to mobilize the community to disrupt King's March 14, 1968, evening appearance in Grosse Pointe, charging that MLK was a "'civil rights agitator' . . . aligned . . . with Communist front groups and causes, [and] parroted their slogans and promoted their anti-American objectives" and denouncing him as a dangerous "TRAITOR."

> Under the guise of "Peace," Martin Luther King has taken up the banner of the Viet Cong by calling for an end of the War in Vietnam on Communist terms. . . . King has long supported the Communist objective of U.S. recognition of the outlaw Chinese Communist regime and its admission to the United Nations. But NEVER has King raised his voice on behalf of the millions living under the brutal tyranny of the Hammer & Sickle. By his promotion of massive civil disobedience and his vile attacks upon law enforcement agencies, King has contributed . . . to the rampant spirit of lawlessness, violent disorder, and "riots" which have stricken many of the nation's cities. . . . King is now preparing—in collaboration with the pro-Castroite Stokely Carmichael and other black power militants—to carry out his plan for the massive disruption of our nation's capital and other major cities. . . . His visit to our city is intended to win support for this program of planned disorder which—it is his hope—will bring our country ever closer to a state of total anarchy, communist revolution, overthrow, and finally conquest. Thus the only AMERICAN response to King's visit can be and IS—LET HIM COME IF HE DARES![120]

Grosse Pointe civil rights activist Jude Huetteman, who had invited King and secured the lecture hall for his talk, received threatening letters and phone calls, including one claiming that her children had been kidnapped. Threats had been directed at school board members who refused to support right-wing efforts to prevent Grosse Pointe High School from hosting King's speech, which could only occur after Huetteman agreed to pay for the million-dollar insurance policy to cover potential damage to the school. Huetteman recalled that when she went over to the school a few hours before King's scheduled speech, she learned that, due to a bomb threat, the high school had "been closed at four o'clock so that the bomb squad could go over it." And that "what was going on outside the school was unbelievable!" The right-wing group had been "circling the block in decorated cars screaming 'King is a traitor' and other slogans. Horns were blaring."[121]

When King arrived for the event, Huetteman let him know about the opposition to his speech and what she had witnessed that afternoon outside the school. King responded calmly: "He nodded knowingly" and told her "he had traveled this path before." She "marveled at his sense of peace," recalling that "we were all to marvel much more before the evening was over." The only comic relief that night came when, as part of the police escort to the school, an officer concerned about King's safety jumped into the front seat with MLK, and Huetteman informed King that "the man sitting on your lap is our chief of police."[122] By the time King arrived at the high school, some two hundred of the Breakthrough reactionaries were picketing outside the building.[123]

Huetteman was so worried about what those who had expressed such hatred for MLK might do to disrupt his talk that she found it difficult to focus on the substance of his speech. As Huetteman put it, she "didn't hear much of the speech; I was concerned with watching for what I knew was going to happen. At the first mention of the war by Dr. King, they started. There was loud heckling." This included repeated, shouted accusations of treason "and some disturbance every few minutes, but that was overshadowed by the 32 times he was interrupted by applause," including several standing ovations from the almost three thousand people who packed the auditorium.[124]

Fearful that the hecklers' bitter attacks on MLK might result in violence, Huetteman "prayed that one of the screamers did not have a gun." The police presence at the event made a difference, for, as Huetteman noted, "police removed one group" of the most disruptive hecklers. She was impressed that even in the face of such bitter denunciation, over the course of the event King "seemed to become more peaceful and controlled," and she cited King's remarks, as the police removed rowdy hecklers, that "I know what my sermon tomorrow will be: 'Father, forgive them, for they know not what they do,'" which led the crowd in the packed high school auditorium to cheer and applaud.[125]

The transcript of King's Grosse Pointe talk affirms that Huetteman was justified in praising the way MLK handled the disruptions. King would not let the hecklers prevent him from giving a substantive speech on "The Other America." This was a revised version of a talk he had given previously, most notably at Stanford University, focusing on the enduring problems of poverty and racism and also raised his objections to the Vietnam War.

Just as King began discussing unemployment, a woman rose up from the audience and denounced him as a "traitor," to which King replied, "I'll just wait until our friend can have her say [applause]. I'll just wait until things are restored . . . and everybody talks about law and order [applause]." King made it clear that he was not trying to prevent his critics from airing their views, at the appropriate time, but that it was wrong that they had "so rudely interrupted" his speech. "It was, King told the crowd, "my understanding that we're going to have a question and answer period, and if anybody disagrees with me, you will have the privilege, the opportunity to raise a question, if you think I am a traitor, . . . to ask me about my traitorness." But King insisted that he would not be intimidated, assuring the audience, which responded with applause, that "I've been in the struggle a long time now, and I've conditioned myself to some things that are much more painful than discourteous people not allowing you to speak, so if they feel they can discourage me, they'll be up here all night."[126]

MLK proved especially effective in responding to "a young man who said he was a veteran of the war, [who] screamed 'Traitor!' With real concern, Dr. King invited him to the platform to explain what made him think that he was traitorous."[127] This heckler came up and spoke briefly, intemperately equating antiwar dissent with treason, asserting that he had been a "communications technician, U.S. Navy, and I fought for freedom. I didn't fight for communists, traitors, and I didn't fight to be sold down the drain."[128] King then calmly but firmly explained why he opposed the war, and insisted such opposition was not done out of disloyalty but rather out of humane concern, including concern for U.S. troops fighting that war. After thanking the veteran for sharing his thoughts, King argued that "I just want to say in response that there are those of us who oppose the war in Vietnam for . . . many reasons. Many of them are moral reasons but one basic reason is that we love our boys who are fighting and just want them to come back home." Since the Vietnam War was not the focus of his speech, King said he did not have time to recount the war's history, but "I'm convinced that it is clearly an unjust war" that damaged the struggle for a more humane and democratic society in the United State, and caused international tensions, "carrying the whole world closer to nuclear annihilation."[129]

Even though the hecklers focused primarily on the war issue, King displayed an awareness of the racial dynamic at work here, since he was speaking to a mostly white audience, in a white suburban community, and to its (and Detroit's) most outspoken, intolerant right-wing foes of the civil rights and antiwar movements. So King closed his Grosse Pointe speech with a powerful appeal for interracial understanding and unity.

> Now let me finally say something in the realm of the spirit and then I'm going to take my seat. . . . In the midst of the hollering and . . . discourtesy tonight, we've got to come to see that however much we dislike it, the

destinies of white and black America are tied together. Now the races don't understand this apparently. But our destinies are tied together. And somehow we must learn to live together as brothers in this country or we're going to perish together as fools. Our destinies are tied together. Whether we like it or not, culturally and otherwise, every white person is a little bit negro and every negro is a little bit white. Our language, our music, our material prosperity, and even our food are an amalgam of black and white, so there can be no separate black path to power and fulfillment that does not intersect white routes, and there can ultimately be no separate white path to power and fulfillment short of social disaster without recognizing the necessity of sharing that power with black aspirations for freedom and human dignity. We must come to see . . . yes we do need each other, the black man needs the white man to save him from his fear and the white man needs the black man to free him from his guilt.[130]

Eloquent and poised as he was during his speech, King admitted at the press conference afterwards that, prior to his Grosse Pointe speech, "he had never experienced such vocal opposition at an indoor meeting."[131] Huetteman thought he "seemed shaken after he left the stage but still managed to be gracious to those of us who were with him."[132] Try as he might to transcend it, the hostility directed at him at Grosse Pointe, and at such close range, was disturbing, demonstrating to King that his outspoken opposition to war had made him as much of a target for right-wing hatred as had his civil rights work. This was likely why, just before leaving Grosse Pointe, King discussed with Huetteman the dangers of such rage and the threat of assassination. He talked "about hate and how it fills a man so nothing else can get into him; and about the inevitable and how it happens no matter how one plots against it." Huetteman was "moved by his sincerity," stating, "He really didn't hate anyone. He couldn't."[133]

Engaged as he was with what turned out to be the final protest movements of his life, the Poor People's Campaign, and Memphis's sanitation workers strike, King, upon leaving Grosse Pointe, did not have time to reflect publicly on his encounter with this suburban audience's hateful right-wing extremists. He would not live long enough to write a word about the ugly slanders they hurled at him as they tried to disrupt his speech. So it would not be King but rather the religious leader who had introduced King at his Grosse Pointe speech, Richard S. Emrich, the bishop of Michigan's

Episcopal Diocese, who wrote the most extensive and revealing indictment of those hecklers who had sought to prevent King from speaking.

Bishop Emrich, in an open letter that appeared in the *Grosse Pointe News* a week after King's speech, offered what he termed "a public apology to Dr. Martin Luther King, for as a guest he had a right to expect other things; and I write it also that the thousands who were not there may feel in their bones the rudeness, arrogance, sickness, and ignorance of our superpatriots." Suggesting that the protesters had revealed themselves to be profoundly illiberal and anti-democratic, Emrich wrote that he had "not seen anything quite like" them since his "student days" when his international studies had landed him in "Nazi Germany." The Bishop noted that these superpatriots

> always appear with flags hiding their un-American activity behind the screen of patriotism. Although they wave the flag and pass as patriots, they have no understanding whatever of the treasured institutions which the flag represents—freedom of assembly, the tradition of Parliament in which one listens while another speaks, the rules of order, respect for the rights of others. They are spiritual and political barbarians. They are arrogant and cruel, having no regard whatever for the Constitutional rights of others, and assuming that they alone know what it means to love one's country. In one sense, it was a good meeting and edifying; for a crowded hall saw at first hand the stature and wisdom of Dr. King contrasted with the rudeness, cruelty, and repulsive arrogance of miserable men and women. We saw extremists in action, and felt the sickness of their souls.[134]

The most important account of MLK's Grosse Pointe speech and its hecklers that was not made public in 1968 derives from the FBI, whose report on this event only came into public view when it was released in response to a Freedom of Information Act request more than a decade later. The report accurately noted that, according to two FBI sources, Breakthrough leader Donald Lobsinger and several others in his group were escorted out of the lecture hall after they denounced King as a traitor and sought to disrupt his speech. But the FBI report was chilling in its indifference to the question of MLK's personal safety. Despite the bomb threat, the hatred directed at King by the extremist hecklers in the lecture hall, and by the large group of hostile picketers outside the school building, the FBI uncritically accepted the characterization by one of its informants that attempted disruption of the speech constituted merely a "minor disturbance."[135] This is quite a contrast, as we have seen, to the fear expressed by Huetteman, and concern by the Grosse Pointe police, that violence might erupt. Nor did the FBI report take note of the threats Huetteman had been subjected to for inviting King to speak at Grosse Pointe or indicate a need to investigate the right-wing militants who displayed such hostility towards King, both at his speech and in the threatening leaflet they had circulated to mobilize protesters to disrupt MLK's talk. (Lobsinger's and Breakthrough members' violent proclivities became even clearer when they were later indicted for assaulting an antiwar priest.[136]) Such FBI indifference and ineptitude, coming just weeks before the tragedy in Memphis, is chilling and helps explain why, despite its constant surveillance of MLK, the Bureau proved unable—and perhaps unwilling—to act in any meaningful way to protect King from assassination.

Although the Grosse Pointe speaking event is remembered by King scholars due to the ugly superpatriot attempts to disrupt it (as well as for King's speech there), that evening in Michigan generated another speech—neglected by historians—that was quite revealing about this time in MLK's life. These were the remarks Bishop Emrich made in introducing King to those in attendance. He began by stating that he was "honored" to have been invited to introduce Dr. King, who "I admire and esteem . . . and love." Emrich praised King as "a brave man who has walked with death, and has been imprisoned for the sake of human rights," who preached love and nonviolence, and refused to countenance hatred, and so had "never said a hateful word about men who have hurt and vilified him."[137] He knew that "if any man hates, his soul is corrupted and he has been inwardly destroyed." King was, in Emrich's estimation "a great leader" in the "struggle for justice. . . . I honor him as a brother in Christ, for I believe his name is written in heaven." Aware that right-wing extremists had, in the weeks leading up to the Grosse Pointe speech, loudly demonized MLK as a traitor, the Bishop powerfully refuted this charge, arguing that King

> sees that hatred and violence could create wounds in America too terrible to heal. And he sees that as an American people we must go forward together, that any other plan is madness. He sees, like the prophets, and like His Lord who wept over the city, that the will of God is justice, that love is the motive and justice the goal, that no unjust society can be stable or endure. He sees that America must become what America is in its

> deepest soul; and all of his actions for social justice are based upon the profound love of this land and his belief in it. He has a dream for America which can be summarized in the familiar words—"one nation, under God, indivisible, with liberty and justice for all."[138]

Yet along with such praise, Bishop Emrich spoke of his "political disagreement" with MLK. He did so diplomatically, explaining that "we must learn to listen to one another and to understand each other as friends, though we may not always agree." Emrich made clear how uncomfortable he was with King's vocal opposition to the Vietnam War. Citing the recent New Hampshire primary, in which the peace candidate Eugene McCarthy came within striking distance of President Lyndon Johnson (who had, of course, escalated the war), Emrich held that the war had left Americans "deeply divided." So near the end of his introductory remarks, the Bishop asked King if his antiwar activism did not weaken his position as a civil rights leader because it "divide[d] your followers" and "set back the cause" of racial justice. "Respecting profoundly your belief in nonviolence, and the love in your heart, was it not a political mistake . . . when you combined the two issues" of Vietnam and racial justice? The bishop also expressed his doubts about the planned civil disobedience for King's Poor People's Campaign encampment in the nation's capital: "I do not understand how if" through such civil disobedience "the city of Washington is tied up, if the City stops, that really can be called non-violence. . . . Does not that open the door for a violence which you deplore?"[139]

While Emrich insisted to King that he raised these doubts respectfully "as one who admires you and is honored to be your friend," they nonetheless attested to the political price of King's decision to openly break with LBJ, the Vietnam War, and Johnson's paltry War on Poverty.[140] There MLK was, in middle America, facing not merely hostile right-wing hecklers but even an admiring liberal religious leader unable to comprehend King's increasingly leftist positions. In his speech King addressed these doubts effectively by discussing how the war was immoral and sapped the resources needed to abolish poverty. He believed it crucial to both end the Vietnam disaster and to launch a Poor People's Campaign, which designed not to tie up Washington but rather to awaken Congress to the need to abolish poverty. Emrich's questions were, however, a reminder of how lonely and isolating it could be for King, in the final year of his life, to champion peace and mass protest against poverty at a time when even liberal allies were often ill-disposed to such mass protest on the left that dissented from LBJ's ostensibly liberal administration.

* * *

King's historic Riverside Church speech tends to be referred to today as "Beyond Vietnam" because King spoke not only about Vietnam but the need to re-think the larger U.S. role on the global stage. This re-thinking had many aspects to it, which were deeply meaningful to antiwar activists during his own century and in ours. These included recognizing White House over-eagerness to intervene militarily in violation of less powerful nations' sovereignty. And interrogating the arrogant yet popular assumption that America's power could reform the politics of societies whose cultures U.S. foreign policy-makers did not even understand. As King scholar Michael Honey put it, "During the U.S invasion of Iraq, we often turned to King's 1967 'Beyond Vietnam' speech to grasp a better understanding of why the U.S continued this path, and the terrible results of America's reliance on guns and bombs to solve human problems. King addressed the government's shocking refusal to understand the history of other cultures, or how its policies of war and neglect of humanitarian concerns can shred people's faith in American democratic ideals."[141]

King thought a revolution in values would be needed to end American militarism. He felt that America must transform itself into a more humane and compassionate nation that would confront poverty and racism, becoming more equal and less profit-driven, before it could cure itself of its use (and subsidizing) of military force for global domination. Tragically, this revolution in values has never come. And, in fact, even on the national holiday named for him, King's advocacy of that revolution is rarely discussed. Nor are his views about nonviolence, his antiwar speeches, or his belief that workers and their labor unions ought to be a key force for social justice and peace. Indeed, generations of Americans who think of MLK as a lofty dreamer would be shocked to learn that in his greatest antiwar speech he had criticized America as "the greatest purveyor of violence in the world today."[142] It is impossible to deny that twenty-first century America, a nation with by far the largest military budget in the world, and where an epidemic of gun violence makes it the global center for mass shootings, would stand to benefit from an encounter with MLK's speeches and writings against war and on behalf of nonviolence.

The final, sad irony of King's advocacy of peace and nonviolence was that his life was ended by violence when an assassin murdered him. It is worth reflecting on the impact that MLK's assassination had on his friend Vincent Harding, who wrote the first draft of King's Riverside Church speech. King's death left Harding with persistent feelings of guilt about his work on that speech. Aware that MLK was already unpopular with racists, Harding believed that the pro-war superpatriot rage and red-baiting provoked by the Riverside speech further poisoned the political atmosphere, compounding the threats to King's personal safety. "It was," as Harding recalled, "one year to the day after this speech that that bullet that had been chasing him for a long time finally caught up with him. And I am convinced that that bullet had something to do with that speech. And over the years that's been quite a struggle for me."[143] Whether or not Harding was right to feel such guilt about the speech, those feelings (and MLK's Grosse Pointe encounter with hateful war hawks) are themselves a testament to how difficult it has been to dialogue with America—the "gunfighter nation"—about its addiction to violence and militarism or for Americans even to consider the nonviolent path that King advocated with such moral force and eloquence.[144]

Abolishing Poverty and Supporting Striking Workers

In March 1968, during the final weeks of his life, Martin Luther King Jr. had been hard at work planning and organizing the Poor People's Campaign (PPC), a march on Washington and encampment there. Activists were slated to deploy civil disobedience aimed at pressuring Congress to vastly expand its assistance to the poorest American of all races, lifting them out of poverty. Amid this work and at the request of Memphis's Black Freedom Movement leaders, King broke away from the PPC to travel to that racially polarized city in support of impoverished, exploited African American sanitation workers who were on strike for better conditions, union recognition, and a living wage.[1]

As I write this chapter, the U.S. power structure of 2025, headed by President Donald Trump, a self-proclaimed billionaire, and his key ally and patron Elon Musk, the world's richest man, are aligned not with what King stood for and gave his life for in 1968 but with those who opposed him. Trump, who during the 2024 presidential campaign had praised Musk for firing striking workers, empowered Musk to fire thousands of unionized government employees with neither cause nor adequate notice. He also empowered the world's wealthiest man to shut down the United States Agency for International Development (USAID) that had provided life-saving food assistance and vaccinations to some of the poorest people on the planet.[2] It is not merely Trump and Musk but also their allies in Congress and the millions of voters who empowered such plutocrats whose behavior attests to how far removed twenty-first century America is from the egalitarian ideals and "Good Samaritan" spirit King embodied, and spoke of so movingly, in his last speech, on April 3, 1968, just hours before his assassination. Despite the MLK holiday and the MLK national memorial in Washington, D.C., many Americans have never learned or have chosen to ignore the lessons King taught about the urgent need to make America a more economically equitable society and one determined to abolish poverty.

Even though King lost his life in Memphis supporting a strike, this has caused little reflection among the American public about MLK's (or its own) relationship to the labor movement. This is not a subject that conservatives have been eager to discuss since they are often anti-union, and King had a long history of supporting racially inclusive labor unions. But it is not just conservatives who say little about King's relationship to the labor movement. It is true of most Americans, including those in the news media, and reflects the decline of organized labor in post-industrial America, with union membership down to 9.9 percent of the labor force in 2024, as compared to 20.1 percent in 1983.[3] Labor history is thus seen as unimportant. Neglect of this history, and of King's role in it, obscures MLK's democratic radicalism, his critical take on American capitalism, and his support for union activism and working-class agency.

King's support of the Memphis sanitation workers in 1968 was consistent with his longstanding desire for an alliance between the labor and Black Freedom movements. To promote that alliance, and raise funds for the freedom movement, King had been speaking to labor union audiences since the 1950s. Michael Honey, a leading King scholar and labor historian, has published an entire book (two hundred pages) of MLK's most memorable labor speeches, titled with the King quote "all labor has dignity" and featuring a cover photo of MLK walking a picket line with striking workers at Atlanta's Scripto factory in 1964.[4] King was close to progressive labor leaders who were open to collaborating with the civil rights movement, most notably A. Philip Randolph, Walter Reuther of the United Auto Workers (UAW), and Ralph Helstein of the United Packinghouse Workers of America (UPWA). King was especially supportive of Randolph (who was both a labor and civil rights leader) and his reformist wing of the labor movement that was working to end racial discrimination in unions. MLK's alliance with civil rights unionists placed him to the left of some mainstream union heads, who had done little to stop discrimination.[5]

MLK saw great potential for the labor movement to serve as an instrument for economic equity. So long as unions did not discriminate racially, they could, in King's view, be a source of meaningful Black activism and influence, given the overwhelmingly working-class character of Black America. Though Blacks accounted for just 10 percent of the general population, they represented "20 percent of the organized work force."[6] King saw the Congress of Industrial Organizations (CIO), in its left-leaning early days during the New Deal era, as offering a model for effective working-class organizing, as he explained in his last book, *Where Do We Go from Here: Chaos or Community?* (1967): "[T]he labor movement . . . was one of the few great institutions where a degree of hospitality and mobility was available to Negroes. When the rest of the nation accepted discrimination and prejudice as ordinary and usual—like the rain . . . —trade unions, particularly the CIO leveled all barriers to equal membership. In a number of instances Negroes rose to influential national [union] office."[7]

King was especially fond of the most progressive labor unions whose rank-and-file was predominantly non-white and closely aligned with the Black Freedom Movement. This was the case, for example, with the Retail, Wholesale and Department Store Union (RWDSU), District 65, whose membership was 90 percent Black and Puerto Rican. When MLK gave an impassioned speech to this union in 1962, his talk in upstate New York connected the racial and class issues that both the labor and civil rights movement confronted. He suggested that the union needed to be a force for egalitarian change, not only on its work-related goals but also in the broader struggle to move America leftward, so that Washington directed its resources away from war to battling poverty and racism. He emphasized the need to confront the "three major social evils, the evil of war, the evil of economic injustice, and the evil of racial injustice," since progress on all three was a prerequisite for a more just society, a theme—as we have seen—MLK stressed increasingly as the decade progressed.[8]

These union members proved receptive. They made financial contributions to the Southern civil rights movement and became prominent supporters of the March on Washington. The union would publish King speeches in its newsletter and later memorialize him by having its contracts provide for a day off to honor MLK on his birthday.[9] The mutual affection between the working-class Black community and King was a key reason why A. Philip Randolph so respected MLK, whom he believed had "roused the poor Negro with results more consequential than any leader before him."[10]

King expressed admiration for labor movement activism on behalf of workers in his first speech as an emerging civil rights movement leader in December 1955. This was his Holt Street Baptist Church speech, delivered at the initial mass meeting to help organize the Montgomery bus boycott. King sought to reassure the Black community, fed up with the city's racially discriminatory bus system, that it had the right to protest such oppressive conditions. King not only invoked the U.S. Constitution but also the American labor movement's tradition of protesting injustice. He urged those who risked their jobs and arrest in joining the boycott not to let "anybody frighten you."

> We are not afraid of what we are doing . . . because we are doing it within the law . . . There is never a time in our American democracy that we must ever think we are wrong when we protest. . . . We reserve that right. When labor all over this nation came to see that it would be trampled over by capitalistic power, it was nothing wrong with labor getting together and organizing and protesting for its rights.[11]

This Holt Street quotation shows King's admiration for labor exercising the right to protest, offering a model for anti-racist champions to emulate. It also demonstrates a critical perspective on the abuse of capitalist power, which held that labor would be "trampled" unless workers organized on their own behalf. Long before his emergence as a civil rights leader, moreover, King showed empathy for those impoverished by the American capitalist system and for those struggling to end such deprivation. Coretta Scott King recalled that while still in graduate school and courting her, MLK spoke "about working within the framework of democracy toward a kind of socialism" in one of their early conversations. "I say this advisedly because I think that people misunderstand the word 'socialism,' but in the sense that Martin used it—he said a kind of socialism has to be adopted by our system because the way it is, it's simply unjust. He looked at the poor and the fact that so many people were in ill health with no way to pay for their medical expenses. He asked, 'How do you catch up on all these things? There's got to be some kind of concern within the nation.'"[12]

The young MLK focused on class, aware that poverty and the inability to afford medical care impacted Americans across racial lines. Because MLK emerged as the most prominent leader battling against that discrimination in the Jim Crow South—where it was most severe and legally ordained—we tend to remember King's egalitarianism on race rather than class. But the truth is that there was often great overlap between race and class in the movements King helped to lead.

The Montgomery bus boycott is not often recognized as a chapter in American labor history. It was true, of course, that most of the bus boycott's leaders, chiefly ministers, came from the Black professional class—as did MLK—and that in Jim Crow Alabama race more than class took center stage. And the boycott's leaders did aim to unite Montgomery's African American community across class lines, making it possible for Black-owned cars to be used to transport Black laborers to work. But in Montgomery's Black community it was members of the working class who primarily rode the city's Jim Crow buses (since they could not afford autos). And it was a working class African American, Rosa Parks—a seamstress—whose arrest for defying racial discrimination on a bus sparked the boycott. It was also Montgomery's most prominent Black labor (and NAACP) leader, E. D. Nixon, whose militance, leadership, and support of Rosa Parks helped make the boycott possible. The solidarity, courage, and endurance of rank-and-file working-class Blacks would prove essential to the boycott's success. Their presence was felt and their voices heard in the mass meetings that sustained the movement in its long struggle against discrimination. An elderly working-class Black woman known as Mother Pollard, rather than King, gave the boycott what MLK biographer Taylor Branch referred to as its "classic refrain." When someone suggested to Ms. Pollard that exhaustion from the bus boycott and her advanced aged dictated that she end her participation in the movement, she indignantly replied, "My feets is tired, but my soul is rested."[13]

Branch recounted memorable stories told by Pollard and other Black working-class elders that strengthened bus boycott movement morale at its mass meetings. Speaking from the floor in those meetings, these elders sometimes inspired and amused the crowd through their "folk wisdom and tales of daily life [working] inside the homes of powerful white people—how the boss lady had slipped them five dollars for the boycott with a warning not to tell the boss man, and later that same day the boss man had slipped them another five dollars with a warning not to tell the boss lady."[14] At one meeting, during a particularly troubled time, when a distracted King was not at his best from the pulpit, Mother Pollard came up to King and hugged him, saying, "Something is wrong. . . . You didn't talk good tonight." And when she asked King what was wrong, and he tried to reassure her, she did not believe him. To "a smiling but flustered King," she said loudly enough for the crowd to hear, "We is with you all the way. But even if we ain't with you, God's gonna take care of you." As she made her way back to her seat, as Branch put it, the crowd "roared," and "King's eyes filled with tears. Later King said that with her consoling words fearlessness had come over him in the form of raw energy."[15]

Such intimate interactions with Black working-class activists reveal MLK's affection and concern for them.[16] They make it easy to understand why King responded positively in mid-March 1968 to the request by Rev. James Lawson—a friend of King's, and SCLC leader, who had mentored students in nonviolence during the sit-in movement of 1960—that he come to Memphis to support the striking sanitation workers. The conditions that ignited the strike of Memphis's 1,300 Black sanitation workers in February were dire. As Michael Honey, author of the definitive history of the strike, explains, two workers had been

> crushed to death by a defective packing mechanism on a [garbage] truck in a city that refused to spend the money to update its equipment, leaving their families with no insurance or even workmen's compensation. The city also sent home workers with no pay when it rained and made them work extra hours without pay when it didn't. They worked in filth and had nowhere to clean up, suffered terrible injuries, and were treated by whites as "boys" almost as servants during slavery times. . . . Working full-time jobs, black sanitation workers lived in poverty and could not adequately feed their families."[17]

But the city's reactionary white mayor, Henry Loeb, refused to negotiate over wages and conditions and refused even to recognize their union. Workers came downtown and sat-in to air their grievances and appeal to the city council, to no avail. The following day, police beat and gassed with mace the nonviolent protesting workers and the ministers who had joined then.

In solidarity with the striking sanitation workers, more than one hundred of the city's Black ministers formed Community on the Move for Equality (COME).[18] This organization resembled many of the citywide civil rights groups of the early 1960s. But unlike those organizations, this movement focused on workers' rights rather than more general anti-discrimination goals and did so together with the American Federation of State, County and Municipal Employees (AFSCME), the national labor union that represented Memphis sanitation workers. This coalition seemed a logical response to a city government that was anti-union, racist, and dismissive of union demands from Black workers. In his capacity as head of COME, Rev. Lawson invited MLK to Memphis to help build this union solidarity movement.

MLK came to Memphis and gave his first speech there on behalf of the striking workers on March 18, 1968. In Black America by this time there was, in the wake of the ghetto rebellions, considerable division over Black Power versus racial integration and over nonviolence versus (mostly defensive) violence. In fact, some critics had claimed that King's approach to leadership was outmoded and would be replaced by these other supposedly more militant ideas about organizing in Black America. This was one reason why the crowd's size of some fifteen thousand, its enthusiasm, as well as the apparent unity of Memphis's Black community so impressed King.[19]

In this first Memphis speech, King fit the Memphis strike and the movement in support of it into a larger analysis of the progression of the Black Freedom Movement. He reviewed with pride the great movement for civil rights that defeated Jim Crow from 1955 to 1965: the Montgomery bus boycott, the sit-in movement, the Freedom Rides, the Birmingham struggle, and the Selma voting rights protest that led to the Voting Rights Act. As MLK explained, each "did a great deal to end legal segregation and guarantee the right to vote. With Selma and the voting rights bill, one era of our struggle came to a close and a new era came into being." The Memphis strike was part of this new era, in which "our struggle is for genuine equality, which means economic equality."[20] With this in mind, King praised the strikers and their supporters for "going beyond purely civil rights to questions of human rights."[21]

This focus on economic inequality and battling working-class oppression required movements built upon and beyond civil rights. "It isn't enough to integrate lunch counters," King told the crowd. "What does it profit a man to be able to eat at an integrated lunch counter if he doesn't earn enough money to buy a hamburger and coffee? . . . What does it profit one to have access to the hotels of our city and the motels of our highways when we don't earn enough money to take our family on a vacation? What does it profit one to be able to attend an integrated school when he doesn't earn enough money to buy his children school clothes?"[22] King then described many of the consequences of economic oppression. From substandard housing, with "wall-to-wall rats and roaches," to "walking the streets in search for jobs that do not exist," to working hard manual-labor jobs for "a wage inadequate for the necessities of life," "smothering in an airtight cage of poverty in an affluent society." With the all-male striking sanitation workers in mind, King spoke of being "tired of our men being emasculated so that our wives and our daughters have to go out and work in the white lady's kitchen . . . leaving us unable to be with our children and give them the time and the attention they deserve. We are tired . . . of being at the bottom"[23]

What this meant, in effect, was that now that the burden of Jim Crow had finally been lifted, King and the movement he helped lead could get back to dealing directly with the issues of extreme economic inequality and poverty that he had expressed such concern about in his days as a young student.[24] After winning voting rights, access to public accommodations, and other major gains thanks to federal civil rights legislation, King called for a movement that could tackle the core economic issues that plagued Blacks in the rural South and urban ghettoes as well as low-income Americans of all races. These were problems that went to the heart of the capitalist system and the inequality that had been endemic to it. King realized that his call for economic equity would be harder to win than the earlier struggles for civil rights. As King had explained in his testimony before a U.S. Senate committee in December 1966, "It was easier to integrate public facilities; it was easier to gain the right to vote because it didn't cost the nation anything. And the fact is that we are dealing with [economic equity] issues now that call for something of a restructuring of the architecture of American society. It's gonna cost the nation something [to wage and win a war on poverty]."[25]

King invoked religious ideals and rhetoric in this first Memphis speech to criticize the exploitation of the sanitation workers and other low-wage workers, who constituted a majority in Black America. Terming it "a crime for people to live in this rich nation and receive starvation wages," King denounced this oppression as sinful, and a sure path to damnation: "Jesus reminded us in a magnificent parable one day that a man went to hell because he didn't see the poor. His name was Dives. . . . Dives went to hell because he sought to be a conscientious objector in the war against poverty."[26] And King warned that "America too, is going to hell if she doesn't use her wealth . . . her vast resources . . . to end poverty and make it possible for all of God's children to have the basic necessities of life." King told the crowd that he could hear God saying that America's technological progress meant little because "I was hungry and you fed me not. . . . I was naked and you clothed me not. . . . The children of my sons and daughters were in need of economic security and you didn't provide it for them. And so you cannot enter the Kingdom of greatness. And that same voice says in Memphis to the mayor . . . to the power structure, 'If you do to it unto the least of these my children you do it unto me.'"[27]

King called unity, solidarity, the key to winning the struggle on behalf of Memphis's sanitation workers. He told the workers that, though the strike had dragged on, they should not despair. They could win a living wage, better conditions, and union recognition if they, and the entire Black community, stood together. Drawing upon his own knowledge of the labor movement, MLK spoke of the need for the workers to obtain power, the kind of power United Auto Workers (UAW) President Walter Reuther had described as "the ability of a labor union like UAW to make the most powerful corporation in the world—General Motors—say yes when it wants it say no." And King urged the union to persist until "you will be able to make Mayor Loeb . . . say yes when he wants to say no." King insisted that moral suasion was not enough: "Never forget that freedom is not something that is voluntarily given by the oppressor. It is something that must be demanded by the oppressed."[28]

King ended his speech with an appeal for even greater resistance via a general strike of all the city's Black workers. His spontaneous call for a general strike could have taken the civil rights movement to a new level of militancy. King thought that teachers, students, workers, and middle-class people in the Black community could shut Memphis down. If "not a Negro in this city will go to any job downtown" that would force the Memphis city government finally to negotiate in good faith. King promised to return to Memphis to support the workers' struggle.[29]

On March 28, King returned to Memphis and led a march in support of the strikers. But this march had to be aborted, revealing that the Memphis movement was not as united as he had thought. A few Black youths, and some street people, smashed store windows, forcing King to abandon the march since he would only lead it if it was nonviolent. These disruptive acts gave the Memphis police an opportunity to attack, turning the march into a rout.

The brutal response by Memphis's racist police sent hundreds of Blacks to the hospital. The police also shot and killed an unarmed Black teen. The hostile news media and politicians blamed King for the violence, falsely depicting him as a coward who had instigated the bloodshed and then fled the scene. All this left King determined to make another attempt to lead a nonviolent march in support of the strike. Despite death threats, King returned to Memphis on April 3, 1968, to help organize and lead that march.[30]

This was the context for the last speech of King's life on the night of April 3. Feeling exhausted and ill, King had not initially planned on giving this speech at all. But when it became evident that the two thousand or so people, at the Bishop Charles Mason Temple, had braved a raging storm to hear MLK, he agreed to come. King spoke in an improvised manner, delivering one his most powerful speeches. Like the "I Have a Dream" speech, this final "Mountaintop" speech is remembered and named for one segment, its dramatic ending. That ending, unlike the dream segment of King's March on Washington speech, centered less on a utopian future free of racism than on MLK's realization that deadly racist violence—"the threats" made to his life by "some of our sick white brothers" since his return to Memphis—might prevent him from living to see that future. He admitted that in the face of such ugly hostility the movement would confront some "difficult days ahead." Though his life was threatened, King expressed a fearless message to the crowd:

> [I]t really doesn't matter with me now because I've been to the mountaintop. . . . And I don't mind . . . I would like to live a long life—longevity has its place. But I'm not concerned about that now. I just want to do God's will. . . . And He's allowed me to go up to the mountain. . . . And I've seen the Promised Land. . . . I may not get there with you. . . . But I want you to know tonight . . . that we as a people will get to the Promised Land. . . . And so I'm happy tonight. . . . I'm not fearing any man. Mine eyes have seen the glory of the coming of the Lord."[31]

These words prophesying his own death, and yet predicting that one day African Americans would reach the promised land, remain haunting and courageous. There is little wonder that they are the most well-known part of the speech. Yet it is also true that while the dream segment in King's March on Washington speech has often been used to depict him as an icon of racial harmony, his final speech in Memphis is almost never used to suggest the opposite: that King was a realist who understood the depth and persistence of American racism and who recognized the hatred bred by that bigotry posed an imminent threat to his own life. His death the following day, at the hands of a racist assassin, suggested that not even the thirteen years of King's life when he devoted his great oratory and charismatic presence to ending such hatred could cure America of its deadly racism and perhaps nothing ever could. King's tragic fate is evidence in support of the critical race theorists' view that racism is a permanent, institutionalized feature of American life.[32] King thought it possible, however, as the motto of his organization the SCLC suggests, to redeem the soul of America. But his assassination by the hate-filled racist James Earl Ray undermines that redemptive hope.[33]

The significance of this last King speech transcends its dramatic conclusion. As a lesson in ethics and morality its section on the "Good Samaritan" is a rebuke to selfishness and self-centeredness that seems endemic to the hyper-individualism bred by American capitalism. In our own time that has taken its most extreme form in the narcissism and transactional governance of Donald Trump and the cadre of compassionless politicians allied with him. King told the Biblical story of the dangerous Jericho road, in which people, fearful of the dangers, failed to help the man lying on the ground. They were paralyzed by their own selfishness and the question it bred: "If I stop to help this man, what will happen to me?" But the ethical thing to do, and the altruistic approach taken by the Good Samaritan, was "If I do not stop to help this man, what will happen to him?" Applied to the Memphis strike, King held that the Good Samaritan's question was "Not, 'If I stop to help the sanitation workers, what will happen . . . to me?' The question is 'If I do *not* stop to help the sanitation workers, what will happen to them?'"[34]

King underscored this need for caring and solidarity by reminding the crowd that such goodness was divinely ordained. He noted that "Jesus ended up saying" that the one who helped "the man in need . . . was the good man, this was the great man because he had the capacity to project the 'I' into the 'thou,' and to be concerned about his brother."[35] King offered a memorable phrase to reinforce this message, terming it "dangerous unselfishness." Caring Memphis citizens needed to demonstrate such unselfishness by joining the next march with the sanitation workers, even if it meant missing work or school to do so.[36] And they would need such caring and courage even more in the days ahead, in the aftermath of King's assassination, as riots broke out in more than one hundred cities and the National Guard occupied Memphis.

This last MLK speech enables us to learn a great deal about his historical sensibility, because three separate sections discuss history in order to make important points about the past, the present, and the Memphis movement. Near the speech's opening, King offered his longest historical excursion, framed by the question of what era he would select if God offered him the choice of living in any period of history. He quickly discussed the attractions of ancient Greece and Rome, the Renaissance, the Reformation, the moment in 1863 "when a vacillating president by the name of Abraham Lincoln [would] finally come to the conclusion that he had to sign the Emancipation Proclamation," and the New Deal era, when President Franklin Roosevelt, responded to the Great Depression courageously.[37] King said, however, he would choose none of those eras but would instead tell God that if he would "allow me to live just a few years in the second half of the twentieth century, I will be happy." He explained his selection of the 1950s and 1960s by referring to the wave of liberation movements he was so happy to witness and participate in. By including the Memphis struggle in this list of movements, King imparted to the crowd the larger historical context of the strike that he so enthusiastically supported; it suggested that the struggle against economic oppression in Memphis was of global historical significance. "I see God working in this period of the twentieth century. . . . The masses of people are rising up. And wherever they are assembled today, whether they are in Johannesburg, South Africa, Nairobi, Kenya, Accra, Ghana, New York City, Atlanta, Georgia, Jackson, Mississippi, or Memphis, Tennessee, the cry is always the same: 'We want to be free.'"[38]

This first historical segment is illuminating in that it displayed King's critical view of the American social order. Here MLK expressed admiration not for the status quo but rather for those rebelling against its oppressiveness. In fact, when he discussed his choice to live not in the Renaissance or other exciting times but rather in his own era of American history, King admitted that it might seem "strange" to choose the current era out of all others because "the world is all messed up." He said, "The nation is sick, trouble in the land, confusion all around. . . . But I know, somehow, that only when it is dark enough can you see the stars."[39] And those stars offering hope were the movements seeking freedom and equality that surged in Memphis and across the United States and the globe.

So unlike those on the political right today, whose slogan is "Make America Great Again," King saw America not as having been great but "sick." And by that he meant sick with racism, violence, and callous indifference to the plight of those suffering from economic oppression. At two other points in the speech King alluded to sickness in America, and both were about such indifference and hatred. The first is when MLK referred to the antiunion mayor of Memphis, who headed the city's segregationist white power structure, as being so hateful and unwilling to treat the sanitation workers fairly that "Mayor Loeb is in dire need of a doctor."[40] Near the speech's dramatic ending, moreover, where King alluded to the imminent danger to his life, he used the word "sick" to refer to those in Memphis so filled with hateful racism that they threatened to kill him. Here he spoke of when he "got into Memphis" and began to hear about "the threats that were out . . . or what would happen to me from some of our sick white brothers."[41]

Though our focus here is on King's "Mountaintop" speech, it would be inaccurate to see his perception of America as sick with racism and violence as some new view that he developed in Memphis in 1968. MLK had been exposed to racist violence in his very first work as a movement leader, when his house was bombed in January 1956, and he and his wife received death threats during the Montgomery bus boycott. MLK lived with such threats from then on. In a 1965 interview, King mentioned that he "seldom" went "through a day without one . . . of these death threats." Such threats were inevitable, King explained, because America "is an extremely sick nation."[42] In a later article MLK diagnosed America's indifference to the discrimination and poverty facing poor Blacks as "a potentially fatal disease" that had yielded the ghetto riots, with their bloodshed and destruction.[43]

This does not mean, however, that King thought America's sickness was incurable. After all, the SCLC, the civil rights organization King founded and led, had adopted the motto "To Save the Soul of America," which indicated that he thought change was possible. And so did the fact that, as we have seen, King so admired the ongoing liberation movements in the United States and globally that he favored living in the modern American era over alternative points in time. If he thought these movements for egalitarian change were doomed to fail, perhaps he would have preferred other historical moments. And right after the Good Samaritan portion of his final speech, King indicated that "in these powerful days, these days of challenge" labor solidarity and anti-poverty activists in Memphis and elsewhere needed, in his words, "to rise up . . . with a greater determination" in "these days of challenge, "to make America what it ought to be. We have an opportunity to make America a better nation."[44]

What greatness existed in America was not, for King, its inequitable social order nor its greed-centered economic system but rather the most liberal ideals of the republic's founders, which had never been adequately implemented, and the protest movements that struggled to push America to finally start living up to them. Thus when, in his final speech, King discussed the Black-led student movement that in 1960 had protested racially discriminatory lunch counters across the South, King argued that "as they were sitting in, they were really standing up . . . for the best in the American dream and taking the whole nation back to those great wells of democracy, which were dug deep by the founding fathers in the Declaration of Independence."[45]

The problem was, however, that those in power, opposed to movements for justice and democratic change, trampled the nation's liberal ideals as they sought to suppress these movements. Thus in his "Mountaintop" speech, as an example of such trampling that made a mockery of the First Amendment, King cited the injunction Memphis city officials obtained to stop the strike supporters from marching. King promised to fight this injunction, which he termed "illegal, unconstitutional." He observed, "If I lived in China or even Russia, or any totalitarian country, maybe I could understand some of these illegal injunctions . . . the denial of certain basic First Amendment privileges, because they haven't committed themselves to that over there. But somewhere I read of the freedom of assembly . . . the freedom of speech . . . That the greatness of America is the right to protest for right. . . . We aren't going to let any injunction turn us around."[46]

Given that MLK had returned to Memphis to help lead a second march in support of the striking sanitation workers, since the first one had been aborted due to violence, King felt compelled to use part of his "Mountaintop" speech to make the case for nonviolence. He did so on two levels. First, King stressed the harm done to the movement when marches departed from nonviolence, since it focused attention on the property damage, distracting the media and the public from the injustice oppressing the sanitation workers: "the refusal of Memphis to be fair and honest in its dealings" with those workers.[47] MLK then offered a memorable history of the Birmingham Black freedom struggle, which demonstrated that nonviolent protest was not only superior ethically to violence but also that its moral force could overpower even the most brutal and repressive foes. Just as nonviolent protest had carried the movement to victory over Bull Connor and his racist police in Birmingham in 1963—despite his use of police dogs and high-powered fire hoses against the demonstrators—those same nonviolent tactics could work in 1968. Which is why, King concluded, "Now we've got to go on in Memphis just like that."[48]

The final and most moving historical section of the "Mountaintop" speech came just moments before the speech's dramatic conclusion. Obviously prompted by the death threats to consider his own mortality, in what we might term his speech's "If I had sneezed" segment, MLK opened with the story of his near-death experience a decade earlier. While in New York City signing his first book, on September 20, 1958, he was stabbed by a mentally ill woman and rushed to Harlem Hospital. The newspaper reportage included a physician's assessment that the blade of the knife had come so close to his aorta that if he had sneezed, he would likely have died. Mentioning all this, combining his anti-elitism with his appreciation for solidarity that transcended racial lines, King said that while in the hospital he received get-well messages from top public officials, but it was not those messages that meant the most to him. The letter that resonated most powerfully came from a young girl, as MLK recalled: "I looked at that letter and I'll never forget it. It said simply, 'Dear Dr. King: I am a ninth-grade student at the White Plains High school. . . . While it should not matter, I would like to mention that I'm a white girl. I read in the paper of your misfortune and of your suffering. . . . That if you had sneezed, you would have died. And I'm simply writing you to say that I'm so happy that you didn't sneeze.'"[49]

King used this letter to frame his discussion of the freedom movement, prefacing this history lesson by saying that "I too, am happy that I didn't sneeze," because if he had, he would have missed the lunch counter sit-ins, the Freedom Rides, the Albany and Birmingham movements, the March on Washington, the Selma voting rights struggle, and the Memphis strike solidarity movement.[50] These earlier struggles were, King pointed out, democratic protests that mattered, that chipped away at oppression, pushing America to finally start living up to the national credo of liberty and justice for all. The lunch counter sit-ins had proven that racial discrimination in stores and restaurants would no longer be tolerated; the Freedom Rides had "ended segregation in interstate travel"; the Birmingham freedom struggle had "aroused the conscience of this nation and brought into being the Civil Rights Bill"; the March on Washington gave MLK the opportunity "to try to tell America about a dream that I had had"; and "the great movement" in Selma paved the way for the Voting Rights Act.[51]

Even when discussing the Albany, Georgia, struggle, which King biographers tend to see as a failure, MLK—who did not mention any such negative assessment—implied that the act of protesting for freedom and justice itself constituted a form of victory.[52] As he put it, "If I had sneezed, I wouldn't have been around here in 1962, when Negroes in Albany, Georgia decided to straighten their backs up. And whenever men and women straighten their backs up they are going somewhere, because a man can't ride your back unless it is bent."[53]

All the history in the "If I had sneezed" segment led back to and ended with Memphis. And, of course, that was the point, to link the movement there on behalf of the striking and impoverished Black workers with this older tradition of effective nonviolent mass protest that embodied the best of American democracy: "If I had sneezed, I wouldn't have been in Memphis to see a community rally around those brothers and sisters who are suffering.... I'm so happy that I didn't sneeze."[54]

Just how wrong conservatives are about MLK as being like them, in their supposed color blindness, is evident from his "Mountaintop" speech's discussion of economics. King stressed here that "we've got to strengthen black institutions."[55] He urged Memphis's Black community to engage in "a 'bank-in' movement," removing its money from "the banks downtown" that supported the city's callous white power structure and depositing their funds instead in a Black-owned bank. This same approach should be used when investing in insurance. "You have six or seven Black insurance companies here in the city of Memphis. Take out your insurance there. We want to have an 'insurance in.'" The idea here was to harness Black economic power on behalf of a more just society.[56]

King urged Memphis's Black community to engage in "economic withdrawal" in their daily lives as consumers and not to purchase goods from discriminatory, exploitative companies and stores. This would give business owners and executives the message that they must "make the first item on your agenda fair treatment where God's children are concerned," and if they refuse, "our agenda calls for withdrawing economic support for you." King got specific here, urging Memphis's Black community not to buy from Coca-Cola, Sealtest milk, Wonderbread, or Hart's Bread: "Up to now only the garbage men have been feeling pain. Now we must... redistribute the pain.... These companies... haven't been fair in their hiring policies," or used their power and influence to "tell Mayor Loeb to do what is right."[57] Though this may sound like a new and more economically militant version of MLK, here it must be recalled that his first role in the freedom struggle back in 1955 was leading a Black economic boycott of Montgomery's buses.

While MLK's most famous critique of religious leaders, his "Letter from Birmingham Jail," came five years before the Memphis strike, King devoted a powerful segment of his final speech to this issue.[58] He praised Rev. James Lawson and Memphis's other Black ministers who organized support for the strike. MLK contrasted their activism on behalf of "a relevant ministry" with the indifference of all too many religious leaders: "So often preachers aren't concerned about anything but themselves." They should be at the forefront of the struggle against poverty. "It's all right," King said, "to talk about long white robes over yonder, but ultimately people want some suits and dresses and shoes to wear down here.... It's all right to talk about streets flowing with milk and honey, but God has commanded us to be concerned about the slums down here and His children who can't eat three square meals a day."[59]

The "Mountaintop" speech is distinct from the "I Have a Dream" speech in many ways. Though drawing upon segments of previous speeches he had given, the Memphis speech was totally improvised since King had not planned on speaking that night. In contrast, MLK had carefully planned his March on Washington speech, though its dream segment was inserted spontaneously. The "Mountaintop" speech was given to a small though enthusiastic crowd of about two-to-three thousand people who had braved a major storm to attend the indoor meeting; some 250,000 had been present at the nationally televised March on Washington.[60] While the "Mountaintop" speech was delivered to a predominantly Black audience rallying in support of a strike by Black workers exploited by Memphis's white mayor, its focus was primarily on economic oppression, poverty, and the rights of labor; the "I Have a Dream" speech was primarily focused on racial discrimination. Where the "I Have a Dream" speech is seen as a high point of MLK's leadership in the freedom movement, the "Mountaintop" speech is associated with the tragedy of King's imminent assassination. But in the American public memory, and especially in news media and during King Day coverage, both speeches are remembered for their dramatic endings rather than for their political content, their radical social criticism. Via soundbites, then, much as MLK's great speech in 1963 is reduced to a lovely dream, his equally powerful speech in 1968 is reduced to a sad prognostication of his imminent assassination, leaving the nation largely clueless about King's insights into the failures of America on race and on class that persist today.

The day after this final MLK speech, there was some good news for the Memphis movement. The injunction preventing the planned march in support of the strikers was challenged successfully in court.[61] And the meetings between King aides and the youths who had disrupted the first march seemed to go well. So it looked like the nonviolent march MLK had helped plan and endorsed so enthusiastically in his "Mountaintop" speech was back on track.

But that night, tragedy struck. As he was getting ready for dinner, Martin Luther King Jr. was shot and killed while standing on the balcony of the Lorraine Motel. Mayor Loeb responded to the assassination by calling in the National Guard, and incredibly, continuing his refusal to settle the sanitation workers' strike. Loeb stonewalled even after Coretta Scott King came to Memphis and led a huge march—more than forty thousand strong—in memory of MLK and urged Memphis's government to grant the union's demands. Outrage over the assassination ignited Black community protests and rioting in more than one hundred cities.[62] The sanitation workers' strike was finally settled with a crucial assist from the Johnson administration, after President Johnson dispatched his undersecretary of labor to get Memphis to recognize the union and raise the workers' pay.[63]

As Americans tried to come to grips with the tragic loss of MLK, conspiracy theories abounded. The convicted assassin, James Earl Ray, an inveterate liar and thief, initially confessed but later claimed he was framed. No grand conspiracy theory was ever proven. Nor was any necessary to explain why Ray, an escaped convict and rabid racist, with the possible help from his equally racist brother and the hope of a financial reward from some segregationist, would assassinate MLK.[64] In fact, the focus on conspiracies has distracted from the deeper roots of this tragedy, which rests with the assassin's violent racism. He essentially inherited anti-Black hatred from his racist working-class father. And then, in an environment of institutionalized racism, Ray encountered no anti-racist intervention by the public school system in which he was educated. To the contrary, he attended an all-white school in an Illinois town so racist that athletic teams from a nearby city were told not to bring Black students with them when they competed in athletic events, a warning they heeded.[65] Ray's murderous racism was a product of the bigoted social order that MLK had given his life to change, as George McMillan, Ray's biographer, reminds us:

> [His story is] the biography of an American, an American assassin. He hated passionately, hated enough to kill, to kill without help, someone he did not know, to slay an abstraction. The geography of that hatred is

> domestic. We cannot deny James Earl Ray his American heritage. The roots of his crime were seeded in our native soil and nourished within our familiar landscape. He shared our common life and *he* believed he shared our common ideals. Our national history, our politics, our economics, our traditions, and our uniquely American social systems and social classes—*these* are the elements that conspired to produce his murderous act. This is an American story.[66]

MLK well understood the danger of assassination in a nation as violent as America. Back in 1963, his response to President Kennedy's assassination made this evident to Coretta Scott King, who recalled MLK's words when he first learned of JFK's fate: "This is what is going to happen to me. This is such a sick society."[67] The frequent death threats merely confirmed MLK's awareness of the dangers he faced. And so did King's intimate acquaintance with the racist right wing, the segregationists who directed hatred and violence at the Black Freedom Movement, resulting in assaults and murder of movement activists. Although MLK is mostly celebrated in the twenty-first century for his dream of an America that reputedly lived up to its liberal ideal that "all men are created equal" by ending racism, King was an astute critic of its illiberal right wing and its fascistic tendencies toward lawlessness and bloodshed. In his last book, MLK warned of the endurance of the racist right wing's hateful vision for America: "The segregationist goal is the total reversal of all reforms, with the reestablishment of naked oppression and if need be a native form of fascism. America had a master race in the antebellum South. Reestablishing it with a resurgent Klan and a totally disenfranchised lower class would realize the dream of all too many extremists on the right."[68]

For King the logic of racism was such that its adherents posed a threat not only to his life but also to the survival of any minority group that was the target of racist hatred. Here again King argued that racism and fascism were intimately connected. Thus, just a few weeks before his assassination, King warned a predominantly white audience in suburban Michigan that racism unimpeded could lead America down the path taken by Nazi Germany: "There must be a recognition on the part of everybody in this nation that America is still a racist country. . . . We must see racism for what it is. . . . It is the notion than one group has all the knowledge, all of the insights, all of the purity . . . all of the dignity. And another group is worthless, on a lower level of humanity, inferior . . . the notion that the very being of a people is inferior."[69] This was the twisted logic that guided the most evil leader in global history, as MLK explained:

> Hitler was a very sick man. [In] one of the great tragedies of human history . . . he took his racism to its logical conclusion. . . . His racism caused him to sickly feel . . . that there was something innately inferior about the Jew, [and so] he ended up killing six million Jews. The ultimate logic of racism is genocide, and if one says that one is not good enough to have a job that is of solid quality . . . to have access to public accommodations . . . to have the right to vote . . . to live next door to him, to marry his daughter because of his race, then at that moment that . . . [racist] is saying that that person is not . . . fit to exist or to live. That is the ultimate logic of racism . . . [which is why] the first thing that must be on the agenda of our nation is to get rid of racism.[70]

Racism at its sickest and ugliest was on display in the extreme segregationists' response to MLK's assassination. In Memphis, as historian Michael Honey documented, such reactionaries welcomed the news of King's death, regarding him as a dangerous subversive who got what he deserved. For these hateful whites, King's murder was the subject of jokes and celebrations. A poll at Memphis State University found that 20 percent of the student body approved of the assassination.[71] At the University of Georgia, racist students celebrated the assassination, chanting excitedly, "They did it! They shot the nigger," and set off firecrackers late into the night as if it was a holiday.[72] This is symptomatic of the record of the American far right on race from King's time to our own, which has been bigoted, deadly, and destructive.

Among the saddest aspects of the assassination is how much was lost for so little. After all, the sanitation workers' demands were modest. These hard-working laborers, doing the dirtiest job in the city, tasks crucial to public health, were merely seeking a living wage, decent working conditions, and recognition of their union—and of themselves as human beings worthy of respect. This was driven home most poignantly in the picket signs they hoisted bearing the message "I am a man." Yet Mayor Loeb obstinately refused to meet their demands. If not for his callous disregard for the welfare of his city's Black workers, the strike would have been settled weeks earlier, or avoided all together, without MLK having ever been invited to come to Memphis—in the face of ugly death threats—in the first place.

It would also have taken precious little effort for the Johnson administration to have leveraged its power on behalf of the sanitation workers in a far more timely fashion. But President Johnson was too lost in his own pettiness, alienated from MLK because of his stance against the war and his criticism of LBJ's anemic War on Poverty. And so the president did nothing to aid Memphis's impoverished garbage men until the racial crisis caused by King's assassination. Had he dispatched his undersecretary of labor to settle the strike earlier, the tragedy in Memphis could have been avoided. And had the FBI directed its resources to protecting rather than discrediting King, this too could likely have avoided the tragedy. Indeed, when you reflect on the FBI's investigative abilities, on display in the Bureau's impressive international manhunt that tracked down the assassin across the Atlantic and brought him back to justice in the United States, it is difficult to believe that the FBI could not have learned of the danger posed when Ray, a bigoted petty thief and escaped convict, obtained a rifle and stayed at a rooming house with a view of MLK's balcony at the Lorraine Motel.

But on some level this kind of mournful speculation is ahistorical, since it fails to consider how MLK was abused, even demonized, in the right-wing news media—especially in the South—and how loathed and feared he was by much of the white power structure. The Memphis press attacked King mercilessly, slandering him as a violence-courting agitator, mocking him as the cowardly "Chicken a la King," who fled the riot he supposedly instigated in the march he led in his prior stay in Memphis.[73] So Mayor Loeb was under no pressure from the local news media to settle the strike or to treat MLK respectfully. And to expect more from the Johnson administration or FBI Director J. Edgar Hoover, given their anti-radicalism, is simply to forget who they were and how intolerant they were of dissent from the Left. And MLK in 1968 was unmistakably a man of the Left, openly criticizing America's being beset by the triple evils of racism, militarism, and selfish materialism (which bred poverty and inequality), leaving those with the power to help MLK acting as if King was a pariah to be feared rather than a democratic champion to be cherished and protected.

The last word on the Memphis struggle and MLK's role in it should go to those who marched with him in his final days, the sanitation workers. The oral histories of these workers find them crediting King with embodying the Good Samaritan ideal he so dramatically promoted in his final speech, selflessly aiding impoverished workers struggling for justice and dignity.

One of these workers, Taylor Rogers, recalled that "even had it been white workers, King would have" come to help. "That's just the kind of person he was. He stopped what he was doin'. He was planning this big march to Washington. All of his staff thought it was outrageous of him to stop and come to Memphis. But he went where he was needed, where he could help poor people."[74] Rogers believed that, had MLK not intervened, the strike would have been lost due to Mayor Loeb's "plantation mentality" and that it took MLK's advocacy, and the assassination, to put enough national pressure on the mayor, forcing Loeb to finally negotiate and settle the strike.[75] Though acknowledging that King could not end all the racial and economic oppression he had battled against, Rogers concluded that King had not "died in vain," since he helped the sanitation workers win their strike, and had paved the way for lasting egalitarian change in Memphis:

> What a lot of people in Memphis don't realize, white folks and people with good jobs, is that black folks wouldn't be in the position they're in now had it not been for King comin' here and dyin.' All the banks hire colored tellers, and school principals. Before that, we didn't have that. [Today] city hall is full of blacks, even to mayor. From the top all the way through. So some of the things he was about happened. And things are still happening. But it's a slow process. I think there's been a big change in Memphis.[76]

* * *

The final chapter of David J. Garrow's pathbreaking study, *The FBI and Martin Luther King, Jr.* (1981), is titled "The Radical Challenge of Martin King." Grounded in exhaustive research in the FBI files and oral history work, Garrow documented the great concern about King's politics—which were seen as radical and subversive—by the FBI and President Johnson in the final year of MLK's life. This view of King reflected the fact that he had engaged in dissident organizing and radical criticism of the Johnson administration on both foreign and domestic policy. As Garrow explains, King's February 1967 speech in Los Angeles and his Riverside Church address that April, his first speeches devoted exclusively to opposing the Vietnam War, "brought about renewed intensification of FBI and White House interest in King, his advisers, and his political plans." Garrow found that this inclination to use FBI resources to monitor a dissident MLK "intensified further" later in 1967 "when the Bureau learned of King's plan to conduct the 1968 Poor People's Campaign. . . . Word of the Poor People's Campaign rang another alarm bell at the White House," reflecting "how hostile the Johnson administration was to King."[77] This presidential and FBI fear of MLK, according to Garrow, attested that these powerful men believed that King "in the last twelve months of his life represented a far greater political threat to the reigning American government than he ever had before."[78]

While the logic of viewing King as a radical in 1967 to 1968 seems quite clear on foreign policy, where his now public and high-visibility opposition to America's anti-Communist crusade in Vietnam was way to the left of millions of Americans who supported the war, it may at first glance seem puzzling that his Poor People's Campaign would also be considered such a radical threat. After all, King advocated nonviolence, so his Poor People's Campaign plan to bring thousands of impoverished Americans to Washington, D.C., for an anti-poverty protest, lobbying campaign, and encampment hardly seems revolutionary—especially since MLK presented it as an alternative to the destructive ghetto riots. But here the political context needs to be kept in mind. LBJ had only a few years earlier launched his so-called War on Poverty, and so the mere existence of King's Poor People's Campaign amounted to a verdict from the Left that Johnson had lost that war. And in the context of American electoral politics, in which conservatives saw LBJ's poverty initiative as a reckless expansion of the welfare state, King's crusade on behalf of yet more expansive aid to the poor seemed wildly radical.

The conservative backlash against the ghetto rebellions of the mid-1960s intensified fears that the federal government had moved too quickly on civil rights, raising unrealistic expectations that, when unfulfilled, bred Black bitterness and violence. Similar anxieties, according to Garrow, help explain why the Poor People's Campaign "touched a sensitive nerve at FBI headquarters," fueling the Bureau's concern about "urban strife" and fear of a "true black revolution."[79]

There was also the matter of MLK's rhetoric, for as we have seen, King linked the war issue to poverty, arguing that Vietnam so drained the federal government's finances that it could not afford a major anti-poverty offensive. King made this precise point in his extensive testimony at a U.S. Senate Committee hearing, and in his Poor People's Campaign (PPC) launch, asserting that "Poor people who are treated with derision and abuse by an economic system soon conclude with elementary logic that they have no rational interest in killing people twelve thousand miles away in the name of defending that system."[80] So in this way King linked his radical antiwar position to his anti-poverty agenda. And the rhetoric King used in organizing the PPC had a defiant edge to it. For example, in his statement announcing the Poor People's Campaign launch in December 1967, King adopted a militant tone, declaring that his Southern Christian Leadership Conference would

> lead waves of the nation's poor and disinherited to Washington, D.C. . . . to demand redress of their grievances by the United States government and secure at least jobs and income for all. . . . We will demand to be heard, and we will stay until America responds. If this means forcible repression of our movement, we will confront it, for we have done this before. If this means scorn or ridicule, we embrace it, for that is what the poor now receive. If it means jail, we accept it willingly, for millions of poor already are imprisoned by exploitation and discrimination. But we hope . . . our campaign in Washington will receive . . . a sympathetic understanding across our nation, followed by dramatic expansion of nonviolent demonstrations in Washington and simultaneous protests elsewhere. . . . We intend to build militant nonviolent actions until the government moves against poverty.[81]

It is easy to see from his Poor People's Campaign launch why the FBI's leadership would be fearful and would connect it with the ghetto rebellions that had rocked American cities. For in this opening statement King voiced his intention "to channelize the smoldering rage and frustration of Negro people into an effective, militant, and nonviolent movement of massive proportions in Washington and other areas."[82] A key reason King had launched this anti-poverty movement was his realization that the civil rights focus and gains of the freedom movement he had led in the South had done very little for the working class and impoverished Blacks of the urban North (as the ghetto riots attested), whose needs were linked intimately to economics. King was finally daring to air publicly his anti-capitalist sentiments. The PPC's launch statement offered a moral indictment of the greed King thought endemic to American capitalism: the United States was "a nation [that] gorged on money while millions of its citizens are denied a good education, adequate health services, decent housing, and even respect." Thus this was in the United States an "age of technological wizardry and political immorality."[83]

MLK had not jettisoned his rhetoric or concern about racial discrimination, but class began to loom large in his public discourse. There was a new focus, as King put it, on "class issues . . . with the problem of the gulf between the haves and have nots." He said that participants in the Poor People's Campaign were "engaged in the class struggle."[84] Privately, he had told the SCLC that "we can't solve our problems now until there is a radical redistribution of economic and political power." In King's view, the movement had shifted from its ostensibly reformist era, which by 1965 had rid the nation of Jim Crow, "into a new era, which must be an era of revolution"—the revolution of values needed if America was to abolish poverty.[85]

King had a moral, even a theological, dimension to his radicalism. One sees this most clearly in a speech he gave to the SCLC convention in August 1967. Here he framed his holistic critique of American capitalism, racism, and militarism, and his call for revolutionary change—breaking away from all three—by first offering a parable of Jesus and Nicodemus. When Nicodemus asked how he could be saved, Jesus did not instruct him to reject any one sin, whether it be lying, stealing, or homicide. Jesus, as King explained, "said something altogether different, because Jesus realized something basic—that if a man will lie, he will steal. And if a man will steal, he will kill. So instead of getting bogged down in one thing, Jesus looked at him and said, 'Nicodemus, you must be born again.'"[86] King deemed this a call for Nicodemus to change his "whole structure," which meant a revolution in values towards a moral life. King applied this same lesson to American politics, economics, and foreign policy: "A nation that will keep people in slavery for 244 years will 'thingify' them, make them things. Therefore they will exploit them and poor people generally, economically. And a nation that will exploit economically will have to have foreign investments . . . and will have to use its military might to protect them. . . . Today . . . we must go from this convention and say, 'America, you must be born again!'"[87]

In this same SCLC convention speech, King called for movement activists to expand and deepen their critical thinking, their questioning of American capitalism, and the inequity It bred. "The movement must address itself to the question of restructuring the whole of American society. . . . We must ask the question, 'Why are there 40 million poor people in America?' And when you begin to ask that question, you are raising questions about the economic system, about a broader distribution of wealth. . . . You begin to question the capitalistic economy." And this in turn leads to questions about who was benefiting from all this inequity: "Who owns the oil?"[88]

Taking King seriously as an economic thinker means placing him in the context of a long African American tradition—stretching back to the Civil War and Reconstruction eras—of activists advocating egalitarian economic change as essential to Black liberation. Formerly enslaved Blacks in Georgia's Sea Islands and other parts of the Union-occupied South had demanded that lands owned by treasonous former slaveowners be redistributed to the now free Black community. Sylvie Laurent's study, *King and the Other America: The Poor People's Campaign and the Quest for Economic Equality* (2018), points to historic precursors to King's increased public emphasis on battling Black economic oppression: first, Frederick Douglass's advocacy of post-Civil War Black empowerment and, later, W. E. B. Du Bois's advocacy for the creation of Black economic cooperatives in the face of the Great Depression, which identified the connections between race and class. Laurent also discusses A. Philip Randolph's understanding that the federal government wished to avoid labor unrest in wartime, which is why he chose to agitate for the end of segregation in the U.S. military and in the industries that supported it.[89] In 1966, Randolph and Bayard Rustin co-authored *A "Freedom Budget" for All Americans*, advocating immediate federal action to guarantee full employment.[90] When a summary of the "Freedom Budget" was issued in pamphlet form in 1967, MLK authored an enthusiastic foreword to it. He argued that "[t]he long journey ahead" towards a truly democratic society "requires that we emphasize the needs of all America's poor, for there is no way merely to find work or adequate housing, or quality-integrated schools for Negroes alone. We shall eliminate slums for Negroes when we destroy ghettos and build cities for *all*. We shall eliminate unemployment for Negroes when we demand full and fair employment for *all*. We shall produce an educated and skilled Negro mass when we achieve a twentieth century educational system for all."[91]

In the PPC, this emphasis on class led King to advocate not just for Blacks but also for the poor across racial lines. As the campaign's launch statement put it, "We . . . look for participation by representatives of the millions of non-Negro poor—Indians, Mexican Americans, Puerto Ricans, Appalachians, and others."[92] Bernard Lafayette, initially a lead organizer for the

PPC, recalled an early conversation with MLK about broadening the campaign beyond the Black community's poor. Lafayette said,

> "Well there are Chicanos who are poor, you want them to be in—?" He [MLK] said, "Yes we want them to be involved." I said "OK. . . . What about the Native Americans?" He said, "Well yeah, Native Americans." So by this time, he turned around and looked at me 'cause he'd anticipated the next question. I said "Well, Dr. King, what about the poor whites? And he said, . . ."Are they poor?" I said, "Well, yes." [King replied] "We want them involved!"[93]

By mid-March 1968 this multiracial coalition was emerging. As Marian Wright Edelman, the civil rights lawyer who played a central role in giving King the idea for a Poor People's Campaign recalled, "This was a very big thing that happened . . . finding common ground among the poor. That didn't make things easy, but it was a big benchmark into the next stage of the civil rights movement, which had to do with economic rights."[94] King made his enthusiasm for this new mode of multiracial organizing against poverty evident in his remarks at a March 14, 1968, PPC meeting with representatives from diverse racial backgrounds: "We assemble here together with common problems—bringing together ethnic groups that maybe have not been together in this type of meeting in the past. I know I haven't been in a meeting like this and it's been one of my dreams that we could come together and realize our common problems. Black people, Mexican Americans, Puerto Ricans, Appalachian Whites, all working together to solve the problem of poverty."[95]

The dream MLK spoke of in this PPC organizing meeting sounded far different from the one he described at the March on Washington in 1963 that conservatives so selectively quote. Here he was not describing some far-off time when racial harmony prevailed but instead constructing a multiracial coalition to mobilize against the class oppression caused by the very economic system, American capitalism, that conservatives idolize. And King, as well as those from all the other racial backgrounds that he addressed at this meeting, worked towards a goal that would also be anathema to conservatives, who loathed the very idea of the welfare state. That goal centered on dramatically expanding the federal government, to lift the poor out of poverty, guaranteeing an annual income to all, along with major steps to achieve full employment.

MLK knew, of course, about conservative opposition to such an expanded federal role in the battle against poverty. He spoke repeatedly about the right-wing backlash against such government intervention, which King viewed as part of an attempted counterrevolution against the civil rights movement. The negative headlines generated by the mid-1960s ghetto rebellions had, in King's view, served as a pretext for the activation of white resentment that had been simmering for years.[96] As to right-wing complaints that the goals of the Poor People's Campaign would vastly expand the already bloated federal government bureaucracy and breed an unhealthy welfare dependence, King was unimpressed. In one of King's statements defending the Poor People's Campaign goal of a guaranteed annual income, he took direct aim at such welfare state-bashing. "[The] thing I think is very necessary to say is that everybody's on welfare in this country. When it's for white people and [the] rich, we call it subsidies. Suburbia was built by federally subsidized credits, and the highways and expressways that take people out there. So I think we gotta see that when it comes to poor people, we call it welfare, handouts doled, but when it comes to rich people, we call it subsidies. And it's the same thing—it's all welfare.[97] With such inequity and hypocrisy in mind, King noted that America had "socialism for the rich, and rugged free market capitalism for the poor."[98]

Ultimately what may have been the most innovative component of the Poor People's Campaign was its idea of bringing poor people, a traditionally powerless group, to Washington, D.C., to confront those in power, primarily Congress, and to stay in town until Congress did something about poverty. This represented a dramatic departure from the norm since, as the iconoclastic journalist I. F. Stone put it back in 1963, the rich don't need to organize a march on Washington since—with their highly paid lobbyists—they "march on Washington all the time."[99] By keeping the poor isolated and out of sight, often in blighted urban neighborhoods but also in shabby rural shacks and trailer parks, America can imagine that poverty had disappeared. This enables politicians to ignore the poor and their suffering, at least until some compassionate author on the left, like Michael Harrington, comes along and publishes an exposé reminding the nation of the existence of this "other America."[100]

This is why on those rare occasions when poor people connect with the political and economic elite it generates headlines. One thinks, for example, of First Lady Eleanor Roosevelt's visits to sites of rural poverty in West

Virginia or her tour of a coal mine during the Great Depression. Or Mississippi Freedom Summer, when elite college students in 1964 did voter registration work with Black sharecroppers in the most impoverished areas of the Mississippi Delta. Their work was part of SNCC's effort—which the organization had been leading since 1961, in the face of white supremacist terror—to finally get America to pay attention to the racist tyranny of that state.[101] And in fact, the genesis of the Poor People's Campaign was connected to a trip Robert Kennedy made to rural Mississippi with his U.S. Senate subcommittee in April 1967 at the suggestion of Marian Wright [Edelman], a leading civil rights attorney in that state. As she later recounted, "I got called to Washington to testify about poverty and what was happening in Mississippi. After describing the "urgent situation" of those in hunger and need in the Delta, "which must be looked into and met," she asked the senators to travel to Mississippi "to come and see for themselves [and New York Senator] Bobby Kennedy came with them." The group was shocked to find "that you have young children in the United States at the present time within the wealthiest nation in the world who are hungry, and their parents are hungry. It's completely unsatisfactory."[102]

The impact of this Mississippi poverty tour on Kennedy was so profound that after he returned to Washington, when Wright told him she was going to stop in Atlanta to see King, Kennedy suggested that she "tell him to bring the poor to Washington." Taking him up on his suggestion, when Wright went down to Atlanta and visited MLK at his SCLC office, her impression was that he was depressed. "I mean he was sitting in his office by himself. And I told him what Robert Kennedy said—he ought to bring the poor to Washington—and he lit up, he just lit up."[103] King reacted this way because he had long been deeply concerned about poverty and economic inequality, and a crusade on behalf of the poor also seemed a way of showing that a nonviolent movement could advance important initiatives on behalf of social justice at a time when the ghetto rebellions and racial violence had led some to claim that MLK and nonviolence had become passé.

Unlike MLK and RFK, however, powerful politicians rarely welcomed such interaction with the poor, particularly when gathered in mass numbers and intent on creating an encampment designed for protest and a sustained anti-poverty lobbying campaign. Even President Kennedy, it will be recalled, initially opposed the March on Washington in 1963, though as a deft politician he reversed himself after the march's leaders refused to cancel.[104] Back in 1941, FDR was so eager to avoid the mass march A. Philip Randolph and his Black March on Washington movement were planning that the president agreed to issue an executive order meeting the movement's demand that he act to stop racial discrimination in the defense industry—which led to the march's cancellation.[105] And in 1932, a panicky President Herbert Hoover called out the U.S. Army to forcibly evict impoverished veterans of World War I and their families, who had come to Washington to demand advance payment of their bonuses to help them survive the onset of the Great Depression. The Army burned down the veterans' tent village on the outskirts of Washington.[106]

It would have taken great leadership to ensure that the Poor People's Campaign did not meet a similar fate. But such leadership was lacking because the month before the PPC came to Washington, D.C., MLK had been assassinated. The SCLC leadership did its best, but its most talented leaders were still in shock over the loss of King and proved unable to unite behind MLK's successor, Ralph David Abernathy.[107] The protesters did spend over a month in Washington, demonstrating and lobbying Congress, but made no headway at a time when there was little support for a new war on poverty. Some of the loudest congressional voices came from the protest's hostile critics, such as Rep. Wayne Aspinal of Colorado, who said that "since the Bonus Army, the World War I veterans, who came to Washington during the Depression demanding a promised bonus, had been evicted from Washington, the poor people [in the PPC] had even less right to come."[108]

The press was hostile and often seemed more interested in reporting on the mud and internal conflicts at the encampment—known as Resurrection City—than on the issues about poverty and inequality raised by the protesters. The loss of King proved especially damaging to the movement, as King aide Andrew Young explained: "When Martin spoke that became the story and it allowed us to control the message. Without Martin to focus the message, the press ignored many of the substantive issues around poverty that we came to highlight. The press had apparently made up its mind to condemn the Poor People's Campaign and Resurrection City before we even arrived in the capital.... With few exceptions, reporters were interested only in dirt-digging—unearthing internal conflict, disputes, and backbiting from our sea of mud."[109]

The Department of the Interior forced the closure of Resurrection City after a month and a half, when the protesters' park permit expired, with police initially deploying tear gas against some of those in the encampment.[110] In light of all the negative press, the vacuum of leadership caused by King's death, and the inability of the protesters to win major action by Congress, the media's dominant view at the time of Resurrection City's eviction was that the Poor People's Campaign had ended in failure.[111]

However, this was not the way at least some of the poor people in the PPC viewed the protest's outcome, and since this movement was theirs as much as anyone's their verdict is worth considering. They understood that their encampment in Washington D.C. had not won Congress over to the goal of waging an expanded war on poverty. But the PPC was not merely about Congress or policymaking for them; it was also about enhancing their own sense of agency—and on that level the PPC did have some success. This can be seen in the response that Mississippi sharecropper Lee Dora Collins gave to the photographer Ronald L. Freeman (who had documented the Poor People's campaign) when he asked whether the results of the PPC had left her disappointed. Collins replied,

> Yes and no. I really enjoyed the whole experience and I learned what we could do if we stuck together. I had never marched like that before. I saw my government turn us down. But the experience lifted my spirits and changed the way I think forever. I got back here and I didn't say "yes sa boss" anymore. Today I have a comfortable home. Most of my children are doing pretty good. . . . That's all I was hoping for when I went to Washington, was to make things better for my family.[112]

Similarly, historian Amy Nathan Wright found that participants in the Poor People's Campaign from one of the most impoverished towns in the Mississippi Delta came away from the protest with advocacy skills that helped them win access to public and private sources of assistance locally.[113]

Andrew Young and some of the movement's other leaders came to rethink their initially negative verdict on the Poor People's Campaign's impact. As Young explained, dazed as he was from the death of his close friend MLK, in May to June 1968 he viewed the Poor People's Campaign's time in Washington as "something to be endured."

> Looking back, I can see that it marked the emergence of a broad-based progressive coalition: poor people who were black, white, brown, and red; religious leaders; union leaders, peace activists. Jobs, peace, and freedom

> would be linked, sustained through a loose, shifting but persistent coalition of organizations. Among the people gathered were some who would go on to head organizations and become members of Congress and elected officials from small southern communities. But in my despair in June 1968 it was difficult to see the possibilities emerging from the Poor People's Campaign. It seemed that despite our marches, press conferences, and civil disobedience, the only image that ever came through in the press was Resurrection City, beset with turmoil, symbolic of the very problems the nation preferred not to face.[114]

Young's reassessment has been echoed in recent scholarship on the Poor People's Campaign. Most notably, in *Power to the Poor: Black-Brown Coalition and the Fight for Economic Justice, 1960–1974* (2013), Gordon K. Mantler showed that the Poor People's Campaign strengthened both Black and Chicano movements for economic justice into the 1970s by introducing their leaders to one another and fostering what would eventually become a fruitful form of coalition politics.[115] Mantler opens his book with an MLK quotation: "When you stand up for justice, you can never fail."[116] Although the protests failed to move a "recalcitrant Congress to expand its antipoverty efforts," the author embraces a broader view.

The MLK quote reminds us that there is another part of the protest that matters, and that is the impact it had on the protesters themselves. Did it educate them in deep and meaningful ways? Did it enhance their morale and strengthen their skills as anti-poverty organizers? Did it leave them better prepared for future political struggles and enable them to persist in their work as organizers for years, decades, or even a lifetime? Mantler suggests it did, and that in this way the Poor People's Campaign had a long-term impact. One could call it a success, even as one might see it as a failure in terms of its immediate goals.

Since MLK did not live to see the Poor People's Campaign's eviction from Washington and Congress's refusal to address the protesters' anti-poverty agenda, we cannot know for certain what he would have said in response. But one suspects that King, with his deep concern about American militarism, and how massive Pentagon spending sapped resources needed to abolish poverty, would have reacted much as radical journalist I. F. Stone did in his scathing article "Billions for Missiles and Pennies for Poverty." Two weeks after the PPC's eviction, Stone noted that "the day the poor were driven out of Resurrection City," June 24, 1968, "deserves to go down in history for its symbolic significance." On that same day the Senate approved $5 billion for its anti-ballistic missile (ABM) system. This was only the "first installment" on this weaponry, likely to spark a new arms race with the Soviet Union, leaving the United States, in the words of Wisconsin Senator Gaylord Nelson, "right back where we started, except out of pocket $50 to $100 billion."[117]

Stone pointed out that this Pentagon program would end up "cost[ing] more than the Poor People's Campaign's 'most utopian demands.'" Linking this spending to the trillion dollars the American warfare state had allocated for armaments since World War II, Stone concluded—echoing MLK on America's misplaced priorities—that such extravagant military spending "has fallen like manna on the country club set and . . . created a new generation of millionaires. We could have cleaned up every slum and solved every racial and social problem with a fraction of the money . . . which went into military hardware, most of it already junked as obsolete."[118] This warning about wasteful spending and obsolescence proved prophetic, for the ABM missile system, seven years and billions of dollars later, would be abandoned as ineffective in deterring an enhanced Soviet nuclear threat.[119]

In the very long term, the Poor People's Campaign ideal has resonated with anti-poverty organizers into the twenty-first century, most notably Rev. William Barber. From his base in North Carolina, Barber organized first a statewide and then a national anti-poverty movement, using the same "Poor People's Campaign" name for the advocacy work he and his movement do on behalf of the poor, whose needs have been so neglected as North Carolina and national politics have drifted rightward.[120]

Admirable as Rev. Barber's anti-poverty work has been, it is hard to imagine King being anything but disappointed that here in the twenty-first century such a movement remains necessary. After all, in launching the Poor People's campaign, MLK sought to win massive federal intervention, a guaranteed annual income funded by Congress, that could end the obscene spectacle of mass poverty in the richest nation on earth. Yet this goal of abolishing poverty seems as distant a dream today as ridding America of racism. According to the most recent data, more than 36 million Americans live in poverty, 11.1 percent of the population.[121] The childhood poverty rate in New York in 2025 stands at 18.1 percent, 25.7 percent in Louisiana, and 26.4 percent in Mississippi.[122]

Since MLK was assassinated before he could even come to Washington with his Poor People's campaign, it would be absurd to attribute this failure to him or even simply to his SCLC, much as critics in the media did at that time. Rather, the failure derives primarily from the lethargy and indifference of the American presidents, Congress, and public about tackling the issue of poverty. On this sad and persistent failure of American capitalism, the last word ought to be left to MLK, in this case the young MLK, who explained to his future wife back in 1952: "[C]apitalism . . . has outlived its usefulness. It has brought about a system that takes necessities from the masses to give luxuries to the classes."[123] For those not inclined, as King was, towards democratic socialism, his conclusion will likely seem too pessimistic about capitalism. But if King was wrong about capitalism, that still leaves us with the question he raised back in 1968, as he organized the Poor People's Campaign: Why does our nation, whose great wealth is fueled by American capitalism (today as back in King's day), allow tens of millions of its citizens, its children, to endure life in poverty? And why is there so little talk today about waging a war on poverty when, according to the latest data, nearly fifty million Americans, including one in five children, are food insecure?[124]

* * *

King Day media coverage, with its focus on the "I Have a Dream" speech at the March on Washington, rarely acknowledges his planned final Washington protest: the Poor People's Campaign. Nor does the MLK Memorial in Washington reference the Poor People's Campaign. The King monument there does include on its north wall a stirring MLK quote related to the need for economic justice. In his Nobel Peace Prize acceptance speech, King spoke of his having "the audacity to believe that peoples everywhere can have three meals a day for their bodies, education and culture for their minds, and dignity, equality, and freedom for their sprits."[125] But the monument bears no quote on his work spotlighting the problem of poverty in affluent America or his organizing on behalf of the poor. The word "poverty" does not appear on the MLK monument.[126] This is not surprising since, in a nation that loves winners and reveres capitalism, there is not much motivation to mention, much less honor, King's ambitious yet unfulfilled quest to abolish the poverty endemic to capitalist America. No 30-foot statue or public history monument in our nation's capital honors MLK's abolitionist ideal, which the United States has done precious little to realize. In fact, you have to travel to Mississippi to find some public commemoration of the Poor People's Campaign, and this takes the form not of a major monument but rather a modest historical road sign identifying the town Marks, Mississippi, as the place where MLK wanted this last march on Washington to begin.

This historical marker in Mississippi is headed "Marks Mule Train and Poor People's Campaign." It reads, in part, as follows: "In March 1968 Martin Luther King Jr. visited Marks to get support for a Poor People's Campaign. He envisioned masses converging on Washington in a plea for anti-poverty projects. King wanted the march to begin in Mississippi, with mules and wagon trains. After King's death on April 4 the SCLC organized the Marks Mule Train which left [for Washington, D.C.] May 13."[127] But this marker does not explain why King wanted the march to begin there. It was because of the shocking poverty he encountered in his visit to Marks, a town located in the poorest county in the United States in 1968. For King, Marks embodied all the problems and all the deprivation of American poverty at its worst.

In King's last interview, and in his final sermon—delivered at the National Cathedral in Washington, D.C.—in March 1968, he discussed his recent trip to Marks and its powerful impact upon him. In both the interview and sermon, King mentioned that the deprivation he witnessed there reduced him to tears.

> I was in Marks, Mississippi the other day and I found myself weeping before I knew it. I met boys and girls by the hundreds who didn't have any shoes to wear, who didn't have any food to eat, in terms of three square meals a day, and I met their parents, many of whom didn't even have jobs. But not only do they not have jobs, they are not even getting an income. Some of them aren't on any kind of welfare, and I literally cried when I heard men and women saying that they were unable to get any food to feed their children.[128]

MLK's words here tell us something quite important about him. He cared, deeply and personally, about the suffering and deprivation of poor people, those marginalized, oppressed, and forgotten by most Americans. The tears he shed in Marks, Mississippi, are a reminder that just focusing on King as a thinker, his social criticism, and ideas for egalitarian change can lead us to miss something important: that it took a compassionate person to feel what he did, to act and think as he did, as a champion of those burdened by economic and racial injustice. And that for MLK this was a role grounded not in abstraction but in direct personal experience, and not just in Marks, Mississippi, in 1968. Such experience dated back to his days as a boy in America's Great Depression, when witnessing the bread lines of the poor in Atlanta led to his early questioning of capitalism.[129]

Although none of us can equal MLK's gifts as an inspiring orator, one would like to believe that all are capable of feeling and acting on the kind of compassion he did. And yet, as I contemplated King's account of poverty, hardships, and sorrow in Marks, Mississippi, came the news that today's Republican-dominated Congress, aligned with and pressured by President Trump, adopted a federal budget plan that would remove federally funded health care from some 15 million low-income Americans and cut off food assistance to some two million poor children in order to subsidize a massive tax break for the rich.[130] This calls to mind MLK's remark, at the New Politics Conference in 1967, that "Victor Hugo could have been talking about . . . America when he wrote that there is always more misery among the lower classes than there is humanity in the higher classes."[131] The time seems ripe, then, to reflect not only on King's social criticism but also on his compassion, the tears he shed for poor families, and the organizing he did so urgently, seeking to banish poverty and to reflect as well on the paucity of such humanitarian concern for the poor, the absence of any King-like ambition to end poverty in America's billionaire-dominated political world.

Next Steps

To push back against the power and pervasiveness of the domesticated MLK image that has become so popular in the United States since the advent of the MLK Day holiday, I have tried in this book to introduce readers new to MLK scholarship on King as the social critic who thought deeply and critically about racism, militarism, and capitalism's fueling of poverty and vast economic inequality. My intent is to show that, politically, King was neither the moderate nor conservative that many Americans today imagine but egalitarian, anti-capitalist, and socially democratic, well to the left of the American mainstream. In making this point I used Vincent Harding's terms: he labeled the domesticated, distorted version of MLK the "convenient hero." This needed to be replaced, Harding insisted, by a historically accurate version of MLK as an "inconvenient hero" who challenged America to rethink its flattering self-image and face its oppressive record on race, economics, and violence.[1]

While the imagery and the point Harding made with it are helpful in provoking us to rethink the simplistic popular image of MLK, the term "hero" is itself problematic, as Harding acknowledged in one of his last interviews.[2] A heroic image can easily lend itself more to the mythical than the historical. If we think of MLK the hero, what comes to mind is the larger than life thirty-foot likeness of King at the MLK Memorial on the National Mall in Washington, D.C., which makes him into a kind of demigod.[3] In defying frequent death threats and even the bombing of his home, by continuing his work leading the freedom movement, King certainly acted courageously. And when you add to such courage his tragic assassination while serving the cause of social justice, the term "heroic" seems appropriate. And yet, if we take King off his pedestal and probe his actual history, there were moments when a hero's courage seemed lacking. This occurred in 1961 after the first two groups of Freedom Riders had been beaten bloody by racist thugs and one bus was firebombed in Alabama. Intrepid young activists from SNCC's Nashville contingent rushed in to save the Freedom

Ride campaign by taking the place of the injured riders. When the SNCC volunteers asked MLK to join them on the Freedom Ride's next leg, he refused, and when they persisted, he said, "I think I should choose the time and place of my Golgotha."[4] This reference to the site of Jesus's crucifixion seemed pretentious to the disappointed students and even led some SNCC activists to mock King as "De Lawd."[5] So was MLK's claim that an arrest during the ride could lead to a long Georgia prison sentence, since he was on probation there, which the students told him was no different than the situation of several of them, whose activism had resulted in probation too.

Upon hearing of this incident, Robert Williams, the dissident NAACP organizer from North Carolina who believed in armed self-defense, sent King an irate telegram denouncing him as a "coward" who should resign his leadership position in the movement.[6] This charge was unfair since King, because he was so prominent and hated by racists, would be the first one targeted and likely killed if violence occurred on the next Freedom Ride.[7] The threats King faced from white supremacists on a daily basis had left him aware that his life was in danger so long as he remained a movement leader. In fact, at the meeting when he refused to join the Freedom Ride, King broke the silence in the room that followed his words of refusal by talking about "what those in the movement should do after he was killed." One Freedom Rider recalled that King "spoke in the most fatalistic of voices: not *if* he was killed, but *when* he was killed. The room became even more quiet. It was as if his violent death was a given, and the only question was when it would happen."[8]

There were many occasions when MLK defied specific, ominous threats to his life, including when he refused to heed the warning by John Doar of the Department of Justice of such a threat and in doing so risked his life leading the march into Montgomery at the end of the trek from Selma in 1965.[9] And, of course, he defied death threats to return to Memphis the day before his assassination. Even so, King's refusal to essentially court death as a Freedom Rider back in 1961 reminds us that MLK was only human, and one can hardly expect him to risk his life heroically every day, on demand, and in this case for an action that CORE, then SNCC, not his own organization had initiated.

In this same humanizing spirit, having now been introduced to MLK's social criticism, and how much more perceptive and searching it was regarding the connections between racism, militarism, and capitalism than anything one hears from most American politicians, we can now take the next step in our engagement with MLK's ideas by reflecting upon the limitations of both his social criticism and his strategy for translating those ideas into action. And in the process, we can consider some of the more important criticisms of and debates about King offered by historians and King's contemporaries as they assessed his successes and failures. In offering my take on all this, the goal is not necessarily to win your agreement with me but rather to highlight these issues and debates, so you may explore them further and make up your own mind by reading more of MLK's writings and speeches as well as the most illuminating studies of MLK and the Black Freedom Movement.

One example of such criticism connects to the final years of MLK's life, when he became more open about his belief in the need for "a revolution in values," to build a more egalitarian America free of racism, militarism, and poverty. But King was not clear on how to achieve such a values revolution, especially in a capitalist society so effective in offering economic inducements to its supporters and in marginalizing and suppressing anti-capitalist discourse—so much so that King had for most of his years in movement leadership personally avoided publicly discussing his anti-capitalist views.

Similar questions about tactics and strategy can be raised about confronting Congress with another mass march in 1968, which is where King left off with the Poor People's Campaign. Was this approach viable, given how Congressional politics had drifted to the right and with Washington's self-serving politicians tending to loath such protests? In addressing this question, King scholar Thomas F. Jackson argued that the PPC demonstrated that despite MLK's anti-capitalism, "King confronted governmental power more than corporate control of the means of production. . . . King overestimated the strength of liberalism and underestimated the power of resurgent conservatism. His solutions . . . looked to the federal treasury . . . to guarantee jobs and income. . . . He expected too much from the federal government and the strategy of protest."[10] But both the values revolution ideal and the Poor People's Campaign came *near the start* of the new economics-centered phase of the movement, so it may be unrealistic to expect King to have devised a whole new strategy. After all, this protest model and Washington-centered strategy had worked in the past, yielding the Civil Rights Act and the Voting Rights Act, and King never lived to see it fail with the Poor People's Campaign, so he would not have been in a position to recognize the need for a new strategy.

This issue of strategy is connected to several other important conceptual questions concerning MLK's leadership and the movement's successes and failures. Historians have long operated under the periodization scheme introduced by MLK himself, and modified by one of King's early biographers, David Levering Lewis, who divided the years of MLK's movement leadership into two distinct eras. The first era, as Lewis explained, "begins with the December 1955 Montgomery bus boycott and ends with the march from Selma to Montgomery, Alabama, in late March 1965."[11] This period was, as Lewis put it, a "decade of innovative protest tactics employed to achieve traditional citizenship rights for Afro-Americans"; it was "partially successful," culminating with the passage of historic federal legislation to protect Black rights: the Civil Rights Act of 1964 and the Voting Rights Act of 1965.[12] The second and final period began with King steering the SCLC northward, in the Chicago demonstrations for jobs and housing during 1966, and ends with the assassination of King in Memphis, on April 4, 1968. This later period was, according to Lewis, marked by "relative failure," three "turbulent years" in which "nontraditional tactics in pursuit of increasingly radical goals for the larger society" proved ineffective.[13]

Lewis avoided a simplistic good/bad dichotomy between the two periods. He acknowledged that "relative success" in the first period, most notably its winning civil rights legislation, "accentuated what yet remained to be done before the poor, the powerless, and the racially disadvantaged could begin to achieve equal opportunity in America." And that the post-Selma period, despite its "relative failure," had to its credit left as its legacy an admirably egalitarian "vision of political power and economic well-being devolving increasingly upon the poor, the powerless, and the racially disadvantaged." Lewis acknowledged that there was "greatness" in both eras: "The greatness of the decade ending with Selma was the nobility of the protesters; that of the times after Selma was in the far-reaching implications of the protest."[14]

Even with Lewis's nuanced explanation, however, these "relative success and failure" categories, though quite a useful introduction to the King years, seem problematic. First, they fail to take into account the regional versus national foci of the two eras. From 1955 to 1965 the SCLC, as its name implied, was a Southern organization, focused primarily on toppling the South's Jim Crow regime. This struggle was so absorbing and exhausting that King—though concerned with, and knowledgeable about, the plight of Blacks in Northern ghettoes and expressing solidarity with organizing against racism up north—had no time to lead mass protest movements outside the South.[15] King recognized that some civil rights issues, such as voting rights—so crucial in the South—were not relevant to Northern Blacks, since they had those rights already, and that for them issues of class and economic oppression, compounded by racial discrimination in the job and housing markets, were central. The Watts riots in Los Angeles enhanced King's understanding of this difference and helped lead him to shift his focus to economic inequality, poverty, and Northern ghettoes, beginning with Chicago, into which he would move not just his political focus but also his residence in 1966.[16]

Admirable as this Northern move was, it was made in part because of King's realization that the SCLC and the freedom movement it helped lead in the South had failed to do enough to prioritize the needs and problems of low-income Blacks in the North. This failure was underscored by the ghetto rebellions/riots that began in Harlem in 1964, whose spread attested to MLK's inability to convince those most disillusioned in Black America that nonviolence offered the best path towards egalitarian social change.

The point here is not to dub MLK a failure in the 1955–1965 era. Most King scholars accurately present this as his time of historic successes: Montgomery, Birmingham, the March on Washington, Selma, and the Civil Rights and Voting Right Acts. Toppling Jim Crow and winning the first major civil rights acts since Reconstruction were indeed epic milestones in the history of democracy. But even those successes had limits, and this was also a time of failures, which King well understood. This is why he was dissatisfied and changed course during 1965 and 1966. Daunting though it was, and costly in terms of lives lost and brutality absorbed in the Southern freedom struggle, it was nonetheless far more difficult to go national, seeking to challenge America's capitalist system and the poverty it bred across racial lines from coast to coast, and to stop a still popular anti-Communist war waged by a powerful and determined president.

So this second period involved significantly greater challenges than the first, and yet due to his assassination, King had less than a third of the time of the first period in which to meet those challenges. Thus, terming the later period a failure seems to hold King to an impossible standard, as if we are expecting him to move at incredible speed, offer a kind of divine intervention, to part the waters, and defeat capitalism, a rightward shifting Congress, and the military industrial complex all at once. Even the American Revolution, with an army led by George Washington, did not manage to prevail in three short years. Indeed, if we judged the early King years on a three-year cycle, MLK would not fare well, since his first major victory after Montgomery did come until the Birmingham struggle, seven years later, in 1963 (though he did loan valuable support to the sit-ins of 1960 and the Freedom Rides of 1961). This is why, in his classic history of King's SCLC, Adam Fairclough's chapter on the 1957–1959 period is titled "The Fallow Years," which contradicts Lewis's conclusion about the 1955–65 era as successful.[17]

Much more scathing criticism of King's leadership in this later period came from radical journalist Andrew Kopkind in his review of MLK's final book, *Where Do We Go from Here: Chaos or Community?* in 1967. Kopkind argued that time had passed King by, making his integrationist idealism and nonviolence seem outdated, losing its appeal to Black America amidst the crisis of the Northern ghettoes in the mid-1960s, which required a more explicitly revolutionary approach of the kind being offered by Black Power advocates, who were gaining Black support while King was losing it. In Kopkind's view,

> Martin Luther King once had the ability to talk to people, the power to change them by evoking images of revolution. But the duty of a revolutionary is to make revolution (say those who have done it), and King made none. By his own admission, things are worse today—for white people and black—than when he began the bus boycott in Montgomery eleven years ago. Last summer in Chicago, he was booed at a mass meeting, and later he understood why: "They were booing because we [in the civil rights movement] were unable deliver on our promises [of freedom and equal opportunity]."[18]

While conceding that King's approach to social change had in the past worked against "Southern feudalism," Kopkind found it ineffective in overcoming the "stonier walls behind the first defenses of segregation. A society infused with racism," backed by "a national system of industrial and technological capitalism [that] was practically invulnerable. Marches and freedom songs were unavailing." Kopkind accused King of being vague in his calls for the restructuring of American society, and of having no idea of how to accomplish such change. Thus Kopkind argued for "King's irrelevancy," deeming him caught between "white anxieties and black anger. . . . Whites have ceased to believe him, or really to care; the blacks hardly listen."[19]

Harsh as it was, Kopkin's review does connect with important problems that troubled MLK in his final years, and that at times seemed so overwhelming that King—as his biographer David J. Garrow documented—suffered bouts of depression.[20] These included how to respond to the surge of Black nationalism, the major ghetto riots—and the lack of faith they represented in the nonviolent ethos he cherished—plus the right-wing backlash that followed the ghetto rebellions, the persistence of poverty in an affluent society, and the escalating war in Vietnam. Indeed, to capture how difficult these last years of King's life were for him, the producers of a recent HBO documentary chose as their title, *King in the Wilderness*.[21] So Kopkind was raising the right questions about how King responded to the difficult political problems he faced as 1960s America became increasingly polarized and inhospitable to the nonviolent movement he had helped lead.

It also seems clear, however, that Kopkind underestimated King's ability to respond creatively—and effectively—as the political ground shifted beneath his feet. That response, as we have seen, involved King embracing a more leftist tone, being more openly critical of the inequity inherent in American capitalism—the mass poverty it bred—and offering scathing dissent on the Vietnam War, especially its sapping resources and focus from domestic social problems. It also involved King's critique of Black nationalism, which he offered in a way that often combined a sympathetic view of its promoting Black pride, culture, and unity, with an insistence that as a political strategy its separatism was a dead end, since it hampered the multiracial coalition building necessary to promote egalitarian change in a white majority nation.

While it is true that, by 1967, the ghetto riots indicated substantial Black disregard for King's advocacy of nonviolence, Kopkind provided no empirical evidence that either the ghetto rebellions or the growing appeal of Black nationalism had ended King's status as Black America's most popular leader. Indeed, the polling data, as historian Jason Sokol points out, attests to the endurance of that popularity:

> Even in the heyday of Black Power, many African Americans still held King in high esteem. Early in 1968, a poll was conducted among blacks in fifteen cities. Fully 72 percent approved of King; only 5 percent disapproved. By contrast, just 14 percent approved of [Black Power advocate] Stokely Carmichael while 35 percent disapproved. According to an additional poll, some 90 percent of African Americans judged that King

had the "best approach" to racial change and said they trusted him more than any other Black leader. Even at King's lowest point, he remained their prince.[22]

On the issue of eroding white support, however, Kopkind was on more solid ground. As we have already seen, when King broke with the Democratic establishment over Vietnam, powerful white liberals formerly allied with him, from Lyndon Johnson's White House to the *New York Times* editorial board, bitterly attacked MLK. The loss of white liberal allies was also an inherent risk, as King became more publicly critical of President Johnson's War on Poverty and LBJ's refusal to follow the Kerner Commission's recommendations for expanding federal programs to combat the racial inequities that had bred the major ghetto rebellions.

The anti-capitalist tone of King's calls for a revolution in values also threatened to alienate moderates. King was well aware of this risk and had been warned about it quite early, in 1965—even before the Voting Rights Act was signed into law. Back then his closest advisor, Stanley Levison, wrote King that the coalition that had yielded the voting rights victory was "a coalition around a fairly narrow objective . . . for moderate change, for gradual improvements, which are to be obtained as it gently alters old patterns. *It is militant only against shocking violence and gross injustice.* It is not for deep or radical change. . . . America today is not ready for a radical restructuring of its economy or social order . . . in order to free the Negro."[23]

Echoing Levison, King biographer David Levering Lewis's explanation of King's declining white support in his final years, confirms the wisdom of Levison's warning and prediction. Lewis concluded that when King's

> immediate scope of objectives was mainly constitutional and regional—desegregation and voting rights in the South—King's allies . . . more often than not came effectively to his assistance. The minimal demands of integrated schools, open public facilities, and access to the ballot were always recognized as legitimate in principle by a majority of Americans. King used the same tactics of conciliatory confrontation when the scope of his objectives was enlarged as he moved northward. The specter of terrible social and economic upheaval was put forward as inevitable, unless swift and profound national advances were achieved in the area of

> human rights and economic opportunity. This time, however, resistance was far greater; many of King's powerful Establishment supporters came to regard him as a major contributor to rather than the antidote for intolerable socioeconomic disorder.[24]

King's willingness to do what he thought was right on the war, poverty, and the failures of the Johnson administration attests that in his final years he followed his conscience rather than public opinion. Even if this came across as too radical for some of his liberal white funders. This seems fitting for King as a moral leader and a pastor, quite the opposite of an opportunistic politician. And it fits as well with the argument made in much of this book in which we see King as a radical social critic. But one needs to be cautious about carrying this argument too far, since, as this book's opening chapter details, as a tactician King often displayed a strong pragmatic streak: as when he avoided criticizing the Kennedy administration in his "I Have a Dream" speech, in order to preserve a fragile alliance with Kennedy that had finally resulted in the introduction of what would become the first major civil rights act since Reconstruction. King had shown this same pragmatism in pulling back from vigorous dissent against the Vietnam War, so as to avoid a break with President Johnson in 1965–1966. And MLK had taken similar actions in reluctantly supporting LBJ's compromise position on the Mississippi Freedom Democratic Party's seating at the 1964 Democratic Party Convention as well as his decision to abide by a federal injunction, which led him to abort the second Selma march.

With this in mind, it seems worthwhile to think in terms of ends and means when we consider how MLK did and did not change politically in his final years. In his first decade as a movement leader, when the focus was on race, as historian Louis B. Harlan put it, "King's goals were the same radical ones of social justice and equal rights that animated SNCC and CORE." This was also true of his criticism of American racism, past and present. But during these early years, when it came to strategy and tactics, King, in Harlan's words, "gave the appearance of greater caution, moderation, and openness to negotiation."[25] This tactical cautiousness and moderation faded, however, in his final years when King proved unafraid of challenging President Johnson in peace marches against the Vietnam War and in the planning of a Poor People's Campaign that mocked the puniness of LBJ's War on Poverty.

And one can see in this a unifying of King's radicalism to include means as well as ends, though in both eras his faith in nonviolent protest endured.

In his final year, King offered powerful arguments about how the tremendous cost of the Vietnam War had made a major war on poverty impossible, hurting Blacks and others stuck in poverty. The relationship between the American warfare state and racial progress was more contradictory, however, than King acknowledged. One of the defenses of the *Brown* decision and rationales for other United States moves towards racial integration, as in the armed forces, had been Cold War America's need to shed Jim Crowism so as to be better be able to line up Cold War allies in Africa and non-white nations across the globe.[26] This mindset led U.S. Attorney General Robert F. Kennedy, in a 1961 speech at the University of Georgia, months after its first two Black students were admitted under federal court order, to argue that the graduation of these students would "without question aid and assist" the U.S. Cold War struggle in Africa, Asia, and South America.[27] So here we have, contrary to King's antiwar argument, a war effort serving to promote, not impede, the struggle for Black progress and racial justice—though it is also true that domestically the Cold War Red Scare enabled segregationists to undermine the civil rights movement by casting its leaders as disloyal subversives.

On a moral and ethical level King's arguments for nonviolence were virtually unassailable. But politically they could lead to contradictions. King was a great admirer of the anti-colonial liberation process, but some of those rebellions involved anti-imperialist violence.[28] And, of course, this was also true of the American Revolution, whose central documents—the Declaration of Independence and U.S. Constitution—conveyed liberal ideals that King invoked so approvingly on behalf of the Black freedom struggle. So there was certainly merit in Malcolm X's insistence that violence was often necessary for revolutionary change and in his skepticism about nonviolence.[29] But on the other hand, it was difficult to argue with King's point that, aside from its moral superiority, nonviolence was the only practical way forward in a society where Blacks were a relatively small minority. MLK, moreover, devoted a great deal of time to arguing that ghetto riots damaged the struggle for racial equality. And yet, ironically, by far the largest wave of ghetto rebellions in 1960s America, sparked by MLK's assassination, resulted in a major racial crisis, prompting the passage of the era's last significant civil rights legislation: the Fair Housing

Act, which Congress had been unwilling to enact prior to the assassination and riots.[30]

The irreverence that MLK encountered from such rivals as Robert Williams and Malcolm X could be harsh—at times unduly so. Yet even King ally Bayard Rustin mocked King's limitations, asserting, "I know Martin very well . . . he did not have the ability to organize vampires to go to a bloodbath. The organizing was done by Southern brutality."[31] The point here is not to diminish MLK but rather to remember that during MLK's political life the Black Freedom Movement's leadership constituted a critically minded community that valued King but questioned his judgments and skill in some areas. That is a far better way to approach MLK than placing him on a pedestal or pretending he was omniscient.

This point was made in a slightly different and illuminating way by Vincent Harding. Although he strongly admired King as an orator and leader, Harding stressed the collectivity of the movement as more central than King himself. It was, Harding recalled, "always about the movement and how we were interacting and learning together in the midst of everything else."[32] King was, in this view, one of many leaders, along with other movement veterans such as Ella Baker, who played a crucial role in helping to launch SNCC and mentor its founders. Baker, as Harding explained, "was a great teacher of the movement. We were all teaching each other . . . learning together about what it meant to be a democratic movement, and that's what it was. It wasn't about Martin or anyone else telling everyone else what to do."[33] This is why Harding viewed the presentation of King as some singular heroic figure as distorting the history of a movement that was a collaborative endeavor, so that "to make King into a hero is to misunderstand what was happening."[34]

Harding's comments connect back to one of the perennial debates about the relationship between MLK and the Black Freedom Movement: Did the movement make MLK? Or did MLK make the movement? At one of the early historical conferences about King, SNCC veteran Robert Parris Moses compared the movement to an ocean and depicted King as just one wave in that ocean.[35] SNCC historian and MLK papers editor Clayborne Carson also depicted the movement as central rather than King and pushed back on what he saw as the historical myth of King as the "Great Man" who "is seen as the decisive factor in the process of social change," whose "unique qualities as a leader are used to explain major historical events."[36] This myth, often transmitted by the mass media, presented King as "not only the preeminent leader of the civil rights movement but also as the initiator and sole indispensable element in the southern black struggles of the 1950s and 1960s." Citing recent historical scholarship exploring "the black struggle as a locally based mass movement rather than a reform movement led by national civil rights leaders," Carson concluded that

> the King myth departs from historical reality because it attributes too much to King's exceptional qualities and too little to the impersonal, large-scale social factors that made it possible for King to display his singular abilities on a national stage. Because the myth emphasizes the individual at the expense of the black movement, it not only exaggerates King's importance but also distorts his actual considerable contribution to the movement. . . . If King had never lived, the black struggle would have followed a course of development similar to the one it did.[37]

At this same conference, however, historian Nathan Huggins dissented from this view, holding it was so movement-centered it risked understating King's importance. Huggins warned that "there is as much danger in romanticizing movements as in romanticizing movement individual leaders."[38] While agreeing that great man mythology is problematic and that "some of what occurred in the 1960s would have occurred without any individual, Martin Luther King included," Huggins deemed it a mistake to write movement history that reflected an unwillingness to credit the leadership role played by extraordinary talents like King. Huggins concluded that "it is foolish to imagine that the individual actors were interchangeable parts and that without the particular personality of Martin Luther King someone else would have served as well. Individuals do make a difference, and when they play such important roles as did Dr. King, we must give them great attention."[39]

This debate is not merely academic, however; it is also political. Early SNCC's organizing style stressed grassroots movement building and communities generating their own leadership from the bottom up, rather than relying upon national leaders. There was something disempowering about emphasizing charismatic leadership. If communities relied on such leaders, there was a danger that if the leader did not appear, or was lost in the struggle, as King was when he was cut down by an assassin's bullet, that might render them passive and waiting on a national leader, a kind of political equivalent to waiting for the messiah. As SNCC veteran Diane Nash put it, "If people think that it was Martin Luther King's movement, then today they—the young people—are more likely to say 'gosh, I wish we had a Martin Luther King here today to lead us. . . .' If people knew how that movement started [from the bottom up] then the question they would ask themselves is, 'What can I do?'"[40]

This is not to suggest that historians drawn to the image of the movement as an ocean and MLK as just one wave (and other waves being the local community movements and the grassroots leaders they generated) took this position because they were biased, or that these scholars distorted history because they were so taken by the SNCC grassroots approach to organizing that they understated MLK's historic role. There is, as Carson indicated, a great body of historical scholarship offering evidence that while the Black Freedom Movement could mobilize for King-centered events, the struggle for racial equality erupted primarily at the local level, constituting a political force of great size and impact nationally because it was a movement composed of hundreds of locally led grassroots movements.[41] Think again back to the 1957 prayer pilgrimage when community organizing was limited and drew a relatively small crowd to Washington. King's eloquent voting rights speech on the Mall garnered relatively little attention. But with the 1963 March on Washington, after the Birmingham struggle had catalyzed local protests across the nation, the stage was set for King's historic "I Have a Dream speech" to generate an unprecedented national TV audience. This was because grassroots organizers helped assemble on the Mall in D.C. the largest protest rally to that point in American history. In this case we could say the movement made Martin. The same could be said of his very first civil rights struggle when he was essentially drafted into the leadership of a bus boycott that local activists had already started.

We could also say the same thing about the struggles in Albany and in Memphis, where large and enthusiastic movement crowds turned out to rally for racial and economic justice. Their impressive presence and solidarity inspired King, and helped ensure that, instead of just delivering a single speech, he would return to help with the movement in their cities.[42] And inspiration was a two-way street. Surely the enormous crowd that came to King's first speech in Memphis, in March 1968—fifteen thousand, the largest indoor rally he had ever addressed in the South—had been drawn at least in part by a desire to hear King.[43] One could offer the same conclusion about the smaller but no less enthusiastic crowd that came out in a severe storm to hear King's final speech on April 3. And in turn, the crowd's presence and emotion, relayed to MLK by his friend and colleague Ralph David Abernathy, who was supposed to speak in his place, convinced an exhausted King to rush from his hotel room to deliver a speech he had intended to skip. There was, at least in these cases, a dialogical quality to King's relationship to the movement, best captured by Vincent Harding's conclusion that King as a protest leader "was created by the movement, and he also created parts of the movement."[44]

As to King himself, like most veterans of the movement, he did not believe he had created the Black Freedom Movement of his time. King was aware that through his oratory, Nobel Peace Prize, and prominence in the victorious struggles for justice in Montgomery, Birmingham, and Selma, and in the legislative achievements represented by the Civil Rights Act and Voting Rights Act, he had become a magnet for media coverage of the movement. He served as, in Garrow's words, a "symbol . . . representative . . . and a trustee of the movement," but King "was never under any illusion . . . that he was the capital-L 'leader' of the movement." He "profoundly believed that" the movement had created him as a protest leader, since it had, first in Montgomery in 1955, "really drafted him, to take up a public role. King was never someone who wanted to be a celebrity . . . never terribly comfortable in the public eye . . . he had a very consciously self-sacrificial understanding of what his calling entailed."[45]

One sees evidence of this from the start of MLK's role as a protest leader in Montgomery. In March 1956, after the biased Alabama judge convicted MLK in a conspiracy trial, and deriding that conviction in front of a mass meeting of the bus boycott rank and file, King said, "'I want to ask you a question. I want to ask you because they said in court that I started the protest. They said that a selfish, power-seeking group who wanted to get publicity started it. Who started the protest?' Audience: 'We did.'"[46]

Near the start of this book, I advocated the advantages of introducing MLK through the issues-oriented approach used in this book. Yet it is also true that to understand fully how King came to be so politically radical and yet in some ways culturally conventional one needs—as a next step in understanding King—to consult the MLK biographies and the rich field of King scholarship. This involves learning about MLK's family background, his youth, his experience in the Black Church, his college and graduate work in theology, the ways, as historian Thomas F. Jackson put it, King "was influenced by and in turn reshaped the political cultures of the black freedom movement and democratic left. [How] his vision of unfettered human rights drew on the diverse tenets of the African American social gospel, socialism, left-New Deal liberalism, Gandhian philosophy, and Popular Front internationalism."[47] It also means learning more about Coretta Scott King, whose left-leaning background and its influence on her husband has not gotten the attention it deserves. For example, one of the most revealing letters the young MLK wrote expressing his anti-capitalist views was sent to Coretta in response to her gifting to him Edward Bellamy's utopian socialist novel *Looking Backward*. And though King biographers often cite his letter they do not stop to reflect upon her role in inspiring King to write that letter.[48] The same can be said concerning her peace activism, which preceded his by more than a decade.

In the realm of intellectual history, the studies of King's religious ideas are by far the richest and most revealing—especially the work of David J. Garrow, Keith D. Miller, Garry Dorrien, Lewis Baldwin and Jonathan Rieder, along with important discoveries made by Clayborne Carson and the Martin Luther King, Jr. Papers Project that he headed for decades. This scholarship revealed that though King explored the ideas of a variety of Christian thinkers in theological seminary and his doctoral program—and was pulled in different directions by the classic social gospel authors and Reinhold Niebuhr's more pessimistic view of human nature—his experience in the Black Church had the most impact on his sermons and political oratory. Miller was the first to show that MLK had a strong knowledge of earlier sermons of Black preachers and freely borrowed from them, adapting them to his own needs.[49] King drew too on the Black Church's Judaic emphasis, its use of the book of Exodus for a model of liberation and resisting evil.[50] King's ability to use the Bible to frame his political speeches helped to give his political oratory both a moral clarity and a familiar reference point that made his speeches all the more powerful. And it was the Christian ethic of love that inclined King towards nonviolence even before his embrace of Gandhism.

There was considerable overlap between King's sermons and his dissident political speeches, as, for instance, with his "Drum Major Instinct" sermon that he preached to his Ebenezer Church in February 1968. This sermon offered criticism of U.S. militarism and nationalist arrogance that was as scorching as anything he ever said at an antiwar rally. It is telling that the editors of the book of his sermons that King published in his lifetime, *Strength to Love* (1963), would—as the King papers' historical researchers discovered—see fit to remove the sharp political edges from several of his sermons, so as to de-radicalize them for a mainstream readership in Cold War America. Among the phrases they removed were King's terming racial segregation "one of the ugly practices of our nation," his advocacy that "capitalism must be transformed by a 'deep-seated change,'" his indictment of colonialism as "evil because it was based on a contempt for life," as well as "many of his anti-military and antiwar statements."[51]

MLK was more radical than not only the editors of his book of sermons but also most of his advisors, especially in his final years, both on Vietnam and in his inclination towards democratic socialism, as documented by King scholars David Garrow, Clayborne Carson, Thomas F. Jackson, and Adam Fairclough, in the reminisces of Coretta Scott King, and in the evidence presented in this book. Yet it is also the case that there is some debate on King's relationship to socialism, and so readers should consider the arguments of those King scholars skeptical of MLK's embracing socialism.

MLK's most recent biographer Jonathan Eig asserts that King "was not a socialist. . . . He condemned capitalism for generating massive economic inequality while arguing that the system could be reformed." In support of this view, Eig cited King scholar Tommie Shelby's assertion that though MLK "called for a fairer distribution of wealth, he did not criticize private ownership of productive assets and natural resources as inherently unjust."[52] Eig's argument is certainly worth considering, though the dichotomy he draws, between reformist organizing to make capitalism less oppressive (i.e. to pressure Washington to guarantee a minimum income to all) and preferring a democratic socialist society that prioritizes people's welfare rather than capitalist profits, seems false. Indeed, much of the history of labor radicalism and the American Left involved working to mitigate capitalist oppression in the here and now and also hoping in the long term to see America abandon capitalism for democratic socialism, a more egalitarian social order.

Shelby is correct about King not rejecting private property outright, but MLK's attacks on the profit motive and the capitalist system's reduction of human beings to commodities certainly reflected a socialist ethos. It seems problematic to expect King to have offered a detailed blueprint for a democratically socialist America, since as a practical political organizer, it was counterproductive for him to speak publicly like a socialist theoretician in a society so at odds with socialism. Indeed, even among his advisors, explicit anti-capitalism proved controversial. This can be seen in a story told in the memoir of MLK's close friend and financial supporter Harry Belafonte, the famed singer, actor, and civil rights activist. Belafonte wrote of an argument in March 1968 between MLK and his moderate advisor Andrew Young, in which King expressed his agreement with young radicals that "it's the system that's the problem, and it's choking the breath out of our lives." When Young dissented, "[I]t's not the entire system. It's only part of it, and I think we can fix this," King replied angrily, "I don't need to hear from you, Andy. You're a capitalist and I'm not. . . . The trouble is that we live in a failed system. Capitalism does not permit an even flow of economic resources. With this system, a small privileged few are rich beyond conscience and all others are doomed to be poor at some level. That's the way the system works. And since we know that the system will not change the rules, we're going to have to change the system." Belafonte concluded, "At heart, Martin was a socialist and revolutionary thinker."[53]

While getting to know MLK better via biographical background and the debates among King scholars is important, so is the larger political context, which means learning about the broad spectrum of individuals and organizations in the Black Freedom Movement with whom MLK interacted. They span from the direct-action radicals of SNCC and CORE to the more conventional politics of the NAACP and the Urban League, plus King's SCLC, and Black Nationalist critics, advocates of armed self-defense, and the anti-war movement. We need to know the names, ideas, and organizing work of prominent figures in all these organizations as well as the grassroots local movements and activists that King interacted with in Montgomery, the sit-ins and Freedom Rides, the Albany, Georgia, Birmingham, Selma, Chicago, and Memphis movements. This gives us King as part of, but not above, the Freedom Movement and his movement colleagues. As Robert P. Moses, SNCC's Mississippi voting rights leader, recalled, sometimes other organizers proved more effective than MLK. Thus Ella Baker and her model of collective leadership influenced early SNCC approaches to decision-making and activism, while MLK's model of charismatic leadership did not, resulting in the differences between the early SNCC's person-to-person organizing style and King's/SCLC's telegenic mobilization model, centered on MLK speeches.

The results of this were visible at the Atlantic City Democratic National Convention in 1964 when it was the former sharecropper Fannie Lou Hamer, energized by the SNCC, and not MLK who gave the most dramatic and memorable speech on voting rights.[54]

This attention to the leaders, organizations, and political culture of the Black Freedom Movement enables us to see what linked MLK to his contemporaries and what distinguished him from them. It also attests that it was not just King but his times that were so unusual—packed with talented anti-racist organizers who sometimes competed with and sometimes cooperated with MLK. With this in mind, the perennial question of whether the movement made Martin or Martin made the movement seems less important than the fact that both were at times such effective forces for freedom, equality, and justice.

* * *

Although understanding MLK's political thought, and its relation to his times, is important and has been a main goal of this book, I hope it is evident by now that King's ideas and the social criticism he popularized through his powerful oratory, writings, and leadership are of more than historical interest. They offer political, ethical, and moral guidance to us in the twenty-first century. As we have seen, his vision was of an America that confronted and worked to overcome its racist past, that abolished poverty, addressed economic inequality, and worked towards a warless world and a society free of violence. This is not to say that MLK was omniscient or that we should revere his every thought. But rather, more than a half century after his death, we should at least begin to hold ourselves up to the high standards of humanity and civilization he articulated.

Doing so in the Trump era is a sobering affair. MLK understood that all the talk of a white "backlash" against the civil rights movement in the 1960s being caused by Black militancy was misleading, since he knew that white resentment of the African American quest for equality was constant, simmering just below the surface, fated to resurface inevitably, unless and until white America came to grips with its racism.[55] And it has resurfaced with a vengeance with Trumpism's white grievance politics, leaving us with the ugly spectacle of a White House demonizing diversity, equity, and inclusion, firing federal employees who embraced those ideals, purging Black history and the history of racism from American historic sites and cultural institutions, even renaming military bases for Confederates.[56] Reading any of MLK's speeches, grounded in African American history, reminds us of how wrong all this is, that white America can run but cannot hide from its racist past; it tells us that we as a nation have lost touch with King's ideals and his critique of American racism.

* * *

In his final years, King spoke repeatedly of how his dream of equality had turned into a nightmare in a nation sick with racism, blighted by vast economic inequality and poverty, and wedded to war and violence. He warned that unless America confronted the triple evils of racial injustice, economic injustice, and militarism the nation was headed towards destruction. That warning is clearly as relevant today as it was in the 1960s. So perhaps the best way to make use of what you learned about King in this book, and to commemorate MLK and his national holiday, is to take that warning seriously, to reflect on King's prophetic jeremiads as much as his lofty dream, to ask ourselves: How did we go so wrong? And how we can work towards the humane, democratic vision that MLK lived and died for?

ACKNOWLEDGMENTS

My interest in African American history was sparked by my most influential teacher at UC Berkeley, the late Leon F. Litwack, and without him this book would not have been possible. My friends and colleagues Michele Mitchell, Michael Meranze, and Bettina Aptheker offered advice and encouragement in their generous responses to the first writings that led to this book, for which I am grateful.

I was fortunate to have MLK scholar Michael Honey and Freedom Movement historian Emilye Crosby as the readers who critiqued my manuscript for UGA Press. Their criticisms and suggestions proved invaluable, and I am thankful to them for sharing their insights. I am indebted to the many King scholars and Freedom Movement historians whose work I so admire and cited in these pages.

This book was strengthened by what I learned about MLK and the movements of the 1960s from my conversations with those who lived through and wrote about those times, including Robert P. Moses, Vincent Harding, Congressman John Lewis, Tom Hayden, Mario Savio, Calvin Trillin, and Charlayne Hunter-Gault.

My thanks as well to my friends and colleagues who encouraged me in this work, including Alrick Brown, Sonia Murrow, Jon Zimmerman, Cynthia Copeland, Stacie Brensilver Berman, Deborah Menkart, Bill Bigelow, Joan Malczewski, Michelle Deutchman, Fabienne Doucet, Pedro Noguera, and Amanda Najib. A special thanks to Fabienne for sharing her knowledge of Haitian Creole. I am grateful to my dean, Jack Knott, and the chairs of my three NYU departments for their support of my work: Sarah Beck, Jennifer Hill, Marc Scott, and Guy Ortolano. And to my former NYU colleague Philip Kunhardt, whose invitation to me to design a teachers packet for the HBO documentary film *King in the Wilderness* was one of this book's points of origin.

The iconic MLK photo on the cover of this book has a special meaning for me. It was taken by the famed photographer Helen Nestor when Dr. King gave a powerful speech at UC Berkeley in May 1967, before a huge crowd of students who admired his work for justice and were thrilled by his recent emergence as a leading critic of the Vietnam war. During my graduate student years at Berkeley in the 1980s, Ronnie Stevenson, an activist I knew and whose tutoring program and organizing in the Black community I much admired, headed a movement to rename the Berkeley student union for Dr. King. And in 1985 the movement succeeded, so Berkeley's Student Union became the Martin Luther King Jr. Student Union. In 2002, Helen Nestor presented a copy of her MLK photo to the university, and it now adorns the student union that bears his name. I am grateful to Ruth Fischer, Helen Nestor's niece, for her permission to use this MLK photo on my book's cover, and to the late Ronnie Stevenson for his work at Berkeley honoring MLK's memory.

A special thanks to Signe Wilkinson, the brilliant Pulitzer Prize–winning political cartoonist, for permission to use her cartoon on the book's back cover. More powerfully than mere words, it conveys the absurdity of suppressing the freedom to discuss racism and discrimination.

I have long admired Vicki Crawford's pioneering scholarship on women in the Black Freedom Movement and in particular on Coretta Scott King. So I was honored that she agreed, despite her busy schedule—as director of the Martin Luther King Jr. Collection at Morehouse College and editor of the King Collection Series on Civil and Human Rights—to write the foreword to this book. I am grateful to her for taking the time to do so, sharing her illuminating and inspiring thoughts about MLK and his legacy.

My thanks as well to my MLK seminar students, past and present, at NYU for their interest and searching questions, which motivated me to constantly push for a deeper understanding of MLK and the Freedom Movement. I am thankful to my colleague Michael Funk, the faculty director of NYU's Martin Luther King Jr. Scholars Program, for inviting me to share my MLK research with NYU's idealistic and talented MLK scholarship students. I am grateful to Benoit Bolduc for his generosity in taking the time to share his knowledge of the French language, media, and culture. And I am grateful to Lucas Koutsoukos Chalhoub for his research assistance at the Bentley Historical Library.

I thank Mick Gusinde-Duffy of UGA Press for his support and faith in this project. I am also indebted to John Gehner for his crucial editing advice.

My sisters Judith and Myra, and my brother Steven, as always, were there for me when I needed them most.

As with all my books, my wife Rebecca Hyman's advice, patience, and love proved essential, as did that of our son Daniel Hyman-Cohen and our daughter-in-law, Lucia Hsiao. This proved all the more important with this book project, which I started and completed while on medical leave, as I recovered from a bout with cancer.

Recovery was made possible by my surgeon Brian L. Schmidt and my doctor, Denise A. Trochesset, to whom I owe not just my thanks but my life. My hope is that much as their medical knowledge helped save me from cancer, MLK's example of love and compassion, and his searching social criticism, can help save America from the cancer of racism.

NOTES

Introduction

1. "The 15 Year Battle for Martin Luther King Day," National Museum of African American History and Culture, https://nmaahc.si.edu/explore/stories/15-year-battle-martin-luther-king-jr-day; David L. Chappell, *Waking from the Dream: The Struggle for Civil Rights in the Shadow or Martin Luther King, Jr.* (New York: Random House, 2014), 91–123.

2. "The 15 Year Battle"; Chappell, *Waking from the Dream*, 91–123; David J. Garrow, "The Helms Attack on King," *Southern Exposure* (March/April 1984): 12–15. A particularly ugly part of the resistance to the King holiday came from former Jim Crow states, which for years "*dishonored* King by naming the holiday for something else . . . in the case of Virginia, calling it "Lee-Jackson-King Day," a title that gave priority to two white men, both slaveholders, who had waged war against the Union in a struggle to preserve human bondage." Adam Fairclough, foreword to *The Domestication of Martin Luther King, Jr.: Clarence B. Jones, Right-Wing Conservatism, and the Manipulation of the King Legacy*, ed. Lewis V. Baldwin and Rufus Burrow Jr. (Eugene: Cascade Books, 2013), xiii.

3. "The 15 Year Battle."

4. Vincent Gordon Harding, "Beyond Amnesia: Martin Luther King, Jr., and the Future of America," *Journal of American History* 74, no. 2 (September 1987): 468–76.

5. "How Donald Trump Perpetuated the 'Birther' Movement for Years," *ABC News*, September 16, 2016, https://abcnews.go.com/Politics/donald-trump-perpetuated-birther-movement-years/story?id=42138176.

6. Rosie Gray, "Trump Defends White-Nationalist Protesters: 'Some Very Nice People on Both Sides,'" *The Atlantic*, August 15, 2017, https://www.theatlantic.com/politics/archive/2017/08/trump-defends-white-nationalist-protesters-some-very-fine-people-on-both-sides/537012.

7. Merlyn Thomas and Mike Wendling, "Trump Repeats Baseless Claim About Haitian Immigrants Eating Pets," BBC News, September 15, 2024, https://www.bbc.com/news/articles/c77l28myezko.

8. Obed Manuel, "Bomb Threats Followed Trump's False Claim About Springfield. Some Haitians May Leave," NPR, September 19, 2024, https://www.npr.org

/2024/09/19/nx-s1-5114047/springfield-ohio-haitian-migrants-trump-safety-concerns.

9. Matt Brown, "Who Is Lorenzo Sewell, the Pastor Who Referenced King's 'Dream' Speech in Inaugural Prayer?" AP, January 20, 2025, https://apnews.com/article/trump-sewell-benediction-king-dream-a9550188ef39184a2d5fd14b67843a28; Cheyenne M. Daniels, "Bernice King: Black Pastor at Trump Inauguration 'Misused' Father's 'I Have a Dream' Speech," *The Hill*, January 23, 2025, https://thehill.com/homenews/race-politics/5102513-bernice-king-donald-trump-inauguration-sermon.

10. "President Trump's Inaugural Address," *U.S. Embassy in Qatar*, January 20, 2025, https://qa.usembassy.gov/president-trump-inaugural-address. Trump was only the latest in a long series of right-wing leaders who misleadingly invoked MLK's memory to back their attacks on racially egalitarian government programs in the name of "color-blindness." This tradition dates back to the 1990s, when prominent figures on the American right, some of whom had vilified King in his lifetime, switched to misusing his memory after he emerged as a revered national hero honored with a national holiday. See Lewis V. Baldwin, "Distorted Characterizations: Images of Martin Luther King, Jr. in the Conservative Mind," in *The Domestication of Martin Luther King, Jr.: Clarence B. Jones, Right-Wing Conservatism, and the Manipulation of the King Legacy*, ed. Lewis V. Baldwin and Rufus Burrow Jr.(Eugene: Cascade Books, 2013), 1–28.

11. Martin Luther King Jr., *"In a Single Garment of Destiny": A Global Vision of Justice*, ed. Lewis V. Baldwin (Boston: Beacon Press, 2012).

12. David J. Garrow, *Bearing the Cross: Martin Luther King, Jr. and the Southern Christian Leadership Conference* (New York: Vintage, 1988), 524.

13. "Looking Back at Martin Luther King, Jr.: An Interview with David J. Garrow," *Telos* (Spring 2018): 201. For evidence of how right Garrow was about this, see MLK's statements on his refusal to hate in Taylor Branch, *At Canaan's Edge: America in the King Years, 1965–68* (New York: Simon and Schuster, 2006), 652–53.

14. Oliver Laughland, "Donald Trump and the Central Park Five: The Racially Charged Rise of a Demagogue," *The Guardian*, February 17, 2016, https://www.theguardian.com/us-news/2016/feb/17/central-park-five-donald-trump-jogger-rape-case-new-york.

15. On Trump's ad, which appeared in *Newsday* in 1989, see https://www.documentcloud.org/documents/6131533-trumpdeathpenaltyad05011989/.

16. Murray Kempton, "The Proof That Trump Is a Self-Made Man," in *Going Around: Selected Journalism*, ed. Andrew Holter (New York: Seven Stories Press, 2025), 394–95.

17. Kimberley Richards, "MLK's Daughter Calls Out Trump's Inauguration Pastor and Those Who Misuse Her Dad's Speech," *HuffPost*, January 24, 2025,

https://www.huffpost.com/entry/mlk-jr-bernice-king-donald-trump-inauguration-lorenzo-sewell_l_6793ad9ee4b0da71b7c16943.

18. Ibid. Also see Dr. Bernice A. King, foreword, in *I Have a Dream*, 60th Anniv. ed. (New York: Martin Luther King Jr. Library, HarperCollins, 2023) xiii-xxiii.

19. Harding, "Beyond Amnesia"; Vincent Harding, *Martin Luther King: The Inconvenient Hero* (Maryknoll, N.Y.: Orbis Books, 1996); Vincent Harding, "The Inconvenient Hero: Martin Luther King," Ikeda Center, November 11, 2010, YouTube, https://www.youtube.com/watch?v=OzaqVxVp3B4. This point was also made by MLK friend and movement colleague Marian Wright Edelman, who complained that Americans who forgot his ideas about battling racism, war, and poverty had "sanitized and trivialized his message and his life." See Marian Wright Edelman, foreword to *The Trumpet of Conscience*, by Martin Luther King Jr. (Boston: Beacon Press, 2010), x. An ironic consequence of this national amnesia about MLK's radicalism is that his (distorted) moderate image rendered him much more popular with white America in the twenty-first century than he had ever been in his lifetime. In 1966, 69 percent of whites had an unfavorable view of King, but by August 2023—the March on Washington's 60th anniversary—81 percent of Americans said that MLK had a positive impact on the United States. See Jenn Hatfield, "How Public Attitudes Towards Martin Luther King Jr. Have Changed Since the 1960s," August 10, 2023, Pew Research Center, https://www.pewresearch.org/short-reads/2023/08/10/how-public-attitudes-toward-martin-luther-king-jr-have-changed-since-the-1960s.

20. Vincent Harding, "The Inconvenient Hero."

21. Harding, "Beyond Amnesia," 469.

22. Garrow, *Bearing the Cross*; Taylor Branch, *Parting the Waters: America in the King Years, 1954–63* (New York: Simon and Schuster, 1988); Jonathan Eig, *King: A Life* (New York: Picador, 2023). Note that, as their titles reveal, the Garrow and Branch volumes are not narrowly biographical but also offer histories of King's civil rights organization (SCLC) and the Black freedom struggle in the era in which King led it. Also note that the best books on MLK's key struggles tend to be quite long. For example, the most deeply researched account of King's role in the Memphis strike is more than six hundred pages. See Michael K. Honey, *Going Down Jericho Road: The Memphis Strike, Martin Luther King's Last Campaign* (New York: W. W. Norton and Co., 2008).

23. Clayborne Carson and Tenisha Hart Armstrong, eds., *The Papers of Martin Luther King, Jr., Vol. 7: To Save the Soul of America, January 1961–August 1962* (Berkeley: University of California Press, 2014).

24. Kurt Knue, "Trump Wins Largest Republican Share of Vote in Clark County, Home of Springfield, in at Least 40 Years," WLWT5, November 11, 2024, https://www.wlwt.com/article/trump-wins-record-share-of-republican-vote-in-clark-county/62863871.

25. Bruno Venditti, "Visualizing Over $1 Trillion in Wealth at Trump's Inauguration," *Visual Capitalist*, January 24, 2025, https://www.visualcapitalist.com/visualizing-over-1-trillion-in-wealth-at-trumps-inauguration; Senator Bernie Sanders, "Welcome to the World of Oligarchy," December 20, 2024, YouTube, https://www.youtube.com/watch?v=79KDKWEOJ1s; Bernie Sanders, "We Are Living in Unprecedented Times," January 31, 2025, YouTube, https://www.youtube.com/watch?v=mL0crkf5Dzw.

26. Todd Gitlin, *Occupy Nation: The Roots, the Spirit, and the Promise of Occupy Wall Street* (New York: Harper, 2012).

27. Honey, *Going Down Jericho Road*; Michael K. Honey, *To the Promised Land: Martin Luther King and the Fight for Economic Justice* (New York: W. W. Norton and Co., 2019); Martin Luther King Jr., *"All Labor Has Dignity,"* ed. Michael K. Honey (Boston: Beacon Press, 2011); Sylvie Laurent, *King and the Other America: The Poor People's Campaign and the Quest for Economic Equality* (Berkeley: University of California Press, 2018); Thomas F. Jackson, *From Civil Rights to Human Rights: Martin Luther King, Jr., and the Struggle for Economic Justice* (Philadelphia: University of Pennsylvania, 2009).

28. Martin Luther King Jr., interview by Sander Vanocur, NBC News, May 8, 1967, Atlanta, *King in the Wilderness*, directed by Peter W. Kunhardt (Kunhardt Films, 2018), transcript, 6.

29. Martin Luther King Jr., "The Casualties of the War in Vietnam," February 25, 1967, *"In a Single Garment of Destiny,"* 160.

30. Honey, *To the Promised Land*; Jackson, *From Civil Rights to Human Rights*; Martin Luther King Jr., *The Radical King*, ed. Cornel West (Boston: Beacon Press, 2015); Laurent, *King and the Other America*. Also see the excellent "Fifty Years Since MLK," ed. Brandon M. Terry et al., special issue, *Boston Review: Forum* (Winter 2018); Jeanne Theoharis, *A More Beautiful and Terrible History: The Uses and Misuses of Civil Rights History* (Boston: Beacon Press, 2018), ix–82.

31. Drew D. Hansen, *The Dream: Martin Luther King, Jr., and the Speech That Inspired a Nation* (New York: Ecco, 2003), 72–76.

32. John Lewis and Michael D'Orso, *Walking with the Wind: A Memoir of the Movement* (New York: Simon and Schuster, 1998).

33. Daniel S. Lucks, *Selma to Saigon: The Civil Rights Movement and the Vietnam War* (Lexington: University Press of Kentucky, 2014).

34. There is some disagreement as to whether MLK became more radical as the 1960s progressed or simply became more open about his socialist and anti-imperialist views (and his view that America was so sick with racism that it would take years to cure it). This will be discussed in chapter 2, but also see David Halberstam, "The Second Coming of Martin Luther King, Jr." *Harper's Magazine*, August 1967, 39–51; David J. Garrow, "The Intellectual Development of Martin

Luther King, Jr.: Influences and Commentary," *Union Seminary Quarterly Review* 40, no. 4 (January 1986): 9; Adam Fairclough, "Was Martin Luther King a Marxist?" *History Workshop* 15, no. 1 (Spring 1983): 117–25; Coretta Scott King, "Thoughts and Reflections," in *We Shall Overcome: Martin Luther King, Jr., and the Black Freedom Movement*, ed. Peter J. Albert and Ronald Hoffman (New York: Pantheon, 1990), 254.

35. Clayborne Carson, *Martin's Dream: My Journey and the Legacy of Martin Luther King Jr.* (New York: Palgrave Macmillan, 2013), 176. Religion played a pivotal role in King's willingness to persist even in the face of murderous threats from racists. During the Montgomery bus boycott, troubled by threats made against his family, King prayed. In his kitchen he heard the voice of Jesus tell him to "fight on" for justice and that he would stand by King through the end of his life, and MLK consequently believed it was his mission to persist in the freedom struggle. For an insightful discussion of this religious inspiration, see David J. Garrow, "King and the Spirit of Leadership," *Journal of American History* (September 1987): 441–47; Gary Dorrien, *Breaking White Supremacy: Martin Luther King Jr. and the Black Social Gospel* (New Haven: Yale University Press, 2018), 255–354.

36. Wesley Hogan, "Freedom Economics," *Reviews in American History* 35, no. 4 (December 2007): 642.

37. Stewart Burns, ed., *Daybreak of Freedom: The Montgomery Bus Boycott* (Chapel Hill: University of North Carolina Press, 1997), 23–24.

38. This King quote is from the speech "Where Do We Go from Here?" that he gave at the SCLC Conference in Atlanta on August 16, 1967. See Graham Davis, "The arc of the moral universe is long but it bends toward justice," January 17, 2011, YouTube, https://www.youtube.com/watch?v=yeVITdHsY6I. The quotation is adapted from the words of abolitionist Theodore Parker. See Tufts, "The Magnet and the Iron: John Brown and George L. Stearns, The Stories Behind the Busts: Theodore Parker," https://exhibits.tufts.edu/spotlight/john-brown-tufts/about/theodore-parker.

39. Martin Luther King Jr., interview by Sander Vanocur, NBC News, May 8, 1967, Atlanta, *King in the Wilderness*, directed by Peter W. Kunhardt (Kunhardt Films, 2018), transcript, 6.

40. Louis P. Masur, *Lincoln's Last Speech: Wartime Reconstruction and the Crisis of Reunion* (New York: Oxford University Press, 2015; George McMillan, *The Making of An Assassin: The Life of James Earl Ray* (New York: Little, Brown, 1976); Clay Risen, *A Nation on Fire: America in the Wake of the King Assassination* (John Wiley and Sons, 2009).

41. Barbara Ransby, *Ella Baker and the Black Freedom Movement*, 2nd ed. (Chapel Hill: University of North Carolina Press, 2024); Ralph Luker, "On Martin Luther King's Plagiarism," *History News Network*, December 21, 2004, https://www.historynewsnetwork.org/blog/9172; Adam Fairclough, *To Redeem the Soul of*

America: The Southern Christian Leadership Conference and Martin Luther King, Jr. (Athens: University of Georgia Press, 1987), 49–50; Chappell, *Waking from the Dream*, 148–74; Bayard Rustin, "Martin Luther King's Views on Gay People," in *Time on Two Crosses: The Collected Writings of Bayard Rustin*, ed. Devon W. Carbado and Donald Weise (New York: Cleis Press, 2013), 192–94; Jonathan Eig, "Rustin and King: Stony the Road They Trod," in *Bayard Rustin: A Legacy of Protest and Politics*, ed. Michael G. Long (New York: NYU Press, 2024), 82–86; John D'Emilio, *Lost Prophet: The Life and Times of Bayard Rustin* (Chicago: University of Chicago Press, 2004).

42. Martin Luther King Jr., *Where Do We Go from Here: Chaos or Community?* (1967; reprint, Boston: Beacon Press, 2010), 2.

Chapter 1. Freedom Dream and Racist Reality

1. Drew D. Hansen, *The Dream: Martin Luther King, Jr., and the Speech That Inspired a Nation* (New York: Ecco, 2003), 81. Hansen offers the closest textual analysis of King's "I Have a Dream" speech, including side-by-side versions of the written text and the actual speech as delivered, so you can see which parts of the speech were improvised. The "I have a dream" segment and most of the speech's closing sections (including the "Let freedom ring" segment) were improvised, not part of his planned remarks. See Hansen, *The Dream*, 79–85.

2. For examples of the brutal racist violence the Black Freedom Movement encountered in Alabama, Mississippi, Georgia, and Florida in the years leading up to the March on Washington, see Taylor Branch, *Parting the Waters: America in the King Years, 1954–63* (New York: Simon and Schuster, 1988), 417–24, 497–500, 509–22, 660–72; David J. Garrow, *Bearing the Cross: Martin Luther King, Jr., and the Southern Christian Leadership Conference* (New York: Vintage Books, 1988), 250–51; John Lewis and Michael D'Orso, *Walking with the Wind: A Memoir of the Movement* (New York: Simon and Schuster, 1998), 140–42, 185–86, 190–91; Anne Moody, *Coming of Age in Mississippi* (New York: Bantam, 1968), 267, 276–85; Rodney L. Hurst, *It Was Never About a Hot Dog and a Coke! A Personal Account of the 1960 Sit-In Demonstrations and Ax Handle Saturday in Jacksonville, Florida* (Livermore: Wingspan Press, 2018).

3. Hansen, *The Dream*, 83–85. The final part of the "I Have a Dream" speech was all the more dramatic since it was unscripted—not part of the text of his planned speech. But it is not correct to see this ending as extemporaneous, since King drew from memory on material from his prior speeches, and the "Let freedom ring" conclusion was borrowed from a 1952 speech by a prominent Black

minister. See Keith D. Miller, "On Martin Luther King Jr. and the Landscape of Civil Rights Rhetoric," *Rhetoric and Public Affairs* 16, no. 1 (2013): 168–69.

4. Eric Foner, *The Second Founding: How the Civil War and Reconstruction Remade the Constitution* (New York: Norton, 2020); Eric Foner, *The Story of American Freedom* (New York: Norton, 1999); Patricia Sullivan, *Lift Every Voice: The NAACP and the Making of the Civil Rights Movement* (New York: New Press, 2010); Charles M. Payne, *I've Got the Light of Freedom: The Organizing Tradition and the Mississippi Freedom Struggle* (Berkeley: University of California Press, 2007).

5. Paul Gottfried, "Martin Luther King, Jr., as Conservative Hero," *Chronicles: A Magazine of American Culture*, April 1, 1997, https://chroniclesmagazine.org/web/martin-luther-king-jr-as-conservative-hero.

6. Hansen, *The Dream*, 1–64, 167–206.

7. Clarence B. Jones and Stuart Connelly, *Behind the Dream: The Making of the Speech That Transformed a Nation* (New York: Palgrave, 2011), 16–17; Hansen, *The Dream*, 207–30.

8. Hansen, *The Dream*, 207–29.

9. Moody, *Coming of Age in Mississippi*, 307.

10. David J. Garrow, *The FBI and Martin Luther King, Jr.* (New York: Penguin Books, 1983), 71.

11. Garrow, *The FBI and Martin Luther King, Jr.*, 101–50, 204–19. Also see Lerone A Martin, *The Gospel of J. Edgar Hoover: How the FBI Aided and Abetted the Rise of White Christian Nationalism* (Princeton, NJ: Princeton University Press, 2023).

12. Garrow, *The FBI and Martin Luther King, Jr.*, 60–61.

13. Barbara Ransby, *Ella Baker and the Black Freedom Movement: A Radical Democratic Vision* (Chapel Hill: University of North Carolina Press: 2003), 175.

14. "King Claims Braden, Wilkinson Jailing Evidence of 'McCarthyism,'" *Chattanooga News-Free Press*, May 2, 1961; Septima Poinsette Clark to Dr. Martin Luther King, May 23, 1961, in *The Papers of Martin Luther King, Jr., Vol. 7: To Save the Soul of America, January 1961–August 1962*, ed. Clayborne Carson and Tenisha Hart Armstrong (Berkeley: University of California Press, 2014), 233; Martin Luther King Jr. to Harry Truman, April 19, 1960, in *The Papers of Martin Luther King, Jr., Vol. 5: Threshold of a New Decade, January 1959–December 1960*, ed. Clayborne Carson et al. (Berkeley: University of California Press, 2005), 437–38.

15. Garrow, *The FBI and Martin Luther King, Jr.*, 63.

16. John D'Emilio, *Lost Prophet: The Life and Times of Bayard Rustin* (Chicago: University of Chicago Press, 2004), 34.

17. Garrow, *The FBI and Martin Luther King, Jr.*, 43, 60; David J. Garrow, "The FBI and Martin Luther King, Jr.," *Atlantic Monthly* (July/August 2002): 85–86. King too was red-baited by segregationists, who published a photo in their racist

newspapers and then posted it on billboards in the South, captioned to indicate that King was attending "a Communist training school" when he was actually attending a commemorative event at the Highlander Folk School in New Market, Tennessee, celebrating its work assisting labor and civil rights organizers. The fact that King connected with Highlander (even having the SCLC run its citizenship education program there), whose interracialism in Jim Crow Tennessee often made it a target of red-baiters, was another indication of how little credence he gave to such red-baiting. So was the fact that King, in his "Letter from Birmingham Jail," praised anti-racist writer and activist Anne Braden as a white Southerner who stood up for Black rights. MLK did so despite frequent charges that she and her husband Carl were Communists. King's cautiousness did prevent him from responding to Anne's request that he circulate a petition against the prosecution of Carl for defying the House Un-American Activities Committee, but MLK later attended a reception on Carl's behalf and signed a petition for his clemency. Similarly, while King refused to break with Levison over his alleged Communist ties, he did end organizer Jack Odell's work in the SCLC due to similar charges. So King's defiance of red-baiting, while impressive for its day, did have its limits, deriving from his concern about protecting the SCLC's reputation. See "Braden, Anne Gamrell McCarthy and Braden, Carl James," The Martin Luther King, Jr. Research and Education Institute, Stanford University, https://kinginstitute.stanford.edu/braden-anne-gamrell-mccarthy-and-braden-carl-james; Ben Wilkins, ed., *Anne Braden Speaks: Selected Writings and Speeches, 1960–2006* (New York: Monthly Review Press, 2022); "Martin Luther King . . . at Communist Training School," *Augusta Courier*, July 5, 1963, https://search.register.shelby.tn.us/media/mlk/mlkviewimage.php?imgtype=pdf&image=ray_material_2011-02-08/attorney_general_file/microfilm_images/000237ag10.tif; "O'Dell, Hunter Pitts 'Jack,'" The Martin Luther King, Jr. Research and Education Institute, Stanford University, https://kinginstitute.stanford.edu/odell-hunter-pitts-jack.

18. Garrow, *The FBI and Martin Luther King, Jr.*, 73.

19. Coretta Scott King, *Coretta: My Life, My Love, My Legacy* (New York: Henry Holt & Co., 2017), 28. Coretta Scott King also defied the Cold War Red Scare's ethos by mentioning in her memoir—with pride—that as a college student she had shared a concert stage with the "world famous baritone Paul Robeson," who "commended" her voice and encouraged her to continue her "voice studies." This was at a time when Robeson was still a political pariah in the United States for being uncritical of the Soviet Union and asserting that Black people would not support a war against the USSR. See Coretta Scott King, *My Life With Martin Luther King, Jr.* (New York: Holt, Rinehart and Winston, 1969), 43.

20. Hansen, *The Dream*, 80–82. This and subsequent references below to Hansen—unless otherwise indicated—are to the text of King's "I Have a Dream" speech as it appears in Hansen.

21. Ibid., 71–80.
22. Ibid., 79–80.
23. Ibid., 80.
24. Ibid.
25. Ibid., 82–83.
26. Ibid., 83.
27. Ibid., 81–82.
28. Ibid., 81.
29. Vincent Harding, "The Inconvenient Hero: Martin Luther King," Ikeda Center, November 11, 2010, YouTube, https://www.youtube.com/watch?v=OzaqVxVp3B4.
30. Hansen, *The Dream*, 72.
31. Ibid., 72–73.
32. Nancy Murr, "Faculty Q and A: Richard Bell on The 1619 Project, Critical Race Theory and Teaching Hard Truths," UC Berkeley OLLI, May 4, 2023, https://olli.berkeley.edu/blog/faculty-qa-richard-bell-1619-project-critical-race-theory-and-teaching-hard-truths; Sarah Schwartz, "Map: Where Critical Race Theory is Under Attack," *Education Week*, July 22, 2025, https://www.edweek.org/policy-politics/map-where-critical-race-theory-is-under-attack/2021/06.
33. Hansen, *The Dream*, 72.
34. Taylor Branch, *Parting the Waters*, 589–90. King's efforts to press Kennedy to issue this Second Emancipation Proclamation against segregation began the first year of JFK's presidency. See Martin Luther King Jr., "Press Conference After Meeting with John F. Kennedy, [October 16, 1961]" and MLK to JFK, December 17, 1961, *The Papers of Martin Luther King, Jr., Vol. 7*, 308–9, 349.
35. Branch, *Parting the Waters*, 590.
36. Ibid.; Thurston Clark, *Ask Not: The Inauguration of John F. Kennedy and the Speech That Changed America* (New York: Holt, 2004), 135–37; Harris Wofford, *Of Kennedys and Kings: Making Sense of the Sixties* (Pittsburgh: University of Pittsburgh Press, 1980), 11–28, 124–77.
37. Martin Luther King Jr., "I Have a Dream," in *A Call to Conscience: The Landmark Speeches of Dr. Martin Luther King, Jr.*, ed. Clayborne Carson and Kris Shepard (New York: Grand Central Publishing, 2002), 82.
38. Ibid.
39. Ibid.
40. Ibid., 86.
41. Ibid., 83.
42. Martin Luther King Jr., *Why We Can't Wait* (1964; reprint, Boston: Beacon Press, 2010), 141–42.

43. Martin Luther King Jr., *Where Do We Go from Here: Chaos or Community?* (1967; reprint, Boston: Beacon Press, 1996), 80.

44. Ibid., 79–80.

45. King, "I Have a Dream," *A Call to Conscience*, 82; Nick Bryant, *The Bystander: John F. Kennedy and the Struggle for Black Equality* (New York: Basic Books, 2006), 264, 277–78.

46. King, "I Have a Dream," *A Call to Conscience*, 84.

47. Ibid.

48. Ibid.

49. Ibid.

50. Ibid., 83

51. Ibid.

52. William P. Jones, *The March on Washington: Jobs, Freedom, and the Forgotten History of Civil Rights* (New York: Norton, 2013); William P. Jones, "You've Been Lied to About the 1963 March on Washington," interview by Shawn Gude, *Jacobin*, August 28, 2022, https://jacobin.com/2022/08/william-jones-interview-march-on-washington-fdr-jfk-king-randolph.

53. Jones, *The March on Washington*.

54. King, "I Have a Dream," *A Call to Conscience*, 86

55. Ibid., 87.

56. For an excellent discussion of King's approach to public speaking and its effectiveness, see Hansen, *The Dream*, 121–33. Prior to the March on Washington speech, the largest event at which King had used the "I have a dream" segment was at a mass rally in Detroit in June 1963. In 1962 he used it in speeches in Albany, Georgia, and Rocky Mount, North Carolina. See Hansen, *The Dream*, 109–13.

57. Lewis and D'Orso, *Walking with the Wind*, 219.

58. "March on Washington Speech: Original Draft of SNCC's March on Washington Speech, Delivered by SNCC's Chairman John Lewis," SNCC Digital Gateway, https://snccdigital.org/inside-sncc/policy-statements/march-washington-speech.

59. Lewis and D'Orso, *Walking with the Wind*, 222–23.

60. King, *Where Do We Go from Here*, 3.

61. Martin Luther King Jr., "Fumbling on the New Frontier," *The Nation*, March 3, 1962, https://nationalhumanitiescenter.org/pds/maai3/overcome/text1/mlkingnewfrontier.pdf.

62. Ibid.

63. Harry Belafonte, *My Song* (New York: Knopf, 2011), 268; Patricia Sullivan, *Justice Rising: Robert Kennedy's America in Black and White* (Cambridge: The Belknap Press of Harvard University Press, 2021), ix–xiv.

64. Belafonte, *My Song*, 269–70; "Robert Kennedy Consults Negroes Here About North," *New York Times*, May 25, 1963; also see "Robert Kennedy Fails to Sway Negroes at Secret Talks Here," *New York Times*, May 26, 1963.

65. John F. Kennedy, "Televised Address to the Nation on Civil Rights," June 11, 1963, John F. Kennedy Presidential Library and Museum, https://www.jfklibrary.org/learn/about-jfk/historic-speeches/televised-address-to-the-nation-on-civil-rights.

66. Bryant, *The Bystander*, 4.

67. John Lewis, "Speech at the March on Washington," August 28, 1963, Voices of Democracy: The U.S. Oratory Project, University of Maryland, https://voicesofdemocracy.umd.edu/lewis-speech-at-the-march-on-washington-speech-text.

68. Ibid. President Kennedy was at least as critical of the SNCC and John Lewis as Lewis was of him. Wrongly thinking that Lewis and the SNCC promoted racial violence in Birmingham in 1963, JFK was caught on tape at a private White House meeting denouncing Lewis and the SNCC as "sons of bitches." See Jonathan Rosenberg and Zachary Karabell, *Kennedy, Johnson, and the Quest for Justice: The Civil Rights Tapes* (New York: Norton, 2003), 172.

69. Lewis, "Speech at the March."

70. "'Freedom!': Black Women Speak at the March on Washington For Jobs and Freedom," The Martin Luther King, Jr. Research and Education Institute, Stanford University, https://kinginstitute.stanford.edu/freedom-black-women-speak-march-washington-jobs-and-freedom. On this sexism and also her anger at not being permitted to join the march leaders' meeting with President Kennedy, see Coretta Scott King, *My Life, My Love, My Legacy* (New York: Henry Holt & Co. 2017), 115–16.

71. D'Emilio, *Lost Prophet*, 346–50. Strom Thurmond's hypocrisy in denouncing Rustin's alleged sexual immorality would only come to light after the white supremacist senator died, when his having secretly fathered a Black daughter was exposed by her. See Esse Mae Washington-Williams and William Stadiem, *Dear Senator: A Memoir by the Daughter of Strom Thurmond* (New York: Harper Perennial, 2006).

72. Clayborne Carson, "Martin Luther King, Jr.: Charismatic Leadership in a Mass Struggle," *Journal of American History* 74, no. 2 (September 1987): 438–47.

73. "Prayer Pilgrimage for Freedom (May 17, 1957)," in *The Martin Luther King, Jr., Encyclopedia*, ed. Clayborne Carson et al. (Westport: Greenwood Press, 2008), 274–75.

74. Emilye Crosby, ed., *Civil Rights History from the Ground Up: Local Struggles, A National Movement* (Athens: University of Georgia Press, 2011).

75. Robert P. Moses, "The Mississippi Freedom Movement in the 1960s," interview by Robert Cohen, NYU Steinhardt, May 5, 2011, YouTube, https://www.youtube.com/watch?v=uaGWx7PxD4k.

76. David Halberstam, *The Children* (New York: Fawcett, 1999), 509, 536.

77. Jonathan Rieder, *Gospel of Freedom: Martin Luther King, Jr.'s Letter from Birmingham Jail and the Struggle That Changed a Nation* (New York: Bloomsbury Press, 2013), 172.

78. Ibid., 178–79.

79. Ibid., 179. MLK also embraced this label of "extremist" for love and for justice in an earlier speech. See Martin Luther King Jr., "Lecture Delivered to Christian Ethics Class at Southern Baptist Theological Seminary Question and Answer Period," April 19, 1961, *The Papers of Martin Luther King, Jr., Vol. 7*, 202.

80. James Reston, "'I Have a Dream . . .'; Peroration by Dr. King Sums Up a Day the Capital Will Remember," *New York Times*, August 29, 1963. Note that all the reformers Reston cited were white, which reflected the parochial way history was usually taught and learned in Cold War America.

81. Robert P. Moses, "The Mississippi Freedom Movement in the 1960s," interview by Robert Cohen, NYU Steinhardt, May 5, 2011, YouTube, https://www.youtube.com/watch?v=uaGWx7PxD4k.

82. King, *Where Do We Go from Here*, 4.

83. Ibid., 11.

84. Ibid.

85. Vincent Harding, introduction, *Where Do We Go from Here*, xviii.

86. Paul Gottfried, "Martin Luther King, Jr., as Conservative Hero," *Chronicles: A Magazine of American Culture*, April 1, 1997, https://chroniclesmagazine.org/web/martin-luther-king-jr-as-conservative-hero.

87. David L. Chappell, "Martin Luther King: Strategist of Force," *African American Political Thought: A Collected History*, ed. Melvin L. Rogers and Jack Turner, (Chicago: University of Chicago Press, 2021), 516–40.

88. King, *Why We Can't Wait*, 162–63.

89. Ibid., 160.

90. "*Playboy* Interview with Martin Luther King, Jr.," January 1965, in *A Testament of Hope: The Essential Writings of Martin Luther King, Jr.*, ed. James M. Washington (New York: HarperOne, 1986), 367. MLK also helped the student body president of Caltech to devise a DEI/affirmative action-style recruitment program in an attempt to attract African American students to that elite university, which in 1959 lacked a single Black undergraduate. See Martin Luther King Jr. to Thomas Jovin, May 17, 1959, in *The Papers of Martin Luther King, Jr., Vol. 5: Threshold of a New Decade, January 1959–December 1960*, ed. Clayborne Carson et al. (Berkeley: University of California Press, 2005), 208-9.

91. Inti Pacheco, Elzaveta Galkina, and Theo Francis, "DEI Didn't Change the Workforce All That Much: A Look At 13 Million Jobs," *Wall Street Journal*, February 7, 2025, https://www.wsj.com/business/dei-impact-us-company-workforce-charts-2e6a6bb7?mod=hp_lead_pos10.

92. James Forman, *The Making of Black Revolutionaries* (Seattle: University of Washington Press, 1997), 377–80; Julian Bond, foreword to *This Is the Day: The March on Washington* by Leonard Freed (Los Angeles: J. Paul Getty Museum, 2013) vi–vii.

93. Forman, *The Making of Black Revolutionaries*, 380.

94. See "John Lewis'[s] Historic Speech at the March on Washington," NowThis Impact, July 28, 2020, YouTube, https://www.youtube.com/watch?v=TCqR9LbT1_w.

95. "Rustin Reading Demands of the March on Washington," Annyole, November 26, 2012, YouTube, https://www.youtube.com/watch?v=zbGWhBhOBog.

96. Murray Kempton, "The March on Washington," September 4, 1963, in *Going Around: Selected Journalism*, ed. Andrew Holter (New York: Seven Stories Press, 2025), 154.

97. There is some controversy around using MLK's books as sources to document his thinking, since he traveled so much, giving hundreds of speeches a year, and thus did not have time to write books solo—and so made use of ghostwriters. This is one reason this study centers on his speeches, statements, and interviews, rather than his books. But in terms of their politics, one does not find major differences between his books and other writings, statements, and speeches, and it is hard to imagine King putting his name to a book whose arguments did not reflect his own. I have mostly used his books when they elaborated on positions he took in his major speeches, and in these cases the overlap between the two types of sources leaves me confident that on these issues the books are credible and useful in understanding King's thinking. On criticism of MLK's books as historical sources, see Gary Dorrien, *Breaking White Supremacy: Martin Luther King Jr. and the Black Social Gospel* (New Haven: Yale University Press, 2018), 264.

98. Brandon M. Terry, "MLK Now," in "Fifty Years Since MLK," ed. Brandon M. Terry et al., special issue, *Boston Review: Forum* (Winter 2018): 11–30.

99. Ibid., 14–15.

100. Ibid.

101. Ibid., 15

102. Ibid.

103. Ibid., 14–16.

104. Ibid., 13.

105. Coretta Scott King, *My Life, My Love, My Legacy*, 113.

106. Ibid.

107. Martin Luther King Jr., "I Have a Dream," *A Call to Conscience*, 82.

108. Coretta Scott King, *My Life*, 115; see Geoffrey Gould, "Dr. King Unequalled in Moving a Crowd," *Asbury Park Press*, August 29, 1963, Newspapers.com, https://www.newspapers.com/article/asbury-park-press-editorial-on-martin-lu/20989079.

109. Andrew Young, *An Easy Burden: The Civil Rights Movement and The Transformation of America* (New York: Harper Collins, 1996), 272.

110. Ibid., 273.

111. Ibid.

112. Ibid.

113. Jeanne Theoharis, *King of the North: Martin Luther King's Life of Struggle Outside the South* (New York: New Press, 2025), 14.

Chapter 2. Against War and Militarism

1. David Halberstam, "The Second Coming of Martin Luther King," *Harper's Magazine*, August 1967, 39–51, https://harpers.org/archive/1967/08/the-second-coming-of-martin-luther-king.

2. David Halberstam, *The Children* (New York: Fawcett, 1999); Halberstam, "Second Coming," 39–51.

3. Halberstam, "Second Coming," 48.

4. Ibid.

5. Coretta Scott King, "Thoughts and Reflections," in *We Shall Overcome: Martin Luther King, Jr., and the Black Freedom Struggle*, ed. Peter J. Albert and Ronald Hoffman (New York: Pantheon, 1990), 254.

6. Jonathan Eig, *King: A Life* (New York: Picador, 2023), 37, 51–52, 79–80; Patrick Parr, *The Seminarian: Martin Luther King Jr. Comes of Age* (Chicago: Lawrence Hill Books, 2018), 1–5, 22–24, 133–39.

7. Coretta Scott King, *My Life with Martin Luther King, Jr.* (New York: Holt, Rinehart and Winston, 1969), 42–43.

8. Jeanne Theoharis, *King of the North: Martin Luther King Jr.'s Life of Struggle Outside the South* (New York: New Press, 2025).

9. On MLK's anti-capitalist views prior to his emergence as a civil rights leader, see Martin Luther King Jr.'s letter to Coretta Scott on July 18, 1952, in *The Papers of Martin Luther King, Jr., Vol. 6: Advocate of the Social Gospel, September 1948–March 1963*, ed. Clayborne Carson et al. (Berkeley: University of California Press, 2007), 123–26. Even earlier, in a 1950 autobiographical essay, MLK attributed his "anti-capitalistic feelings" to his witnessing the hardships working-class people experienced during the Great Depression and "how I questioned my

parents about the numerous people standing in breadlines when I was about five years old." Martin Luther King Jr., "An Autobiography of Religious Development," September 12–November 22, 1950, in *The Papers of Martin Luther King, Jr., Vol. 1: Called to Serve, January 1929–June 1951*, ed. Clayborne Carson, Ralph E. Luker, and Penny A. Russell (Berkeley: University of California Press, 1992), 359–63. Also see Thomas F. Jackson, *From Civil Rights to Human Rights: Martin Luther King, Jr., and the Struggle for Economic Justice*, (Philadelphia: University of Pennsylvania Press, 2009) 1–50, 82, 359; Martin Luther King Sr. and Clayton Riley, *Daddy King: An Autobiography* (New York: William Morrow and Co., 1980), 147. Best-selling socialist author Michael Harrington, upon meeting King in 1960, was startled to learn that this Southern minister shared his democratic socialist politics. Like King, Harrington realized it was necessary in Cold War America—owing to its anti-radicalism—to avoid bringing MLK's views to public attention, lest he be red-baited and marginalized. See Michael Harrington, *Fragments of A Century* (New York: Dutton, 1973), 166–67.

10. David J. Garrow, "From Reformer to Revolutionary," *Martin Luther King, Jr. and the Civil Rights Movement: Controversies and Debates*, ed. John A. Kirk (New York: Red Globe Press, 2007), 176–83.

11. Ibid., 179.

12. Vincent Harding, interview by MARHO, in *Visions of History*, ed. Henry Abelove et al. (New York: Pantheon, 1983), 226.

13. Martin Luther King Jr., *Where Do We Go from Here: Chaos or Community?* (1967; reprint, Boston: Beacon Press, 2010), 13.

14. Ibid., 3.

15. Martin Luther King Jr., *"In a Single Garment of Destiny": A Global Vision of Justice*, ed. Lewis V. Baldwin (Boston: Beacon Press, 2012), 52–111.

16. Clayborne Carson, "Rethinking African-American Political Thought in the Post-Revolutionary Era," in *The Making of Martin Luther King and the Civil Rights Movement*, ed. Brian Ward and Tony Badger (New York: NYU Press, 1993), 117.

17. Ibid.

18. Ibid., 115–16.

19. Adam Fairclough, "Review," *American Historical Review* 124, no. 3 (June 2019): 1104; Martin Luther King Jr., *Stride Toward Freedom: The Montgomery Story* (1958; reprint, Boston: Beacon Press, 2010), 82; Melvin Arnold to Rev. Martin Luther King, May 5, 1958, The Martin Luther King, Jr. Research and Education Institute, Stanford University, https://kinginstitute.stanford.edu/king-papers/documents/melvin-arnold.

20. Jackson, *From Civil Rights*, 323.

21. Gary Dorrien, *Breaking White Supremacy: Martin Luther King Jr. and the Black Social Gospel* (New Haven: Yale University Press, 2018), 355.

22. Martin Luther King Jr., "Letter from Birmingham City Jail," in *A Testament of Hope: The Essential Writings of Martin Luther King, Jr.*, ed. James M. Washington (New York: HarperOne, 1986), 293.

23. Jonathan Rieder, *Gospel of Freedom: Martin Luther King, Jr.'s Letter from Birmingham Jail and the Struggle That Changed a Nation* (New York: Bloomsbury Press, 2013), 60–61.

24. "You Have Been the Conscience of Our Nation," *UC Berkeley News*, January 16, 2017, https://news.berkeley.edu/2017/01/16/you-have-been-the-conscience-of-our-nation/; Peter Hartlaub, "Martin Luther King Jr.'s '67 Speech Left Mark on UC Berkeley," *SF Gate*, May 16, 2014, https://www.sfgate.com/bayarea/article/Martin-Luther-King-Jr-s-67-speech-left-mark-on-5475925.php; "King—You Take It Because It's Right," and "King's Dual Commitment: The War and Civil Rights," *Daily Californian*, May 18, 1967.

25. Halberstam, "Second Coming," 51.

26. Ibid.

27. John Herbers, "Vietnam Moratorium Observed by Foes of the War; Opponents React," *New York Times*, October 16, 1969.

28. "Martin Luther King, Jr. Anti-War Poster," Alexander Historical Auctions, https://www.alexautographs.com/auction-lot/martin-luther-king-jr.-anti-war-poster_D954CDC929.

29. Daniel S. Lucks, *Selma to Saigon: The Civil Rights Movement and the Vietnam War* (Lexington: University of Kentucky Press, 2014), 196.

30. Martin Luther King Jr., "A Time to Break Silence, 1967," in *A Testament of Hope: The Essential Writings of Martin Luther King, Jr.*, ed. James M. Washington (New York: HarperOne, 1986), 231–44; Martin Luther King Jr., "Beyond Vietnam," in *A Call to Conscience: The Landmark Speeches of Dr. Martin Luther King, Jr.*, ed. Clayborne Carson and Kris Shepard (New York: Grand Central Publishing, 2002), 133–64.

31. On King's labor movement speeches, see Martin Luther King Jr., *"All Labor Has Dignity,"* ed. Michael K. Honey (Boston: Beacon Press, 2011).

32. John Lewis and Michael D'Orso, *Walking with the Wind: A Memoir of the Movement* (New York: Simon and Schuster, 1998), 377.

33. James Peck remarks at NYU 50th Anniversary Commemoration of MLK's Riverside Church speech, April 18, 2017, New York University Department of Teaching and Learning.

34. Vincent Gordon Harding, "Beyond Amnesia: Martin Luther King, Jr., and the Future of America," *Journal of American History* 74, no. 2 (September 1987): 469.

35. David Thelen, "Introduction: A Round Table: Martin Luther King, Jr.," *Journal of American History* 74, no. 2 (September 1987): 436.

36. Vincent Harding and Daisaku Ikeda, *The Courage to Dream: On Rights, Values, and Freedom* (London: I.B. Tauris, 2016), 148–51.

37. Harding, *Visions of History*, 219–41.

38. Clayborne Carson, *In Struggle: SNCC and the Black Awakening of the 1960s* (Cambridge: Harvard University Press, 1981), 188.

39. "Harding, Vincent Gordon," The Martin Luther King, Jr. Research and Education Institute, Stanford University, https://kinginstitute.stanford.edu/harding-vincent-gordon; Harding and Ikeda, *The Courage to Dream*, 150.

40. Tom Hayden, "Bob Moses," *The Nation*, July 2, 2003, https://www.thenation.com/article/activism/bob-moses.

41. Jonathan Eig, *King: A Life* (New York: Picador, 2023), 424.

42. Ibid.

43. Lucks, *Selma to Saigon*, 90–91.

44. "Dr. King Declares U.S. Must Negotiate in Asia," *New York Times*, July 3, 1965.

45. Adam Fairclough, "Martin Luther King, Jr. and the War in Vietnam," *Phylon* 45, no. 1 (1st Quarter, 1984): 25–26.

46. Nick Kotz, *Judgment Days: Lyndon Baines Johnson, Martin Luther King, Jr., and the Laws That Changed America* (New York: Mariner, 2005), 345, 352–53.

47. Lucks, *Selma to Saigon*, 141.

48. Ibid., 170–73.

49. Ibid., 169–212. On King's nonviolence, see Kenneth L. Smith and Ira G. Zepp, *Search for the Beloved Community: The Thinking of Martin Luther King Jr.* (Valley Forge: Judson Press, 1998), 51–69; David J. Garrow, "The Intellectual Development of Martin Luther King, Jr.: Influences and Commentary," *Union Seminary Quarterly Review* 40, no. 4 (January 1986): 9–11; Dorrien, *Breaking White Supremacy*, 265–72.

50. James Fraser, email message to author, April 4, 2017.

51. Fairclough, "Martin Luther King, Jr. and the War in Vietnam," 26.

52. Ibid., 28; Kotz, *Judgment Days*, 344, 359.

53. Kotz, *Judgment Days*, 359–69; Eig, *King*, 482.

54. Lucks, *Selma to Saigon*, 187–88.

55. Fairclough, "Martin Luther King, Jr. and the War in Vietnam," 28.

56. Coretta Scott King noticed this male dominance, and, at an early conference of King scholars, said, "The next time we have a conference on [MLK] I want to see more women scholars. . . . We have yet to deal with how Martin Luther King saw women and dealt with women and women's roles." Coretta Scott King, "Thoughts and Reflections," *We Shall Overcome*, 255. Fortunately, this neglect of Coretta has begun to be addressed in the work of women King scholars. See Vicki Crawford, "Coretta Scott King and the Struggle for Civil and Human Rights: An Enduring

Legacy," *Journal of African American History* 92, no. 1 (Winter 2007): 106–17; Jeanne Theoharis, *King of the North: Martin Luther King Jr.'s Life of Struggle Outside the South* (New York: New Press, 2025). Jonathan Eig's *King: A Life* pays more attention to her activist trajectory than have prior MLK biographies.

57. Coretta Scott King, *My Life, My Love, My Legacy* (New York: Henry Holt & Co., 2017), 148–49.

58. Bernard Lafayette, interview, *King in the Wilderness*, directed by Peter W. Kunhardt (Kunhardt Films, 2018), transcript, 43.

59. Coretta Scott King, *My Life, My Love, My Legacy*, 149.

60. Martin Luther King Jr., press interview, *King in the Wilderness*, directed by Peter W. Kunhardt (Kunhardt Films, 2018), transcript, 43.

61. King, *"In a Single Garment,"* 150.

62. Ibid., 151.

63. Ibid., 152.

64. Ibid., 156–57.

65. Ibid., 152–53.

66. Ibid., 152–53.

67. Ibid., 154.

68. Ibid., 155.

69. Julian Bond, *Vietnam: An Anti-War Comic Book*, illus. T. G. Lewis (1967), Civil Rights Teaching, https://www.civilrightsteaching.org/resource/vietnam-anti-war-comic.

70. King, *"In a Single Garment,"* 161–62.

71. Ibid., 160.

72. Ibid., 156, 160.

73. David J. Garrow, *Bearing the Cross: Martin Luther King, Jr., and the Southern Leadership Conference* (New York: Vintage, 1988) 549.

74. Martin Luther King Jr., "Remaining Awake Through a Great Revolution," sermon delivered at the National Cathedral, Washington, D.C., March 31, 1968, in *A Knock At Midnight: Inspiration from the Great Sermons of Martin Luther King, Jr.*, ed. Clayborne Carson and Peter Holloran (New York: Warner Books, 1998), 221–22.

75. Joanna Shenk, *The Movement Makes Us Human: An Interview with Dr. Vincent Harding on Mennonites, Vietnam, and MLK* (Eugene: Wipf and Stock, 2018), 17.

76. Calvin Trillin, *Jackson, 1964: And Other Dispatches from Fifty Years of Reporting on Race in America* (New York: Random House, 2016), 11.

77. Andrew Young, *An Easy Burden: The Civil Rights Movement and the Transformation of America* (New York: HarperCollins, 1996), 427–29.

78. King, "Beyond Vietnam," *A Call to Conscience*, 141–42.

79. Ibid., 142–43.
80. Ibid., 143.
81. King, "Beyond Vietnam," *A Call to Conscience*, 144.
82. Ibid., 141, 144.
83. W. Jason Miller, *Origins of the Dream: Hughes's Poetry and King's Rhetoric* (Gainesville: University Press of Florida, 2015), 1–54, 213–16.
84. Ibid., 214.
85. Brandon M. Terry, "MLK Now," in "Fifty Years Since MLK," ed. Brandon M. Terry et al., special issue, *Boston Review: Forum* (Winter 2018): 11–12.
86. King, "Beyond Vietnam," *A Call to Conscience*, 146–49.
87. Ibid.
88. Ibid., 157.
89. Ibid., 156.
90. Ibid., 156–58.
91. Garrow, *Bearing the Cross*, 394.
92. King, *"All Labor Has Dignity,"* 58.
93. King, "Beyond Vietnam," *A Call to Conscience*, 159.
94. Ibid., 156–57.
95. "Dr. King's Error," *New York Times*, April 7, 1967.
96. "Dr. King's Disservice to His Cause," *Life*, April 27, 1967.
97. Taylor Branch, *At Canaan's Edge, America in the King Years, 1965–68* (New York: Simon and Schuster, 2006), 595; David J. Garrow, *The FBI and Martin Luther King, Jr.* (New York: Penguin, 1983), 180.
98. Gene Roberts, "Dr. King and the War," *New York Times*, April 14, 1967.
99. Branch, *At Canaan's Edge*, 595.
100. Andrew Young remarks in "The Promised Land (1967–68)," *Eyes on the Prize 2: America at the Racial Crossroads, 1965-1985*, directed by Orlando Bagwell et al. (Blackside, 1990), aired February 5, 1990, on PBS.
101. King, *"In a Single Garment,"* 57–75.
102. "Martin Luther King at the UN for an Anti-Vietnam War Demonstration (15 April 1967)," United Nations, YouTube, https://www.youtube.com/watch?v=YpGFOiSTs3Q.
103. Martin Luther King Jr., "A Testament of Hope," *Playboy, January 1969, in A Testament of Hope: The Essential Writings of Martin Luther King, Jr.*, ed. James M. Washington (New York: HarperOne, 1986), 317–18.
104. Ibid., 318.
105. Jill Lepore, "The Tug of War," *New Yorker*, September 2, 2013, https://www.newyorker.com/magazine/2013/09/09/the-tug-of-war.
106. James Fraser, email message to author, April 4, 2017.

107. Fairclough, "Martin Luther King, Jr. and the War in Vietnam," 34.

108. "Martin Luther King at the UN," YouTube, https://www.youtube.com/watch?v=YpGFOiSTs3Q.

109. The tensions between these two movements are explored with great insight in Simon Hall, *Peace and Freedom: The Civil Rights and Antiwar Movements in the 1960s* (Philadelphia: University of Pennsylvania Press, 2005).

110. "Face to Face Interview with Martin Luther King, Jr., July 28, 1967," in *A Testament of Hope*, 408.

111. Ibid.

112. Garrow, Bearing the Cross, 555, 558.

113. Branch, *At Canaan's Edge*, 668.

114. Ibid., 670. For MLK's 1968 speech at Santa Rita Prison, see "Martin Luther King at Santa Rita Prison (1968)," AfroMarxist, January 15, 2024, YouTube, https://www.youtube.com/watch?v=m8K8N2Ao5nw.

115. King, *"All Labor Has Dignity,"* 141.

116. Ibid.

117. "Dr. King to Weigh Civil Disobedience if War Intensifies," *New York Times*, April 2, 1967.

118. Halberstam, *The Children*, 538. LBJ also expressed his anger at MLK's antiwar activism by seeking "retaliation through the tax code," instructing the IRS commissioner to audit King and the SCLC (Taylor Branch, *At Canaan's Edge: America in the King Years, 1965–68* [New York: Simon and Schuster, 2006], 659–60.)

119. "Detroit's Infamous Right-Wing Extremist Died and Hardly Anyone Knew—Until Now," *Detroit Free Press*, July 9, 2020.

120. Sylvia Hodges, "Grosse Pointe Citizens Reflect on MLK Legacy," *The Tower Pulse*, January 19, 2017, https://thetowerpulse.net/24931/features/grosse-pointe-citizens-reflect-on-mlks-legacy.

121. Jude Huetteman, "The Night Martin Luther King Jr. Came to Grosse Pointe," *Detroit Free Press*, March 9, 2018.

122. Ibid.

123. "Capacity Audience Hears Dr. Martin Luther King Lecture at High School," *Grosse Pointe News*, March 21, 1968.

124. Ibid.

125. Ibid.

126. Martin Luther King Jr., "The Other America," March 14, 1968, Grosse Pointe Historical Society, https://www.gphistorical.org/mlk/mlkspeech.

127. Huetteman, "The Night."

128. King, "The Other America."

129. Ibid.

130. Ibid.

131. Huetteman, "The Night."

132. Ibid.

133. Ibid.

134. Richard S. Emrich, letter to the editor, *Grosse Point News*, March 21, 1968.

135. SAC Detroit to Director FBI, March 15, 1968. FBI file 100-16800-137, Archives.gov, https://www.archives.gov/files/research/jfk/releases/docid-32989763.pdf.

136. "Detroit's Infamous Right Wing Extremist" *Detroit Free Press*, July 9, 2020.

137. Bishop Emrich, introduction of Dr. King at Grosse Pointe South High School, March 14, 1968, Richard S. M. Emrich Papers, Bentley Historical Library, University of Michigan.

138. Ibid.

139. Ibid.

140. Ibid.

141. Michael Honey, letter to author, April 25, 2025.

142. King, "Beyond Vietnam," *A Call to Conscience*, 143.

143. "Vincent Harding, Civil Rights Author and Associate of Dr. King, 82, Dies," *New York Times*, May 21, 2014.

144. Richard Slotkin, *Gunfighter Nation: The Myth of the Frontier in Twentieth-Century America* (New York: Athenium, 1992).

Chapter 3. Abolishing Poverty and Supporting Striking Workers

1. David J. Garrow, *Bearing the Cross: Martin Luther King, Jr., and the Southern Christian Leadership Conference* (New York: Vintage, 1988), 575–624; Michael K. Honey, *Going Down Jericho Road: The Memphis Strike, Martin Luther King's Last Campaign* (New York: W. W. Norton and Co., 2007).

2. Andrea Hsu, "A Pattern Emerges in Elon Musk's Federal Shakeup: Break First, Ask Questions Later," NPR, February 26, 2025, https://www.npr.org/2025/02/26/nx-s1-5308659/federal-employees-musk-trump-chaos.

3. "Union Members—2024," Bureau of Labors Statistics, U.S. Dept. of Labor, January 28, 2025, https://www.bls.gov/news.release/union2.nr0.htm.

4. Martin Luther King Jr., *"All Labor Has Dignity,"* ed. Michael K. Honey (Boston: Beacon Press, 2011).

5. Ibid., xiii–xxxvi.

6. Martin Luther King Jr., *Where Do We Go from Here: Chaos or Community?* (1967; reprint, Boston: Beacon Press, 2010), 148.

7. Ibid., 149.

8. Martin Luther King Jr., "Speech to the Retail, Wholesale and Department Store Union, District 65," September 8, 1962, in *"All Labor Has Dignity,"* ed. Michael K. Honey (Boston: Beacon Press, 2011), 58.

9. Ibid., 55–56.

10. Murray Kempton, "The Clarity of A. Philip Randolph," July 6, 1963, in *Going Around: Selected Journalism*, ed. Andrew Holter (New York: Seven Stories Press, 2025), 152.

11. Martin Luther King Jr., "Address to the First Meeting of the Montgomery Improvement Association Mass Meeting," December 5, 1955, in *A Call to Conscience: The Landmark Speeches of Dr. Martin Luther King, Jr.*, ed. Clayborne Carson and Kris Shepard (New York: Grand Central Publishing, 2002), 11.

12. Coretta Scott King, "Thoughts and Reflections," in *We Shall Overcome: Martin Luther King, Jr., and the Black Freedom Struggle*, ed. Peter J. Albert and Ronald Hoffman (New York: Pantheon, 1990), 254. For additional evidence of King's disdain for capitalism, see David J. Garrow, "The Intellectual Development of Martin Luther King, Jr.: Influences and Commentary," *Union Seminary Quarterly Review* 40, no. 4 (January 1986): 9; Adam Fairclough, "Was Martin Luther King a Marxist?" *History Workshop* 15, no. 1 (Spring 1983): 117–25; Andrew J. Douglas and Jared A. Loggins, *Prophet of Discontent: Martin Luther King Jr. and the Critique of Racial Capitalism* (Athens: University of Georgia Press, 2021), 33–54.

13. Taylor Branch, *Parting the Waters: America in the King Years, 1954–63* (New York: Simon and Schuster, 1988), 149.

14. Ibid., 163–64.

15. Ibid., 163–64. For other expressions of admiration and love from working-class Black people to MLK during the Montgomery bus boycott, see Stewart Burns, ed., *Daybreak of Freedom: The Montgomery Bus Boycott* (Chapel Hill: University of North Carolina Press, 1997), 224, 228, 232.

16. This is not to say that there were no tensions and failures in relationships between the Montgomery movement's middle-professional class leadership and the Black working class during the bus boycott. Rosa Parks's biographer, Jeanne Theoharis, shows that Parks's economic needs were neglected by the movement's leaders, including King, and she was not asked to speak at movement meetings. See Jeanne Theoharis, *The Rebellious Life of Mrs. Rosa Parks* (Boston: Beacon Press, 2013), 116–64.

17. King, *"All Labor Has Dignity,"* 167–68.

18. Honey, *Going Down Jericho Road*, 219–20.

19. Adam Fairclough, *To Redeem the Soul of America: The Southern Christian Leadership Conference and Martin Luther King, Jr.* (Athens: University of Georgia Press, 1987), 371. This was the largest indoor rally MLK had ever spoken to in the

South. The movement's crowd estimate of fifteen thousand might seem overstated since it exceeded the seating capacity of Mason Temple, but "by 7 pm many" who could not find seats "crowded into the doorways and aisles—and they would stand for the next four hours" (Honey, *Going Down Jericho Road*, 292, 296).

20. Martin Luther King Jr., Memphis Speech, March 18, 1968, *"All Labor Has Dignity,"* 175.

21. Ibid., 174.

22. Ibid., 175–76.

23. Ibid., 176.

24. Garrow, *Bearing the Cross*, 475–526.

25. Martin Luther King Jr., testimony, Subcommittee on Executive Reorganization, Senate Committee on Government Operations, U.S. Congress, December 15, 1966, *King in the Wilderness*, directed by Peter W. Kunhardt (Kunhardt Films, 2018), transcript, 33.

26. Martin Luther King Jr., Memphis Speech, March 18, 1968, *"All Labor Has Dignity,"* 173

27. Ibid., *"All Labor Has Dignity,"* 172–74.

28. Ibid., 177.

29. Ibid., 178.

30. Ibid., 179–82.

31. Martin Luther King Jr., "I've Been to the Mountaintop" speech, Memphis, April 3, 1968, *A Call to Conscience*, 222–23.

32. Victor Ray, *On Critical Race Theory: Why It Matters and Why You Should Care* (New York: Random House, 2022), ix–32.

33. Despite the many conspiracy theories about the assassination, the evidence is overwhelming that James Earl Ray assassinated Martin Luther King Jr. See Gerald Posner, *Killing the Dream: James Earl Ray and the Assassination of Martin Luther King, Jr.* (New York Random House, 1998).

34. King, "Mountaintop" speech, *A Call to Conscience*, 219.

35. Ibid., 217–18.

36. Ibid., 217–18.

37. Ibid., 208.

38. Ibid., 209.

39. Ibid.

40. Ibid., 211.

41. Ibid., 211, 222.

42. "*Playboy* Interview with Martin Luther King, Jr.," January 1965, in *A Testament of Hope: The Essential Writings of Martin Luther King, Jr.*, ed. James M. Washington (New York: HarperOne, 1986), 355.

43. Martin Luther King Jr., "Showdown for Nonviolence," *Look*, May 1968, in Chuck Fager, *Uncertain Resurrection: Dr. King's Poor People's Campaign, 1968*, (Durham: Kimo Press, 2017), 3.

44. King, "Mountaintop" speech, *A Call to Conscience*, 219.

45. Ibid., 221.

46. Ibid., 213.

47. Ibid., 211.

48. Ibid., 211–13.

49. Ibid., 220–21.

50. Ibid., 221

51. Ibid., 221.

52. For a convincing critique of this assumption that the Albany movement was a failure, see J. Todd Moye, "Focusing Our Eyes on the Prize: How Community Studies Are Reframing and Rewriting the History of the Civil Rights Movement," in *Civil Rights from The Ground Up: Local Struggles, A National Movement*, ed. Emilye Crosby (Athens: University of Georgia Press, 2011), 157–64.

53. King, Mountaintop" speech, *A Call to Conscience*, 221.

54. Ibid., 221–22.

55. Ibid., 216.

56. Ibid. King made a similar point about the need for Black economic and political power in his final interview. See *Martin Luther King, Jr.: The Last Interview and Other Conversations* (Brooklyn: Melville House, 2017), 95–98.

57. King, *A Call to Conscience*, 214–16.

58. Jonathan Rieder, *Gospel of Freedom: Martin Luther King, Jr.'s Letter from Birmingham Jail and the Struggle That Changed a Nation* (New York: Bloomsbury Press, 2013), 169–85.

59. King, *A Call to Conscience*, 214.

60. Honey, *Going Down Jericho Road*, 415; Drew D. Hansen, *The Dream: Martin Luther King, Jr., and the Speech That Inspired a Nation* (New York: Ecco, 2003), 48.

61. Andrew Young, *An Easy Burden: The Civil Rights Movement and the Transformation of America*, (New York: HarperCollins, 1996), 463–64.

62. Clay Risen, *A Nation on Fire: America in the Wake of the King Assassination* (New York: John Wiley and Sons, 2009).

63. Honey, *Going Down Jericho Road*, 427–96.

64. David J. Garrow, "Triumphant in Death," *Salon*, April 28, 1998, https://www.davidgarrow.com/File/DJG%201998%20SalonJERayObit28April.pdf; David J. Garrow, "The Assassin's Name is James Earl Ray," *New York Times*, April 2, 1997, https://www.nytimes.com/1997/04/02/opinion/the-assassin-s-name-is-james-earl-ray.html.

65. George McMillan, *The Making of An Assassin: The Life of James Earl Ray* (Boston: Little, Brown, 1976), 60.

66. Ibid., 1.

67. Garrow, *Bearing the Cross*, 307.

68. King, *Where Do We Go from Here*, 12.

69. Martin Luther King Jr., "The Other America," March 14, 1968, Grosse Pointe Historical Society, https://www.gphistorical.org/mlk/mlkspeech.

70. Ibid.

71. Honey, *Going Down Jericho Road*, 462–64.

72. Robert Cohen, *Confronting Jim Crow: Race, Memory and the University of Georgia in the Twentieth Century* (Chapel Hill: University of North Carolina Press, 2024), 229.

73. Honey, *Going Down Jericho Road*, 368.

74. Michael K. Honey, *Black Workers in Memphis: An Oral History of Segregation, Unionism, and the Freedom Struggle* (Berkeley: University of California Press, 1999), 301.

75. Ibid., 297.

76. Ibid., 301.

77. David J. Garrow, *The FBI and Martin Luther King, Jr.* (New York: Penguin, 1983), 207.

78. Ibid., 208.

79. Ibid., 207,

80. Martin Luther King Jr., "Statement by Dr. Martin Luther King Jr.," December 4, 1967, 4, https://www.crmvet.org/docs/6712_mlk_ppc-anc.pdf.

81. Ibid., 1.

82. Ibid.

83. Ibid., 2, 4.

84. Matthew Miles Goodrich, "The Forgotten Socialist History of Martin Luther King Jr.," *In These Times*, January 15, 2018, https://inthesetimes.com/article/martin-luther-king-jr-day-socialism-capitalism.

85. Garrow, *The FBI and Martin Luther King, Jr.*, 214–15.

86. Martin Luther King Jr., "Address to the Tenth Anniversary of the Southern Christian Leadership Conference, Atlanta, Georgia, August 16, 1967," in *The Rhetoric of Black Power*, by Robert L. Scott and Wayne Brockriede (New York: Harper and Row, 1969), 162-63.

87. Ibid., 163. MLK used this same politically charged religious frame for his last speech. See Keith D. Miller, *Martin Luther King's Biblical Epic: His Final, Great Speech* (Jackson: University Press of Mississippi, 2013).

88. King, "Address to the Tenth Anniversary," *The Rhetoric of Black Power*, 161–62.

89. Sylvie Laurent, *King and the Other America: The Poor People's Campaign and the Quest for Economic Equality* (Berkeley: University of California Press, 2018), 1–75.

90. *A "Freedom Budget" for All Americans: Budgeting Our Resources, 1966–1975, to Achieve "Freedom from Want"* (New York: A. Philip Randolph Institute, 1966).

91. Martin Luther King Jr., foreword to *A "Freedom Budget" for All Americans: A Summary*, by A. Philip Randolph and Bayard Rustin (New York: A. Philip Randolph Institute, 1967).

92. King, "Statement," 4, https://www.crmvet.org/docs/6712_mlk_ppc-anc.pdf.

93. Bernard Lafayette, interview, *King in the Wilderness*, directed by Peter W. Kunhardt (Kunhardt Films, 2018), transcript, 56.

94. Marian Wright Edelman, interview, *King in the Wilderness*, directed by Peter W. Kunhardt (Kunhardt Films, 2018), transcript, 56.

95. Martin Luther King Jr., remarks at PPC planning meeting, March 14, 1968, *King in the Wilderness*, directed by Peter W. Kunhardt (Kunhardt Films, 2018), transcript, 56.

96. King's critical view of white backlash in the mid-1960s was very much in accord with the best historical scholarship that emerged decades later. The point being that white resistance to racial integration preceded, and was not an effect of, Black militancy and ghetto riots. This Black turbulence merely served as a pretext for further expression and amplification of white racist resentment and resistance that had already been strong and that had deep historical roots. See Thomas Sugrue, *The Origins of the Urban Crisis: Race and Inequality in Postwar Detroit* (Princeton: Princeton University Press, 2014).

97. Martin Luther King Jr., statement, *King in the Wilderness*, directed by Peter W. Kunhardt (Kunhardt Films, 2018), transcript, 57.

98. Thomas F. Jackson, *From Civil Rights to Human Rights: Martin Luther King, Jr., and the Struggle for Economic Justice* (Philadelphia: University of Pennsylvania Press, 2009), 346.

99. I. F. Stone, "The Rich March on Washington All the Time," *I. F. Stone's Weekly*, May 3, 1963, 1.

100. Michael Harrington, *The Other America: Poverty in the United States* (New York: Macmillan, 1962).

101. See Robert P. Moses, "The Mississippi Freedom Movement in the 1960s," interview by Robert Cohen, NYU Steinhardt, May 5, 2011, YouTube, https://www.youtube.com/watch?v=uaGWx7PxD4k.

102. Edelman, *King in the Wilderness*, transcript, 49.

103. Ibid., 50.

104. Garrow, *Bearing the Cross*, 271, 278.

105. Herbert Garfinkel, *When Negroes March: The March on Washington Movement in the Organizational Politics for FEPC* (New York: Free Press, 1959); "FDR

Signs Order Banning Discrimination in the Defense Industry," *History,* June 24, 2025, https://www.history.com/this-day-in-history/fdr-executive-order-8802-desegregates-defense-industries.

106. Paul Dickson, "The Bonus Army," Bill of Rights Institute, https://billofrightsinstitute.org/essays/the-bonus-army.

107. Young, *An Easy Burden,* 477–92.

108. Ibid., 484.

109. Ibid., 483; Calvin Trillin, "Resurrection City," *New Yorker,* June 15, 1968, https://www.newyorker.com/magazine/1968/06/15/resurrection-city.

110. Young, *An Easy Burden,* 483, 489.

111. Fairclough, *To Redeem the Soul of America,* 386–90.

112. John Edwin Mason, "Seeing Resurrection City, Seeing the Poor," in *Resurrection City, 1968,* by Jill Freedman (Bologna: Damiani, 2018), 14.

113. Amy Nathan Wright, "The 1968 Poor People's Campaign, Marks, Mississippi, and the Mule Train: Fighting Poverty Locally, Representing Poverty Nationally," in *Civil Rights History from the Ground Up: Local Struggles, a National Movement,* ed. Emilye Crosby (Athens: University of Georgia Press, 2011), 131–34.

114. Young, *An Easy Burden,* 488–89.

115. Gordon K. Mantler, *Power to the Poor: Black-Brown Coalition and the Fight for Economic Justice* (Chapel Hill: University of North Carolina Press, 2013), 5–14, 121–53.

116. Martin Luther King Jr., March 10, 1968, epigraph, *Power to the Poor.*

117. I. F. Stone, "Billions for Missiles and Pennies for Poverty," *I. F. Stone's Weekly,* July 8, 1968.

118. Ibid.

119. "Safeguard ABM System to Shut Down: $5 Billion Spent in 6 Years Since Debate," *New York Times,* November 25, 1975.

120. "Bishop Barber, Rev. Theoharis, Religious Leaders and Low-Wage Workers Bring Direct Action Back to DC for a National Moral Monday," Poor People's Campaign, https://www.poorpeoplescampaign.org/direct-action-back-to-dc-for-a-national-moral-monday.

121. "National Poverty in America Awareness Month," U.S. Census Bureau, January 2025, https://www.census.gov/newsroom/stories/poverty-awareness-month.html.

122. "Child Poverty by State 2025," World Population Review, https://worldpopulationreview.com/state-rankings/child-poverty-rate-by-state.

123. Martin Luther King Jr. to Coretta Scott, July 18, 1952, The Martin Luther King, Jr. Research and Education Institute, Stanford University, https://kinginstitute.stanford.edu/king-papers/documents/coretta-scott.

124. Maureen Dowd, "Leaving Hungry Pols to Help Hungry Kids," *New York Times,* December 6, 2025, https://www.nytimes.com/2025/12/06/opinion/charity-holiday-gift-hunger.html.

125. "Quotations," Martin Luther King Jr. Memorial, District of Columbia, National Park Service, https://www.nps.gov/mlkm/learn/quotations.htm.

126. Ibid.

127. "Marks Mule Train and Poor People's Campaign, Mississippi Freedom Trail," The Historical Marker Database, https://www.hmdb.org/m.asp?m=174171.

128. *Martin Luther King, Jr.: The Last Interview,* 113. Also see Martin Luther King Jr., "Remaining Awake Through A Great Revolution," sermon delivered at the National Cathedral, Washington, D.C., March 31, 1968, in *A Knock at Midnight: Inspiration from the Great Sermons of Martin Luther King, Jr.,* ed. Clayborne Carson and Peter Holloran (New York: Warner Books, 1998), 214. There were apparently *two* occasions when the poverty and hunger King witnessed in Marks reduced him to tears. The first, described in MLK's account in the text above, was when he spoke with desperate, jobless parents who told him they lacked the funds to feed their hungry children. The second, according to Ralph David Abernathy, occurred when King, at a daycare center, witnessed hunger stalking impoverished children. "Tears came down his face. And he had to leave the room" when he saw that all that was available to feed hungry children at lunch time was a single apple, which was divided into small slices for children who had no lunch. Ronald L. Freeman, *The Mule Train: A Journey of Hope Remembered* (Nashville: Rutledge Hill Press, 1998), 89.

129. Martin Luther King Jr., "An Autobiography of Religious Development," in *The Papers of Martin Luther King, Jr., Vol. 1: Called to Serve, January 1929–June 1951,* ed. Clayborne Carson, Ralph E. Luker, and Penny A. Russell (Berkeley: University of California Press, 1992), 359.

130. Josh Bivens, "House Budget Bill Would Kick 15 Million People Off Health Insurance and Damage Local Economies," *Working Economics Blog,* Economic Policy Institute, June 3, 2025, https://www.epi.org/blog/house-budget-bill-would-kick-15-million-people-off-health-insurance-and-damage-local-economies; Josh Bivens, Hilary Wething, and Monique Morrissey, "Cutting Medicaid to Pay for Low Taxes on the Rich Is a Terrible Trade for American Families," Economic Policy Institute, February 28, 2025, https://www.epi.org/publication/cutting-medicaid-for-low-taxes-on-the-rich-is-terrible-for-american-families; "2025 Budget Impacts: House Bill Would Cut Assistance for Children, Raise Costs for Families," Center on Budget and Policy Priorities, https://www.cbpp.org/research/federal-budget/2025-budget-impacts-house-bill-would-cut-assistance-for-children-raise.

131. For King's speech at the National Conference for New Politics, Chicago August 31, 1967, see "#MLK: The Three Evils of Society," The Martin Luther King, Jr. Center for Nonviolent Social Change, YouTube; https://www.youtube.com/watch?v=6sT9Hjh0cHMl; "Speech: The Three Evils of Society," January 17, 2024, *Black Agenda Report*, https://www.blackagendareport.com/speech-three-evils-society-martin-luther-king-jr-1967.

Next Steps

1. Vincent Harding, *Martin Luther King: The Inconvenient Hero* (Maryknoll, N.Y.: Orbis Books, 1997).

2. Joanna Shenk, *The Movement Makes Us Human: An Interview with Dr. Vincent Harding on Mennonites, Vietnam, and MLK* (Eugene: Wipf and Stock, 2018), 13.

3. Martin Luther King, Jr. Memorial, National Park Foundation, https://www.nationalparks.org/explore/parks/martin-luther-king-jr-memorial.

4. Taylor Branch, *Parting the Waters: America in the King Years, 1954–63* (New York: Simon and Schuster, 1988), 467; H. Brevy Cannon, "Bond: King Not Joining Freedom Riders Led to First Rift Within Civil Rights Movement," *UVA Today*, January 26, 2011, https://news.virginia.edu/content/bond-king-not-joining-freedom-riders-led-first-rift-within-civil-rights-movement.

5. John Lewis and Michael D'Orso, *Walking with the Wind: A Memoir of the Movement* (New York: Simon and Schuster, 1998), 164.

6. "Williams, Robert Franklin," The Martin Luther King, Jr. Research and Education Institute, Stanford University, https://kinginstitute.stanford.edu/williams-robert-franklin.

7. Note that less than a year before the Freedom Rides, King, with some reluctance, caved in to Atlanta student pressure to join their sit-in at Rich's department store. After their arrests, the students were allowed out on bail but King was not. On the basis of a traffic violation, the judge kept King in jail, and he was transferred in shackles in the middle of the night to a rural Georgia prison, leading Coretta, pregnant at the time, to fear for his life. So King had ample reason to exercise some caution, given the way segregationists targeted him even more eagerly than they did student activists.

8. David Halberstam, *The Children* (New York: Fawcett, 1999), 273.

9. Andrew Young remarks in "The Promised Land (1967–68)," *Eyes on the Prize 2: America at the Racial Crossroads, 1965-1985*, directed by Orlando Bagwell et al. (Blackside, 1990), aired February 5, 1990, on PBS. Young took Doar's warning seriously and—without consulting King—had numerous ministers, dressed in

blue suits like King, walk at the head of the march from Selma as it entered Montgomery to confuse any potential sniper.

10. Thomas F. Jackson, *From Civil Rights to Human Rights: Martin Luther King, Jr., and the Struggle for Economic Justice* (Philadelphia: University of Pennsylvania Press, 2009), 7, 23.

11. David Levering Lewis, "Martin Luther King, Jr. and the Promise of Nonviolent Populism," *Black Leaders of the Twentieth Century*, ed. John Hope Franklin and August Meier (Urbana: University of Illinois Press, 1982), 277.

12. Ibid., 278.

13. Ibid.

14. Ibid.

15. See Jeanne Theoharis, *King of the North: Martin Luther King Jr.'s Life of Struggle Outside the South* (New York: New Press, 2025).

16. David J. Garrow, *Bearing the Cross: Martin Luther King, Jr., and the Southern Christian Leadership Conference* (New York: Vintage, 1988), 439.

17. Adam Fairclough, *To Redeem the Soul of America: The Southern Christian Leadership Conference and Martin Luther King, Jr.* (Athens: University of Georgia Press, 1987), 37–56.

18. Andrew Kopkind, "Soul Power," *The New York Review of Books*, August 24, 1967.

19. Ibid.

20. Garrow, *Bearing the Cross*, 571.

21. *King in the Wilderness*, directed by Peter W. Kunhardt (Kunhardt Films, 2018).

22. Jason Sokol, *The Heavens Might Crack: The Death and Legacy of Martin Luther King, Jr.* (New York: Basic Books, 2018), 17.

23. Stanley D. Levison to Martin Luther King Jr., April 7, 1965, quoted in David J. Garrow, foreword to *Seeing Through Race: A Reinterpretation of Civil Rights Photography*, by Martin A. Berger (Berkeley: University of California Press, 2011), x.

24. Lewis, "Martin Luther King, Jr.," *Black Leaders of the Twentieth Century*, 302.

25. Peter J. Albert and Ronald Hoffman, eds., *We Shall Overcome: Martin Luther King, Jr. and the Black Freedom Struggle* (New York: Pantheon, 1990) 65.

26. Mary L. Dudziak, *Cold War Civil Rights: Race and the Image of American Democracy* (Princeton: Princeton University Press, 2011).

27. Patricia Sullivan, *Justice Rising: Robert Kennedy's America in Black and White* (Cambridge: The Belknap Press of Harvard University Press, 2021), 100.

28. This was an issue King avoided in his speeches on anti-colonialism. He would, for example, praise Nkrumah for endorsing nonviolence but not mention the use of revolutionary violence by the Mau Mau in Kenya. See Martin Luther King Jr., "The Birth of a New Nation," in *"In a Single Garment of Destiny": A Global Vision of Justice*, ed. Lewis V. Baldwin (Boston: Beacon Press, 2012), 69.

29. Kelly M. Nims, "The Necessary Violence of Frantz Fanon and Malcolm X in Global Black Revolution," in *African American Literature in Transition, 1960–1970: Black Art, Politics, and Aesthetics*, ed. Shelly Eversley (Cambridge: Cambridge University Press, 2022), 202–3.

30. David L. Chappell, *Waking from the Dream: The Struggle for Civil Rights in the Shadow of Martin Luther King, Jr.*, (New York: Random House, 2014), 3–27.

31. John D'Emilio, *Lost Prophet: The Life and Times of Bayard Rustin* (Chicago: University of Chicago Press, 2004), 337.

32. Shenk, *The Movement Makes Us Human*, 13.

33. Ibid., 12.

34. Ibid., 13.

35. Robert Parris Moses, "Comment," *We Shall Overcome*, 69–76.

36. Clayborne Carson, "Martin Luther King, Jr.: Charismatic Leadership in a Mass Struggle," *Journal of American History* 74, no. 2 (September 1987): 448.

37. Ibid., 448–51. Also see Emilye Crosby, ed., *Civil Rights History from the Ground Up: Local Struggles, a National Movement* (Athens: University of Georgia Press, 2011).

38. Nathan Huggins, "Martin Luther King, Jr.: Charisma and Leadership," *Journal of American History* 74, no. 2 (September 1987): 481.

39. Ibid., 478, 481.

40. Garrow, *Bearing the Cross*, 625.

41. Crosby, *Civil Rights History*.

42. Pat Watters, *Down to Now: Reflections on the Southern Civil Rights Movement* (New York: Pantheon Books, 1971), 15.

43. Fairclough, *To Redeem the Soul of America*, 371–72; Sokol, *The Heavens Might Crack*, 16.

44. Shenk, *The Movement Makes Us Human*, 13.

45. Kenneth D. Johnson, "Looking Back at Martin Luther King, Jr.: An Interview with David J. Garrow," *Telos* 182 (Spring 2018): 206.

46. Stewart Burns, ed., *Daybreak of Freedom: The Montgomery Bus Boycott* (Chapel Hill: University of North Carolina Press, 1997), 216.

47. Jackson, *From Civil Rights to Human Rights*, book jacket.

48. See Coretta Scott's inscription to MLK in the Bellamy book, accompanying King's August 31, 1952, letter to her in *The Papers of Martin Luther King, Jr., Vol. 6: Advocate of the Social Gospel, September 1948–March 1963*, ed. Clayborne Carson et al. (Berkeley: University of California Press, 2007), 124–27.

49. Keith D. Miller, *Voice of Deliverance: The Language of Martin Luther King, Jr., and Its Sources* (Athens: University of Georgia Press, 1992), 1–11.

50. Ibid., 13–28; Keith D. Miller, *Martin Luther King's Biblical Epic: His Final, Great Speech* (Jackson: University Press of Mississippi, 2013), 71–111.

51. "Strength to Love," The Martin Luther King, Jr. Research and Education Institute, Stanford University, https://kinginstitute.stanford.edu/strength-love.

52. Jonathan Eig, *King: A Life* (New York: Picador, 2023), 480–81.

53. Harry Belafonte, *My Song* (New York: Knopf, 2011), 328.

54. Robert P. Moses, "The Mississippi Freedom Movement in the 1960s," interview by Robert Cohen, NYUSteinhardt, May 5, 2011, YouTube, https://www.youtube.com/watch?v=uaGWx7PxD4k.

55. Martin Luther King, Jr., *Where Do We Go from Here: Chaos or Community?* (1967; reprint, Boston: Beacon Press, 2010), 11–13.

56. Ibram X. Kendi, "Trump's Attacks on Black History Betray America," *New York Times*, June 2, 2025; John McWhorter, "The Future of Black History is Here," *New York Times*, May 18, 2025; Brian Bennett, "Trump Announces 7 Military Bases Reverting to Names Honoring Confederates," *Time*, June 10, 2025.

INDEX

THE MOREHOUSE COLLEGE KING COLLECTION SERIES ON CIVIL & HUMAN RIGHTS

The Drum Major Instinct: Martin Luther King Jr.'s Theory of Political Service
Justin Rose

Reclaiming the Great World House: The Global Vision of Martin Luther King Jr.
edited by Vicki L. Crawford and Lewis V. Baldwin

Dr. Martin Luther King Jr. and the Poor People's Campaign of 1968
Robert Hamilton

Prophet of Discontent: Martin Luther King Jr. and the Critique of Racial Capitalism
Andrew J. Douglas and Jared A. Loggins

Not Dreaming: Martin Luther King Jr.'s Critique of America
Robert Cohen

www.ingramcontent.com/pod-product-compliance
Lightning Source LLC
Chambersburg PA
CBHW020012100926
51241CB00021B/227
9780820380643